ART OF TH. _ _

3rd edition

The essential guide to business affairs for
television, film and new media producers

BY DOROTHY VILJOEN

pact producers
alliance for
cinema and
television

Published by PACT (Producers Alliance for Cinema and Television)
45 Mortimer Street London W1W 8HJ England

Tel +44(0)20 7331 6000 Fax +44(0)20 7331 6700
E-mail enquiries@pact.co.uk
Web www.pact.co.uk

Art of the Deal
first published 1991 by the Independent Programme Producers Association
50-51 Berwick Street London W1A 4RD England. Second edition published
1997 by PACT (Producers Alliance for Cinema and Television)
45 Mortimer Street London W1N 7TD England

This third edition published in 2002 by PACT (Producers Alliance for Cinema
and Television) 45 Mortimer Street London W1W 8HJ England

ISBN 0-9529586-3-5

Designed and produced by Visiontime Limited
Tel +44(0)20 8566 7375 E-mail enquiries@visiontime.co.uk
Printed and bound in England

Dorothy Viljoen is a freelance consultant on film and television business affairs, working with independent producers in the UK and Europe. Since 1989 she has been business affairs adviser to PACT.

With over 35 years experience of working in television in the UK, Dorothy Viljoen is an acknowledged expert with an extensive knowledge of the industry, and production, over and above her expertise in business affairs. Previously she has worked as Programme Administrative Officer for the Independent Broadcasting Authority (now the Independent Television Commission), Deputy Head of the Programme Planning Secretariat of the Independent Television Companies Association, Head of Scripts for the ATV Network, Head of Rights Negotiations for Central Television and Director of Business Affairs and Head of the London office of D.L. Taffner, the US producer/distributor.

Dorothy lectures widely in the UK and Europe on business affairs. She is specialist expert on negotiating skills for the EAVE course of the EU Media Programme and for the AVEA course in Southern Africa and works as business affairs consultant to Film Makers Ireland.

Her previous publications include *The Key to the Negotiation of Audio-Visual Co-Production Contracts* published by the Council of Europe Press in 1994.

Thanks are owed to The Council of Europe for permission to reproduce extracts from *The Key to the Negotiation of Audio-Visual Co-Production Contracts* in Chapters 20 and 21 written by the author and published by the Council of Europe Press in 1994.

To Richard Mawrey QC for permitting the reproduction of his very lucid material on contracts contained in Chapter 2.

To John McVay, Chief Executive of PACT, to all the PACT and Producers Rights Agency staff and to the previous Chief Executives of PACT who commissioned and promoted the earlier editions of the book, Paul Styles, John Woodward and Shaun Williams.

To friends and colleagues in the film and television industry too numerous to mention who have been unfailingly generous with their time and advice on all aspects of production and deal-making.

To Leon, Nina and Tessa Viljoen, who claim to have suffered serious neglect and hardship during the writing of the three editions but have nonetheless remained immensely supportive throughout!

Dorothy Viljoen
London
March 2002

The first edition of *Art of the Deal* was published in August 1991, the second in April 1997. Before writing this preface for the third edition, being published in 2002, it was revealing to review the introductions to the two previous editions. How straightforward the UK television industry was in 1991. There were only four UK terrestrial television channels, the newest being the ten-year-old Channel 4. British Satellite Broadcasting had just merged with Sky Television to provide the first UK satellite service, but the effects of the technological developments which brought about the satellite service had otherwise barely begun to be felt. By 1997 a fifth terrestrial service, Channel 5, had been launched, the BBC had introduced UK Gold and ITV's cable service SuperChannel had opened and closed. Apart from these developments the structure of the industry remained the same as in 1991. The introduction of digital channels was being contemplated but had yet to come about, and only a few technical buffs were speculating on the possible effects of the Internet, broadband and other emerging technologies on existing transmission and viewing patterns.

Now, only five years on, there are over 70 television channels available to UK viewers. All the terrestrial broadcasters, with the exception of Channel 5, operate digital channels. Twelve channels are dedicated to feature films and five to sport. Deal structures now have to anticipate programmes being relayed from many different platforms and in various formats, including reception on home computers, mobile phones, digital watches, fridge doors and so forth. Deals need to take account of versioning for interactive and enhanced usage, the launch of programme-related websites, programme spin-offs marketed through e-commerce and other uses, all of which were still in the realms of science fiction ten years ago.

The irony, or maybe the consequence, of this proliferation of channels is that it is happening at a time when the overall size of the television audience, not only in the UK but in Europe and the USA, is falling year on year. Further, the huge cost of setting up the new channels, coupled with a drop in advertising revenue, means that production budgets are being squeezed ever more tightly. The pressure is on to find cheap ways of delivering a large audience and it is now almost impossible to finance any major drama or documentary programme without raising some form of co-finance. The task for producers of striking commercially viable deals is increasingly difficult and absolutely critical to survival.

The film industry, without the statutory and financial structures imposed on the broadcasters, has always been far more fluid than television. Since 1997 the UK film industry has to some extent been regenerated, not least through the welcome introduction of lottery funding. The Film Council has replaced British Screen and the Arts Council and has a much sharper commercial focus. Channel 4 has set up a separate division, FilmFour, and the BBC has BBC Films, both significant financiers of the development and production of feature films. At a time when television programmes are becoming increasingly formulaic, many producers see feature films affording greater opportunities for creative expression. The essential deal-making required to finance feature films is, however, much more complex and legally heavy duty than that required for television, and the ability to drive these complex deals is an essential qualification for any feature film producer.

For all independent producers there has never been a more challenging time. It is a hugely competitive and overcrowded marketplace. Survival of the fittest is the name of the game and being fit means not only being able to make good programmes, but, perhaps more importantly, being able to do good deals. Previous editions of the book have concentrated heavily on the terms of trade of UK broadcasters but this edition has been comprehensively rewritten to address a global film and television market in which national broadcasters are just one type of programme supplier, and, to use similarly unattractive current jargon, producers are content providers. The art of the deal from the producer's point of view now lies in ensuring that all the contracts will allow the production the widest forms of exploitation and that the producer benefits from whatever form that exploitation may take.

As with the previous editions, this book is not a legal handbook but is aimed primarily at producers and their business affairs executives to advise on appropriate commercial terms which need to be negotiated for production deals. It covers the rights and entitlements which a producer must ensure are obtained from those supplying materials and services to enable the producer to have the greatest possible creative freedom to develop and market the production.

There is an important distinction, which is not always recognised, between the role of a lawyer, which is primarily to ensure that contracts are watertight and legally binding, and that of a producer which is to ensure that the deals are appropriate for the production. It is the intention that the guidelines contained in this book will enable producers and business affairs executives to effectively negotiate these deals, which form the bedrock of any successful production.

Dorothy Viljoen
March 2002

C1

COPYRIGHT Chapter 1

The law of copyright is the legal foundation of every film and television programme. Copyright subsists in nearly all the individual creative elements which together make up a programme. The completed programme has its own separate copyright as does the actual broadcast of the programme. Producing a programme without owning the necessary rights of copyright has been likened to building a house without any entitlement to the land on which it is built. The importance of properly addressing and contracting for copyright materials in the production of films and television programmes cannot be overemphasised, since the problems that can arise when this is neglected can be insuperable.

This chapter gives a brief explanation of the principles of copyright law as it relates to the film and television industry. Practical application when commissioning, contracting for and acquiring rights in programme materials are dealt with in subsequent chapters.

KEY TOPICS & ISSUES

C1

WHAT IS COPYRIGHT?   1

Copyright is property, intellectual property, and only the owner of the property is entitled to copy it, issue copies to the public, perform, show or play it in public, broadcast it or adapt it. If any of these things is done without the permission of the copyright owner it is infringement of copyright and the infringer may be liable for payment of damages to the owner or, in certain circumstances, to punishment by fine or imprisonment.

Copyright in the UK and European Union   1.1

Copyright throughout the United Kingdom (England, Scotland, Wales and Northern Ireland) is governed by the Copyright, Designs and Patents Act 1988 (CDPA) which came into effect on 1 August 1989, succeeding the 1956 Copyright Act. Subsequently the European Commission has implemented copyright directives to harmonise copyright legislation between the EU member states and these have had some far-reaching implications for copyright in film and television productions, particularly in relation to provisions for the term of copyright and the first owner of the copyright.

There is a fundamental philosophical difference between the basis of UK copyright law and the copyright laws of many European countries. Whereas copyright was introduced into UK law primarily to protect the economic rights of the creators of original works, in many European countries it was established primarily to protect their creative and artistic rights. Harmonisation has, therefore, been somewhat problematic since the practical effect of the different approaches can sometimes be difficult to reconcile, particularly over such matters as moral rights.

Under the CDPA various matters relating to copyright are dealt with by the Copyright Tribunal which comes under the auspices of the Lord Chancellor's Department. Its principal responsibility is for approval of copyright licensing schemes, but it also has powers in relation to disputes for equitable remuneration for rental and lending rights. It also has the power to give consent when a performer cannot be identified and to establish royalty rates in respect of copyright material having a revived term.

International copyright: 1.2
Berne Convention and Universal Copyright Convention

Copyright material is safeguarded internationally principally by the Berne Convention and the Universal Copyright Convention (UCC). Most countries are members of one or the other. (China is not a member of either.)

The Berne Convention was established in the late 19th century by the major publishing countries and fundamentally provides that member countries give reciprocal copyright protection to the copyright works of nationals of other countries which are published in their countries. The UCC has slightly lower standards of reciprocal protection but provides that works carrying the © symbol, the year of first publication and the name of the copyright owner, will be afforded the same rights of protection allowed to nationals of its own territory.

USA   1.3

Copyright law in the USA used to be different in a number of significant respects from that of the UK and it could be something of a minefield to acquire US-originated copyright material, particularly since the term of copyright was split into two consecutive terms of 28 years each and copyright could not straightforwardly be acquired for the

C1

duration of the combined terms. Over recent years, however, there have been significant changes in the law and in 1989 the USA joined the Berne Convention. Thus, copyright protection in the USA is now much more in line with the protection afforded in the UK.

To have protection in the USA, there used to be a requirement that copyright be registered at the Library of Congress in Washington and carry a copyright notice. This registration can still be made, but it is optional as is the bearing of the copyright notice (see also *Paragraph 6.2*).

1.4   The Internet and copyright

At present the same copyright laws apply to the Internet and digital developments as apply to any other form of publishing/reproduction/duplication of copyright material. Just because the material is disseminated through the galaxies does not mean that terrestrial laws do not apply: they do. To be effective, legislation related to the Internet will need to be observed internationally and copyright law is currently being developed to keep pace with the Internet and digital developments through World Intellectual Property Organisation (WIPO) treaties which are being adopted by many countries. The aim is to provide consistent protection of copyright works and performances disseminated in digital form. Further, it is likely that in the near future, digital technology will provide the means of encrypting data to prevent the unauthorised use of material recorded in digital form. This may effectively prevent much unauthorised use of copyright material over the Internet and other dissemination of electronic material.

2   WHAT MATERIAL IS PROTECTED BY COPYRIGHT?

The 'intellectual properties' in which copyright subsists are:

2.1   Original literary, dramatic, musical or artistic works

Firstly, for any of these works there is no qualitative test as to what constitutes copyright material. Works without any discernable literary or artistic merit can attract copyright protection.

To qualify as original the work need not be novel. The most commonplace material can qualify but it must be the person's own work, the creation of which has required a combination of skill, labour, experience and judgement. Ideas and suggestions are not original works protected by copyright.

i   **A literary work** is any work which is written, spoken or sung (excluding dramatic or musical works – see below). A literary work can be anything from a detailed shopping list or letters to great literary tomes. Literary works can also include tables or compilations (for example programme schedules and railway timetables) and, importantly, computer programmes and databases. The key criterion for copyright protection is that the work must be in recorded form, either written down or recorded on any media. In this connection bear in mind that, for example, an interviewee will hold the copyright in the material spoken in a recorded interview, albeit the recording may not have been transcribed. Thus, the producer needs to obtain written permission from the interviewee for the reproduction of the recording in a programme. See *Chapter 9, Paragraph 1.5*.

ii   **A dramatic work** is one which can also include a work of dance or mime.

iii   **A musical work** means a work consisting of music, but it does not include any words or action intended to be sung, spoken or performed with the music which attract their own separate copyright/performers' rights. Lyrics are treated as a literary work.

iv   **Artistic works** mean paintings, drawings, diagrams, maps, charts, plans, engravings, etchings, lithographs, woodcuts or similar works, sculptures or collages, works of architecture (a building or a model for a building), works of artistic craftsmanship and photographs.

Films/programmes and sound recordings   2.2

Films/programmes mean recordings on any medium from which a moving image may be produced.

There has been a major test case as to whether copyright subsisted in the style or technique used in a film and whether infringement of copyright could be claimed against the maker of a film having a different subject matter but employing strikingly similar style or technique. The case went to the Court of Appeal which ruled that style and technique were not protected by copyright law.

Sound recordings are defined as:

i   a recording of sounds from which the sound may be reproduced; and

ii   a recording of a literary, dramatic or musical work from which sounds reproducing the work may be produced.

For both films/programmes and sound recordings the underlying rights material need not be original provided that the film or the sound recording is an original production.

Broadcasts and cable programmes   2.3

Broadcasts are defined as transmissions of visual images which are:

i   capable of being lawfully received by members of the public; and

ii   are transmitted for presentation to members of the public.

Cable programmes mean any programme included in a cable programme service. A cable programme service means a service which consists wholly or mainly of sending visual images, sounds or other information by means of a telecommunications system for reception at two or more places or for presentation to members of the public.

Again, the material being broadcast or included in the cable service does not need to be original, but it is infringement of copyright to copy the material being transmitted, in other words, piracy.

Published editions   2.4

Published editions mean the typographical arrangement of a published edition of a literary, dramatic or musical work. The underlying material need not be original but the layout, design and graphics must be originally created for the edition.

Performers' rights   2.5

In addition to the protection given to the above works, the CDPA gives performers protection by requiring their consent to the exploitation of their performances. In this context a performance means a dramatic performance, including dance or mime, a reading or recitation of a literary work, a musical performance or a performance of a variety act. It even extends to a busker's performance. The performer's consent is required for the recording of the performance, broadcasting it live and showing or playing it to the public.

3 WHO IS THE OWNER OF THE COPYRIGHT?

Under copyright law, as a general rule, the first owner of the copyright is not the individual who commissions the material to be created but the person who actually creates the original material – be it a script, artwork, design, graphics, music and so forth. It will be seen, therefore, that it is essential for a producer to ensure that the necessary rights of copyright are obtained from originators of programme materials, albeit the material may have been produced at the instigation and expense of the producer.

Always be aware that the grant of rights of copyright is one of the very few forms of contract which, under UK law, has to be in writing and signed by the owner for the agreement to be legally binding. An oral agreement will not suffice.

The first owners of works protected by copyright are:

3.1 Original literary, dramatic, musical or artistic works

In the case of all such works (which the producer will be commissioning for a production) the creator is generally the first owner of the copyright, except when the work is carried out by any employee in the course of his or her employment, in which case (subject to any agreement to the contrary) the employer is the copyright owner.

Freelances

When commissioning freelance staff the producer must enter into a written agreement with the freelancer whereby copyright in the work will be assigned or licensed to the producer. An example of this is provided in standard form PACT (Producers Alliance for Cinema and Television) production agreements.

Employer/employees

Albeit the employer is the owner of the copyright in an employee's work, as there is no precise definition as to what constitutes an employee, it is advisable, if an individual is employed in any creative capacity, for the employer to enter into an agreement with the individual providing for the assignment of his/her copyright in the work to the employer.

Joint ownership

It is frequently the case that there are two creators of the original work. Screenplays, for example, are quite frequently written by two (or more) writers. The copyright is owned by the originators jointly and any person wishing to acquire copyright or other rights in the work must enter into an agreement with each (or all) of the original creators, even if their contribution was a very minor one.

Qualifying person

To qualify for protection under the CDPA it is necessary to be a 'qualifying person', and it is, therefore, customary in agreements for literary and creative works for the original author to have to warrant that they are a qualifying person. A qualifying person is a citizen, subject, resident of or domiciled in any EEA member state. (Countries in the EEA are: Austria, Belgium, Denmark, Finland, France, Germany, Greece, Iceland, Republic of Ireland, Italy, Liechtenstein, Luxembourg, Netherlands, Norway, Portugal, Spain, Sweden, UK.) Alternatively, the author may qualify if he or she is not a citizen, subject, resident of or domiciled in an EEA state but in a state to whom the UK gives reciprocal protection, which includes the USA.

3.2 Films/programmes and sound recordings

For both films/programmes and sound recordings the first owner of the copyright is the person by whom the arrangements necessary for making the film/programme or sound recording are undertaken and this ownership is shared with the principal director of the film/programme or sound recording.

In nearly every case where the production is being wholly or majority funded by a single financier/broadcaster the standard agreement for production will provide that copyright in the completed film/programme (and the associated sound recording) is vested with the financier/broadcaster.

For many years there has been considerable debate in the UK about this treatment of ownership of copyright in film/programmes. Ownership of copyright is generally regarded as an asset, although the commercial valuation of this asset is largely subjective and speculative, since the value depends on the unknown factor of the long-term commercial life of the production. The 'bottom line' of the debate about ownership is that, in order to raise production funding from any source, most, if not all, of the rights of copyright which have any commercial potential almost always have to be assigned or licensed to the production financiers. It is generally only possible for the producer to retain sole ownership of the copyright if the production is being funded from so many different sources that no one financier is in a position to be able to demand ownership.

The provision for the director to be shared owner of the copyright in the film/programme was recently introduced in the EU copyright directives. In practical terms, within the UK and in other countries with a similarly highly commercial film and television industry, a condition of a director's contract will be an assignment of his/her share of the copyright in the production/soundtrack to the parties responsible for financing the film (see *Chapter 9, Paragraph 1.1*).

Broadcasts and cable programmes   3.3

The owner of the copyright in a broadcast is defined in the CDPA as the person making the broadcast if he or she has any responsibility for its contents, or the person providing the programme who makes, with the person transmitting it, the arrangements for its transmission. In the case of a cable service the owner is the person providing the cable service in which the programme is included.

Published editions   3.4

The owner of a typographical arrangement of a published edition is the publisher.

Performers' rights   3.5

The performer has to give consent to the reproduction of his or her performance.

Assignment or licensing of rights of ownership   3.6

As will be seen in subsequent chapters, in practice rights of copyright are assigned or licensed by the first owner to the producer for the purpose of production. Assignment is when the owner (the assignor) of the copyright grants the purchaser (the assignee) all the rights, irrevocably, in perpetuity. Licensing is when the owner (the licensor) grants the purchaser (the licensee) a licence in certain rights of copyright in the material for a fixed term and the licence may be revoked and the rights revert to the original owner in certain specified circumstances.

Unknown ownership   3.7

When the term of copyright was extended in UK law (see *Paragraph 4* below) provision was included in the legislation to provide that where reasonable enquiries as to ownership of copyright material prove fruitless, exploitation of the work may go ahead without constituting an infringement of the revived copyright.

4   TERM OF COPYRIGHT

As a general rule the term of copyright commences on the date of creation of the copyright work. In 1995 UK law was amended to bring the term in line with other European countries. The effect of the resulting extension on existing copyright materials is detailed in *Paragraphs 4.7* and *4.8* below. For copyright works created since 1996, the term is as follows:

4.1   Original literary, dramatic, musical and artistic works

The term of copyright in these works by UK nationals and nationals of the European Economic Area (EEA) states is the lifetime of the author and 70 years thereafter. For a work of joint authorship it is 70 years from the death of the last surviving author.

4.2   Films/programmes

Copyright in a film/programme expires at the end of 70 years from the end of the year in which the last surviving of the following dies:

i   the principal director;

ii   the author of the screenplay/script;

iii   the author of the dialogue; and

iv   the composer of music commissioned specially for the film/programme and used in it.

This does not mean that any of these people (with the exception of the principal director) have any claim on the copyright of the film: it is simply the mechanism which the European Union (EU) arrived at to determine the date of termination of the term of copyright in films/programmes. In practice, it is going to be extraordinarily difficult to establish the date of death of the last survivor and, thus, when the term of copyright expires. But this virtually insoluble problem will be for future generations to deal with.

4.3   Sound recordings

The term of copyright in a sound recording is 50 years from the end of the year of production or later release of the recording. The exception is when the soundtrack is dubbed onto a film/programme when its term of copyright is the same as the film/programme itself.

4.4   Broadcasts and cable programmes

The term of copyright is 50 years from the year of first broadcast or showing.

4.5   Published editions

The term of copyright is 25 years from the year of first publication of the edition.

4.6   Performers' rights

Performers' rights in their performances run for 50 years from the end of the year of the performance or the later release of a recording of the performance.

4.7   Extension of the term of copyright

The provision for copyright to subsist until 70 years after the death of the author only came into effect in the UK from January 1996. Previously, for works by UK nationals first published in the UK, copyright subsisted until 50 years after the death of the author. In the case of films/programmes, the term of copyright was 50 years from the end of the year in which the film/programme was completed or 50 years from the end of the year of its first public release, whichever was the later.

The change to the term of copyright was brought about by the implementation of an EU directive introduced to harmonise the term of copyright of the different member states. Prior to harmonisation, there had been some significant variations in the term of copyright: for example, in Germany it was already 70 years. In certain countries extensions to the term were granted in respect of the period covering both world wars, during which copyright owners had been deprived of the opportunity to fully exploit the rights in their works. The directive provided that if a work was still in copyright anywhere in the EU the copyright was to be revived for the 70-year term throughout the European Economic Area. The practical effect of the rather cumbersome legal wording customarily used in assignments of copyright – that the assignment is "for the full period of copyright and all extensions and renewals thereto" – suddenly became hugely relevant!

The ownership of extended copyrights (i.e. works which had not fallen into the public domain but would shortly do so at the time of the new legislation) went to whoever was the owner of the copyright on the date the legislation came into effect.

For materials in which the copyright had not expired and for which it was then extended for a further 20 years, any agreement which was in existence for the duration of the original copyright period continued throughout the extended copyright period.

Any exploitation of a production containing a copyright work produced under a contract signed before 1 January 1996 and not expiring before the end of the original period of copyright was deemed licensed by the copyright owner for the extended period, this continued exploitation being subject to the negotiation of a royalty payment. (If negotiation failed, a royalty payment would be imposed by the Copyright Tribunal).

Revived copyright terms   4.8

The extension of the term of copyright brought back into copyright a number of works which had been in the public domain, i.e. in which the copyright had expired under the '50 years after death' term. Works of authors who died between 1925 and 1945 (including Beatrix Potter, J.M. Barrie, Thomas Hardy and Rudyard Kipling) enjoyed a 'revived term' of copyright of between two months and 20 years, depending on the date of the author's death.

General rules for treatment of 'revived copyright' materials were agreed as follows:

i   In the case of works which were already in the public domain, in the absence of existing agreements specifying who was to be the owner of the revived copyright, ownership went to the last owner of the copyright;

ii   If a film or programme included or was an adaptation of a revived copyright work and that work was included or adapted at a time when it was in the public domain, the revived copyright is not infringed by exploitation of the film or programme (provided the revived copyright work was included in the film or programme before July 1995 or pursuant to arrangements made before that date); and

iii   Where the owner of a revived copyright work cannot be identified or found by reasonable enquiry, exploitation does not constitute infringement.

RIGHTS OF COPYRIGHT   5
Owner's rights   5.1

Under the general definition of rights of copyright, the owner of the copyright has the exclusive right to copy the work, issue copies of the work to the public, perform, show or play the work in public, broadcast the work or include it in a cable programme service, make an adaptation of the work or do any of the above in relation to an adaptation. Copyright is infringed by a person who, without the agreement of the copyright owner, does, or authorises anyone else to do, any of these things.

In its practical application, copyright is not necessarily treated as a single right, but a bundle of different types of exploitation rights, as described below. Rights of copyright (whether singly or as a bundle) can be assigned or licensed territory by territory.

5.2   Literary works

With substantial literary works such as books or scripts, the right of copyright can be divided into a number of exploitation rights, principally publishing, television, theatrical feature film, live stage, radio, merchandising, translation, even operatic, ice spectacular and animation rights. The copyright owner can separately license or assign each of these individual rights for the various different forms of exploitation.

5.3   Musical works

Exploitation rights for musical works can, for example, be divided between the right to perform the work to a live audience, record the work, either at a live performance or otherwise, the right to perform and record the work for inclusion in a film or programme for theatrical and/or television release and release on video, to make an audio recording either singly or as part of an album, to perform it on radio, or to make a copy, an arrangement or transcription of the music.

5.4   Artistic works

For artistic works the rights include the right to make a copy in three dimensions of a two-dimensional work and a copy in two dimensions of a three-dimensional work; the right to make a copy by making a photograph of the image, for inclusion in a film or television programme. The right to make an animated adaptation of the original work can also be granted.

5.5   Film/programme rights

The separate copyright in a completed production can be split between different forms of exploitation rights, principally theatrical rights, standard (terrestrial) transmission rights, cable and satellite rights (see *Paragraph 5.6* below), video rights, DVD rights, cable and satellite subscription services, video-on-demand, on-line and Internet rights and interactive rights. The merchandising rights in a film, including the right to publish a book of the film if it is not based on an existing published book, can all be granted separately.

5.6   Cable and satellite rights

Cable and satellite rights are the rights to license a film/programme for satellite or cable showing. These rights were the subject of an EU copyright directive which set out rules governing pan-European cable and satellite broadcasting. When granting cable or satellite rights the definition of the country from which the broadcast is made is, in both cases, where "the programme carrying signals are introduced into an uninterrupted chain of communication".

There is, however, an exception for satellite broadcasts which emanate from countries which fail to give adequate protection to copyright holders and performers. In such cases, if the broadcasts are uplinked from a European Economic Area state, or are commissioned by a person established in such a state, the broadcast is treated as being made in that state. This is intended to discourage broadcasters from moving offshore to countries with a lenient copyright regime to avoid copyright liabilities.

The directive further provided that satellite broadcast licences for programmes carried by a pan-European service (e.g. BBC World, Discovery, ARTE) have to be negotiated under the law of the country in which the broadcaster is "established". Fees are expected to reflect the size of the broadcast 'footprint' and the audience reached within it.

The retransmission of an existing satellite or terrestrial broadcast channel service by a cable operator situated outside the country in which the broadcaster is based (e.g. the UK broadcasters' overspill into the Benelux countries which is generally described in UK production contracts as being the Simultaneous European Cable Right) is considered as a separate broadcast and, as such, triggers a new right for remuneration for the producers of the programmes included in the rebroadcast.

However, claims for remuneration may only be made against cable operators by producers and other rights holders through collecting societies (i.e. organisations set up for the purpose of collecting revenues in respect of exploitation of copyright materials and dispersing the revenues to the copyright owners). Broadcasters are exempted from this and can make claims directly to the cable operator, both for the rights in their own programmes and those of third parties which they may have acquired. Producers, therefore, have the choice of obtaining remuneration either by putting the management of their cable retransmission rights in the hands of a collecting society or of granting the rights to a broadcaster in return for suitable payments.

Sound recording rights   5.7

Recording rights in sound recordings can be separately licensed (e.g. for use with a film or television programme, on video and for audio release on record).

Lending and rental rights   5.8

The rental right is the right to rent copies of the work to the public, generally video rental. It has not yet been conclusively determined whether video-on-demand falls within the scope of lending and rental rights or the 'availability right' (see *Paragraph 5.9*). The lending right is the right to make available copies of the work for non-commercial purposes for showings in places which are open to the public. Lending and rental rights have applied to all films and programmes produced after July 1994.

The lending and rental right is a right vested in the authors of any and all copyright work included in a programme (but not sound recordings); in the producers and performers of sound recordings; in the performers in a programme; and in the film producer and director in relation to the first recording of a programme.

In practice, this means that for a programme to be rented or lent as described above, the author/performer must have assigned the rental and lending rights in his or her work/performance in return for certain consideration and the assignment of these rights is now a standard condition of all production contracts.

Authors and performers have an unwaivable right to remuneration from the exercise of the rental or lending rights. The usual practice is to provide that the fee payable under the contract for the work/performance represents equitable pre-payment in respect of lending and rental rights.

There are certain practical problems in relation to the disbursement of lending and rental rights income since few video distributors/outlets keep separate accounting streams for sales and rental revenues. In the first instance, the party that contracts with the author or performer, which in almost every case will be the producer, is primarily liable for payment of revenues from lending or rental rights. So, to the extent that rental and lending rights may not have been pre-purchased, this matter requires careful treatment by producers when licensing video rights.

5.9   Availability right

At the time of writing two new copyright treaties are introducing into UK law a new right in respect of literary and artistic works which will give the owner the exclusive right of authorising the use of the work in "such a way that members of the public may access these works from a place and at a time individually chosen by them". This covers use of copyright material in interactive on-demand services such as those available over the Internet using digital technology. Currently this is being described as the 'availability right' and is likely to become very significant with the rapid development of on-line technology.

5.10   Moral rights (droit moral)

Moral rights were introduced into UK law in 1989, partly to bring it in line with the laws of most other EU countries, which had long had protection for an author's moral rights. In most European countries it is an inalienable right, but in the UK it can be waived.

There are currently two types of moral rights:

Rights of paternity

Rights of paternity give the author or director the right to be identified as the creator of the work or director of the film/programme. This right is not enforceable unless it has been specifically asserted, i.e. put in writing and signed by the author or director. Having thus asserted the right, the author or director has the entitlement to receive a credit (unless the first owner of the copyright is the author's or director's employer).

In practice, the paternity right is generally covered by the standard credit provisions contained within industry agreements. Contracts frequently contain an acknowledgement that the author's and director's rights of paternity will be met by the fulfilment of the credit provisions. If, however, a producer did not want to accord an author or director credit, and the author or director had written to request one, the producer would be legally bound to accord it.

Rights of integrity

This moral right is more complex than the right of paternity. It gives the authors of literary, dramatic, musical or artistic works, and the directors of films/programmes, the right not to have their work subjected to derogatory treatment. Treatment means any addition to, deletion from, alteration to or adaptation of the work. Derogatory treatment involves distortion or mutilation of the work or treatment prejudicial to the honour or reputation of the author or director. As yet there has been no test case as to what constitutes derogatory treatment and in theory it could be any editing or other adaptation of the work which the author did not like.

As will be appreciated, this moral right can be a sensitive issue. The expression moral rights is itself emotive, and the rights it bestows on the creators of copyright material goes to the heart of creative endeavour. However, the exigencies of commercial production and distribution do not accommodate this sensitivity. All UK (as well as Commonwealth and US) production financiers insist that moral rights waivers are secured in each and every production contract involving an assignment or licensing of copyright material. Without this waiver producers run the risk of their overall editorial control being challenged, and programmes cannot be sold unless purchasers are permitted to adapt the material to fit the schedules and other requirements of their markets. Productions can be put at risk or in limbo by an author or director claiming that even very minor cuts or additions to his or her work constitute derogatory treatment, and could take the producer and/or the broadcaster and/or the distributor to court. (There was an interesting case relating to *The Asphalt Jungle*, which had been filmed in black and white and was subsequently colourised. The case was brought on grounds that the colourisation of the film, without authorisation from the director, infringed his moral rights. The director's case was upheld.)

When planning to co-produce with other European partners, producers should bear in mind that in many countries, most notably France, the law does not allow for moral rights to be waived, and critical issues such as approval of fine cut, can be extremely delicate if a continental European writer or director is to be engaged on the production. The audio-visual tradition in most European countries, heavily based on 'auteur' films, is very different to the highly commercial traditions of the English language production market, as are the copyright laws of many other European countries, and it can sometimes be very difficult to reconcile the different perspectives and laws.

Performers' moral rights

New EU copyright directives currently being processed are likely to confer moral rights on performers, both the right to be identified as the performer and the right to object to any distortion, mutilation or other modification prejudicial to the performer's reputation. These moral rights are likely to have particular significance for the digital manipulation of performances. It is likely that, as with other production agreements, it will become standard practice for performers' contracts to contain a moral rights waiver.

REGISTERING COPYRIGHT   6
UK   6.1

As a general rule copyright only exists when a work has been recorded in writing, on tape or any other media. In the UK there is no requirement to register copyright in order to establish ownership, and there is no legal mechanism for doing so. Proof that the work has been recorded in one form or another is sufficient to establish copyright. In order to provide such proof, if it is ever needed, some copyright owners take the precaution of lodging the documents or recordings with a solicitor or a bank and PACT (Producers Alliance for Cinema and Television) offers a registration service for its members.

A producer should not set too much store on the value of lodging copyright material in this way. It does not provide any protection against infringement of copyright, nor serve to prove that if a very similar work is subsequently produced by someone else, that other work is necessarily infringing the copyright. It is merely a mechanism by which it is possible to prove conclusively that that particular copyright work was in existence at a certain date. This proof may be useful if the matter were ever to go to court, but short of that the value of these procedures lies more in the psychological reassurance they give the copyright owner rather than practical assistance.

Although in the UK there is no requirement to place a © copyright notice on copyright material, it is always a wise precaution to do so, particularly as it is required for productions being shown in UCC countries (see *Paragraph 6.3* below). The notice should give the year the work was originated and the name of the rights owner. This

C1

notice serves to warn any potential infringer that the owner of the copyright is conscious of his or her rights of ownership and is, therefore, likely to take measures to protect them. NB: More information about the protection of ideas is given in *Chapter 8*.

6.2 USA

In the USA there used to be a legal requirement that copyright works had to be registered with the Library of Congress in Washington to attract copyright protection. Since the USA joined the Berne Convention, in accordance with that convention there is now no legal requirement for this registration. It is, however, very much custom and practice in the USA for copyright works to be registered since, if copyright material is to be used as evidence in a US court, it must have been registered. This requires the completion of a Form PA which can be obtained from the Register of Copyrights at the Library of Congress. As explained in *Paragraph 7.4* it is also usual to register titles in the USA.

6.3 Universal Copyright Convention (UCC)

To qualify for copyright protection in countries which are members of the UCC, the work has to show a © copyright notice giving the year the work was created and the name of the owner. Since many films and television programmes are distributed internationally, this UCC copyright notice should always be included in the end credits. Similarly, if programme material is being sent outside the UK it should bear a copyright notice.

6.4 Trade mark registration

Trade mark registration is not a form of registration of copyright material as such. It is, however, a form of protection for the owner of an established trade name and/or logo or image against others using the same or very similar name, logo or image. By obtaining trade mark registration of the name/logo it is possible to prevent anyone else from using the same or very similar name and/or logo in that same trading category. Thus, it is increasingly being used by those who have created television formats which do not attract protection under copyright law.

Trade marks are registered through a patents agent and there are many different categories ranging from those covering audio-visual productions to others for food stuffs, stationery, clothing and so forth. The list is very long. It is only possible to register a trade mark when you are demonstrably trading in that category. For example, you would not be able to register a programme name in a food category unless you could demonstrate that you were actually marketing a food bearing that name/logo. Registration is done territory by territory, with a fee paid for each registration in each territory and in each category. Thus, to obtain worldwide protection is costly. It takes approximately six to nine months to obtain registration, since the application has to be checked to ensure that there are no clashes with other registered marks, but some provisional protection is afforded while the application is being processed.

7 MATERIAL NOT PROTECTED BY COPYRIGHT

7.1 Public domain material

The term 'public domain' is commonly used to describe literary or other copyright materials which are not protected by the copyright laws. The reason is either because they do not qualify for copyright protection, or the term of copyright in the material has expired, or because the material is of a factual nature relating to actual events and real people and situations and as such not protected by copyright. This is not to say that, for example, a newspaper article about a factual event does not of itself attract copyright (it does), but the happenings it describes are not protected by copyright.

Fair dealing   7.2

In certain circumstances copyright material can be used without the permission of the copyright owner. For production of films/programmes, these circumstances are as follows:

i   Copyright material can be used for criticism or review of the material or of another work (or performance of a work) provided that this usage is accompanied by a sufficient acknowledgement; and/or

ii   Copyright material (excluding still photographs) can be used for the purpose of reporting on current events. At the time of writing no acknowledgement is required in connection with the reporting of current events by means of a sound recording, film, broadcast or cable programme, although this may be changed under a forthcoming copyright directive.

'Fair' is the operative word in relation to such usage. The usage must be for genuine criticism or review or for reporting of real current events, and the amount of material used should not constitute a disproportionate amount of the programme.

Incidental inclusion   7.3

The Copyright, Designs and Patents Act 1988 contains provisions whereby the 'incidental inclusion' of artistic works (including music) within a programme does not constitute infringement of copyright. Except in the case of the filming of live events, where the camera shot or sound microphone may inadvertently record an 'artistic work', it would be unwise for producers to rely on this provision since in almost every case the incidental inclusion of copyright material in a recorded programme can be avoided.

Titles/domain names   7.4

There is no copyright in a title, whether it be the title of a book, film or anything else. However, there can be the risk that if a very well-known title is used on another film or programme it could be 'passing off' (see *Paragraph 7.6* below). In the USA it is considered essential to do a title search for any feature film to ensure that the title is not one used previously. Titles can be checked with the Motion Picture Association of America (MPAA) and registered with the MPAA Title Registration Bureau.

As explained in *Paragraph 6.4*, it is possible to get a measure of protection for a programme title by obtaining trade mark registration for the title in the category for audio-visual works, and in other categories if the programme is being merchandised.

Domain names for websites and e-mail addresses can be registered with Internet service providers (see *Chapter 11*).

Ideas and formats   7.5

Ideas are not protected under copyright law since they are not considered to meet the requirement of being an original work requiring skill, labour and effort. Similarly, formats are not protected by copyright since it is considered that a format is too nebulous to be described as a dramatic work and too imprecise to be protected by literary copyright. Obviously programmes are based on ideas and formats which are considered to be of value within the film and television industry and methods of contracting for them are dealt with in *Chapter 7*.

7.6 Passing off

'Passing off' is a legal remedy which can sometimes be used to take action against the unauthorised use for commercial gain of a title or other material not protected by copyright law. If, for example, a game show were to be mounted with a very similar title and format to an existing and well-known game show to the extent that 'the man in the street' thought it was the same show, then the originators of the original show could bring an action in passing off.

C2

CONTRACTS Chapter 2

During the course of setting up production the producer will have to enter into dozens, sometimes hundreds, of contracts. These may include major contracts for underlying rights in copyright works such as books and screenplays; contracts with broadcasters/ financiers/co-producers; contracts with directors, designers, cast, composers; routine standard form contracts for technical services, facilities, goods, locations; contracts with distributors for the exploitation of the completed production. The list can seem endless.

(Producers in Scotland should be aware that Scottish contract law is different in some respects to English contract law. It is advisable to contract under Scottish law for productions being filmed in Scotland, employing Scottish cast and crew.)

This chapter sets out to explain what constitutes a legally binding contract and what does not.

KEY TOPICS & ISSUES

C2

1 WHAT CONSTITUTES A CONTRACT?

Firstly, the word 'contract' and the word 'agreement' mean exactly the same thing and can be used interchangeably: 'contract' just sounds more formal.

Basically a contract is a promise, or a set of promises, between two or more parties which the law will enforce. In general, the law will enforce promises where:

i   the parties intend their agreement to be legally binding or act in such a way as to give that impression;

ii   there is agreement between the parties, which means that the offer of one party has been accepted by the other; and

iii there is what lawyers call 'consideration' for the contract (consideration does not apply in Scottish law).

As a general rule a contract does not have to be in writing: in law an oral agreement is just as binding as a written agreement. Sam Goldwyn had a point, however, when he said that "an oral agreement ain't worth the paper it's written on" since there is obviously far less scope for argument about what (if anything) has been agreed if it is in print. (A small number of contracts are required by statute to be in writing: most importantly for producers are assignments of copyright, which must be made in writing.)

2 INTENDING THE CONTRACT TO BE LEGALLY BINDING

Normally it will be obvious from the discussion as to whether or not the parties intend the agreement to be legally binding. If, for example, A says to B "I'll pay you £25,000 to write a script for my film" and B replies "Fine, I'll start today", there is a concluded contract and it is no good either A or B later saying "I didn't really mean it". When negotiations are being conducted in writing, take the precaution of putting 'subject to contract' at the top of each letter.

If one or both of the parties does not intend the agreement to be binding until a written contract incorporating all the terms and conditions has been signed, this must be stated clearly at the time the initial offer is made or accepted. If A adds "I'll get my lawyer to send you a contract" or B "I'll ask my agent to negotiate the deal", that will do the trick.

3 A CONCLUDED AGREEMENT

For there to be a concluded agreement, there must be an offer from A and an acceptance of that offer from B.

3.1 Making an offer

An offer is when A states that he is willing to enter into a binding contract with B, to whom the offer is made.

It is very important to make the intention clear. A can be making an offer to contract or be merely inviting offers from B. For example, if A says "I will pay you £10,000 for the book rights" and B says "Done" that is acceptance of the offer, and agreement. But if A merely says "How much will the book rights cost me?" and B says "£10,000" that does not constitute an offer and there is no agreement: B cannot force the agreement on A. If A says "If I paid you £10,000 would you give me the book rights?" that is not an offer, but an enquiry, and acceptance by B of that figure would not constitute an agreement.

An offer can be expressed as being open for a fixed time or this can be obvious from the offer itself. (For example, an offer that "I will pay you £2,000 to direct the recording of a live concert on Saturday" cannot remain open after the event.) An offer can also be made subject to a condition. (For example, "if the BBC commits to production I will pay you £2,000 to direct it".)

Otherwise an offer will remain open until:

i   the person making the offer withdraws it and notifies the person to whom it was made;

ii   the person to whom the offer was made rejects it; or

iii (generally) either party dies or becomes insane.

Acceptance of an offer   3.2

An offer can be accepted by words or by action. Silence or inaction cannot constitute acceptance even if the person making the offer says that it will: for example, "If I don't hear from you I shall take it that you have accepted these terms" has no legal validity.

Words

The person making the offer can stipulate the way in which it must be accepted, but unless he or she does so, any communication of acceptance will do. A written offer can be accepted orally and vice versa.

Action

If action by the person to whom the offer is made clearly shows an intention to accept the offer, verbal communication of acceptance may be unnecessary. For example, if A writes to B "I will pay you £10,000 for the rights to your script: if this is acceptable please send the script to me" and B simply puts the script in the post without any covering letter or other communication, there is a concluded contract between them.

Acceptance is the final and unqualified agreement to the terms of the offer. An 'acceptance' which introduces new terms or tries to change the terms of the offer is not an acceptance at all. It is a 'cross-offer'. A cross-offer is a rejection of the offer coupled with the making of a new offer. For example, if B says "I will accept the offer of £2,000 provided I also get 10% of profits from the production", that is not acceptance, but a cross-offer and it is only if A accepts the new offer in full that there is an agreement.

CONSIDERATION (PAYMENT) IN RESPECT OF A CONTRACT   4

For a contract to be enforceable, there must be 'consideration'. Consideration means that both parties agree to do something. Lawyers spend a great deal of time arguing what might or might not constitute consideration. 'Agreement to do something' can take many forms, but basically A's undertaking to pay B a certain sum of money in return for B's work on a production means that both parties have agreed to do something. That is the consideration and the contract is, therefore, enforceable.

Consideration need not involve payment, and if it does the value of the payment has no relevance: a peppercorn charge is as valid as a commercial rate. If consideration takes the form of rendering services or granting rights these too may be minimal. Consideration can be negative: agreement to refrain from doing something in return for something can be consideration. It does not necessarily have to be agreement to do something to the direct benefit of the other party.

When negotiating terms producers should always firmly bear in mind the contractual requirement that each side must be agreeing to do something and ensure that that 'something' is clearly expressed in the contract as being the consideration: for example,

"In consideration of the services you render/the rights you grant/the facilities you supply, I will pay you/will engage you/will accord you credit".

5 VARIATIONS TO A CONTRACT

There is no reason why the terms of a contract cannot be changed, providing both parties agree the variation, and the revised terms contain consideration. The usual procedure is to draw up a variation agreement which refers to the original agreement and sets out the change which has been agreed.

6 TERMINATION OF CONTRACTS

Contracts can be set aside or declared invalid if:

i there is a genuine mistake in it;

ii it covers illegal activities; or

iii it was entered into under economic duress.

But a producer would need to seek expert legal advice in all of these cases.

7 WITNESSING SIGNATURES

There is no requirement under UK law that signatures to contracts should be witnessed – but it might be useful if there were any likelihood that the signatory might later try and claim that he or she did not sign it. (Deeds are a form of contract used for certain specific purposes, usually when there is no obvious consideration. Deeds require signatures to be witnessed.)

8 REVIEWING CONTRACTS

Producers will frequently be in a position of having to check contracts which have been drafted by their own lawyers or which have been issued by the other party. Obviously the contracts need to be read carefully and checked for factual accuracy. Three key pieces of advice when checking contracts are as follows:

8.1 Definitions

One of the clauses which is most frequently skipped over since it tends to look like legal boilerplating is the clause containing the Definitions, which generally appears as Clause 1. Defined terms are those in the contract which start with a capital letter. It is not possible to exaggerate how important it is to check the precise wording of the definition because this gives the term its meaning when the contract is being applied. For example 'Primary Rights' might be defined as 'UK terrestrial television rights', or it might be defined as 'worldwide television rights of all descriptions'. **Never make assumptions about how a term is being defined. Always check.**

8.2 Future approvals and agreements

Never accept an agreement where the wording provides that something has to be mutually approved or mutually agreed by the parties at a future date without providing a mechanism for the approval and agreement procedure and a clear course of action if the parties do not mutually approve and/or do not mutually agree. In practice, contracts are almost never referred to when things go right, only when things go wrong. If they are going wrong, to expect to be able to reach mutual approval/agreement on anything is usually unrealistic.

Understanding contracts 8.3

Do not accept a contract when, after careful checking, you cannot understand what the wording is saying. Do not put off seeking clarification for fear of appearing ill-informed or stupid. Contracts must clearly and unequivocally state what the arrangements are and what procedures are to be followed. If the wording is not clear to the producer, the chances are that, if it were ever to go to court, it won't be clear to the judge either. There is a saying by a Danish philosopher that if you don't understand something, and still don't understand it after reasonable enquiry, it is because it is either wrong or false. The truth of this saying has often been borne out by the consequences of obscure wording in contracts.

SETTING UP A PRODUCTION COMPANY Chapter 3

It is a requirement of all the UK broadcasters, when commissioning an independent production, that the production company is set up as a limited company. In fact this is to the advantage of the producer since the producer's personal liabilities are then limited if something goes drastically wrong with production. In the case of feature films, and sometimes major television productions, it is usual practice to set up a separate limited company just for that production, often referred to as a 'special purpose vehicle'.

Production companies are frequently set up by two or more producers working together, each with individual projects. It is important in these circumstances to have a written agreement to address such issues as how each producer's projects are to be dealt with, both in respect of the financial return to the company and to the individuals themselves. It is also important that the agreement sets out arrangements for the treatment of projects if the producers decide to disband the company.

KEY TOPICS & ISSUES

1 WHAT IS A COMPANY?

1.1 Different types of company

There are four types of company:

i   a private company limited by shares, where the members' liability is limited to the value of the shares they own;

ii   a private company limited by guarantee, where members' liability is limited to the amount they have agreed to contribute to the company's assets if it is wound up;

iii   a private unlimited company, where there is no limit to the members' liability; and

iv   a public limited company (plc), where the company's shares may be offered for sale to the general public and members' liability is limited to the value of the shares held by them.

In the vast majority of cases, a production company will be the first type of company, where liability is limited to the share value, which is generally, although not necessarily, £100. It is the arrangements for this type of company which are addressed here.

1.2 Limited liability company

A limited company is a separate legal entity, in effect a separate person. All contracts for production are entered into in the name of the limited company, and it is, therefore, the company which is liable for all contractual obligations, undertakings and warranties. If the company is in breach of any of its obligations, it is the company which is liable, not the 'company's officers' (i.e. the director(s) and secretary) or shareholders. The company's officers may be liable only if they have acted fraudulently or negligently. Similarly, if the company is unable to meet payment obligations it can be wound up by its creditors and its assets sold off to pay the debts, but the company's directors will not be personally liable, unless they have acted unlawfully or wrongfully (or have specifically agreed to accept liability, for example, by giving personal guarantees). Thus, in the case of a production company, the directors' personal property is not at risk if a production goes down and the company is unable to honour the terms of the various contracts for production.

1.3 Who can form a limited company

A limited company can be formed by one or more persons (in law 'person' can mean either an individual or a company). There must also be a company secretary. The same person can be both a director and company secretary, provided there is another director. A sole director cannot also be the company secretary. No formal qualifications are required in order to be secretary of a limited company.

1.4 Who can be a company director

There are no restrictions on who can be a company director save that they cannot be an undischarged bankrupt or have been disqualified by a court from holding a directorship. In the case of people who are not of British nationality it is advisable to check with the Home Office Immigration and Nationality Department to ascertain entitlement to be a director of a British-registered company.

1.5 How to set up a limited company

An accountant or solicitor is often engaged to advise and assist in setting up a limited company, but it is not absolutely essential. An 'off-the-shelf' company (that is one which has already been incorporated) can be acquired through company formation agents whose names and addresses can be found in the Yellow Pages. Alternatively, an individual can incorporate a company by obtaining the necessary forms from Companies House and sending them to the Registrar of Companies accompanied by a Memorandum of Association and Articles of Association. Specimen Memoranda and Articles of Association can be obtained from legal stationers, or from accountants, solicitors and company formation agents. The Memorandum of Association sets out the company's name, the address of the registered office and what the company will do. These Memoranda of Association tend to be very widely drafted to cover all manner of activities, but do check the wording to ensure that it specifically covers what it is intended the company's main activities will be. The Articles of Association set out rules for running the company's internal affairs. The Companies House standard registration fee is currently £20 and there is a premium service whereby the company can be incorporated on the same day as the documents are received for a cost of £80.

Company name 1.6

The proposed company name needs to be checked with Companies House since a company cannot be registered in the same name as another company. Use of certain words is restricted and names likely to cause offence are not allowed. It is also important to ascertain whether the proposed name is similar to any other name already on the register since if it is too like another name, an objection can be made within the 12 months following incorporation and the company may be directed to change the name.

Registered address 1.7

Every company must have a registered address. It does not have to be the address of an accountant or solicitor, but it must be an effective address, recognised by the Post Office, and one from which correspondence is regularly collected, not least because this is the address to which all legal documents will be served.

Company identification 1.8

The company name should be displayed on the outside of its premises, even if the premises are the director's home. The company's name must be shown on all its business letters and other documentation such as bills, orders and so forth. Letters must also show the company's place of registration and registration number.

The names of company directors do not have to be included on its business letters, but if a company chooses to do so it must state the names of all its directors. It cannot be selective about which names it shows.

Company accounting 1.9

The real drag of having a limited company, particularly one that may only be used occasionally for certain projects, is that annual accounts must be filed at Companies House. Every company has an accounting reference date which, in the first instance, is 12 months from the date of incorporation of the company. (It can thereafter be changed). The first set of accounts must be submitted no later than ten months from the first accounting reference date. Thereafter they must be submitted annually. There are automatic financial penalties of between £100 and £1,000 for late submission of accounts. Companies House also has the right to strike the company off the register and impose penalties on the directors if accounts are not filed.

(More detailed information on setting up a company can be obtained from the Companies House website on www.companies-house.gov.uk)

2   RESPONSIBILITIES OF DIRECTORS

It is very easy to set up a company and almost anyone is entitled to do it. The responsibilities of a company director are, however, similar to those of a trustee and not to be taken at all lightly since, as explained above, whilst a limited company does provide a means of safeguarding an individual's personal property, this protection may not be afforded to a director if he or she has been fraudulent or negligent, or could be deemed not to have shown the "duty of care, diligence and skill owed to the Company".

Directors are under an obligation to act in what they consider to be the company's best interests and those of its creditors and shareholders and not their own. If they are majority shareholders, they must not manage the company to the detriment of minority shareholders. A conflict should not be permitted to arise between a director's personal interests and those of the company, and directors must take proper care of and not appropriate the company's property. As a general rule companies are prohibited from making loans and guarantees available to directors in excess of £5,000.

Directors have responsibility for ensuring the proper management of the company: for attending board meetings; preparing profit and loss accounts in respect of each financial year and ensuring they are properly signed and filed; and for maintaining a record of the directors and their interests.

A director is not necessarily an employee of the company, although any fees paid by the company in respect of a director's services are liable to Schedule E income tax and National Insurance contributions. If a director is an employee then this should be subject to a separate employment contract between the director and the company.

3   AGREEMENTS BETWEEN DIRECTORS/SHAREHOLDERS

3.1   Special purpose vehicle

If a company is being set up as a 'special purpose vehicle' for a single production the arrangements agreed for the production in terms of individuals' roles, responsibilities and entitlements from the production will largely govern the way in which the company is run. Similarly, if the company has been set up for a co-production, the co-production agreement between the parties will effectively dictate the company arrangements.

3.2   General purpose production company

This type of company is one which is being set up to handle all productions brought in by the producers who set up the company. The aim is to obtain sufficient commissions and, therefore, revenues to be able to establish and maintain a company with the infrastructure to support major commissions on an ongoing basis by, for example, engaging permanent development, production management, accountancy and business affairs staff. It is very important that a written agreement is drawn up at the outset, not least since one of the difficulties for a production company is that projects can be in development for many years, during which time circumstances may change out of all recognition. In addition to addressing how the company is going to function day to day and the directors' entitlements to benefits from the various productions, the agreement must also deal with such issues as whether the directors can take on freelance work if the company hits a lean patch, and where the ownership of copyright in individual projects will vest if the company is disbanded. Always remember that agreements are not needed when things go right, but are vital when things go wrong and relationships may have become so soured that it is virtually impossible to reach a mutually satisfactory agreement on anything.

Financial

As a general rule, the more simple and straightforward the agreement, the more likely arrangements will work satisfactorily. Agreements with elaborate formulas for relative levels of shares, revenues and profits, depending on who has done what in relation to a particular production, rarely work in practice. It can also be a delicate matter unstitching them when it seems that the formula is inappropriate. The most equitable arrangement is for the directors (producers) to throw in their lot with the company and have an agreement which determines that, from all revenues from all sources received by the company, each producer will receive the same level of salary, expenses and other entitlements and any remaining net profits are shared equally.

This 'swings and roundabouts' approach can, though, come under some pressure if one director is far more effective then the other(s) in bringing in commissions. It is, therefore, sometimes agreed that each director will have an automatic entitlement to a bonus, being a share of the production fee, from each commission which they bring in. This type of arrangement must be subject to the approval of all the shareholders and, given the responsibilities placed on company directors, the bonus should be paid only when the company has sufficient funds to pay it, after meeting its commitments to salaries, overheads and so forth.

In this connection it may be possible to provide that the bonus can be deferred and recouped from future production fees, when sufficient funds are forthcoming.

It is sensible to address what to do in the event that the company does not have the financial resources to pay the salaries. In these circumstances each director may be entitled to take on freelance work, subject to an agreement to share equally the ongoing company overhead costs. The question then arises as to whether, when working as a freelance, the director is on a 'loan out' agreement from the company with fees for freelance work being paid back through the company and with the company being responsible for tax and National Insurance, or whether the freelance work is undertaken on a self-employed basis. As a general rule, if the directors' intention is to create an established production company, freelance work should be undertaken through the auspices of the company (and even if it is an individual freelance engagement it may be possible to obtain a 'produced in association with XXX company' credit).

Development work

The ability to develop projects is essential to the survival of a production company. The board should establish a fund, topped up as projects move into production, to meet direct costs associated with development work such as the acquisition of rights in such necessary development materials as options, treatments, special research and so forth. The fairest formula would be to provide that, annually, each of the directors has equal entitlement to the fund for their individual projects, but decisions as to which projects the company is funding should be taken, and recorded, at board meetings.

Directors' exclusivity

If the directors are serious about wanting to establish a viable production company, they should be prepared to accept an arrangement whereby the company is exclusively entitled to their services and the projects they propose for production. If the other directors do not agree that a particular project is one for the company it may be that the director should be allowed to take unpaid leave of absence to develop it on a freelance basis, but this does rather conflict with the principle that the interests of the company should be paramount.

Ownership of copyright on termination

If the directors are employees of the company (or are deemed to be employees since there is no precise legal definition of an employee), the company, as the employer, owns the copyright in the products of their services. It is, therefore, necessary for the agreement to address what happens to the copyright in the event that the company is disbanded or one of the directors wishes to leave the company. It is essential that this is dealt with formally since, as is explained in *Chapter 1*, assignment of copyright is one of the very few contracts which, under UK law, has to be in writing, and signed, to be legally binding. There must, therefore, be no room for argument which could result in companies or individuals blocking any further exploitation of a project by withholding signature on assignment of copyright. In the first instance it should be recorded in the board minutes which director has originated which project (albeit the other director(s) may have had input).

Where the company is being disbanded, the director who initiated the project can be entitled to acquire the company's copyright in the project and proceed to production without further obligation. In the case of a director leaving the company, it would be reasonable for them to be entitled to acquire copyright in the projects they have developed. This should be subject to an obligation, in the event that a project proceeds to production, to repay the company the direct costs of the development work and also a share of the production fee and of net profits from sales of the production, in recognition of the company's contribution to the indirect costs of development, including the director's salary whilst he or she was working on it. It may also be appropriate for the company to receive a 'developed in association with A.N. Other Company' credit on any production.

OPTION AGREEMENTS   Chapter 4

To hold an option is to have an agreement with the owner of a copyright work whereby, in return for a payment (or other 'consideration'), the owner grants the option holder, for a limited period, the exclusive opportunity to acquire certain rights in the work for a fixed price.

Options benefit the producer and the owner. It is essential for producers to acquire, at the beginning of development work, a hold on rights in a copyright work, which might form the basis, or an integral part, of a production. However, at this early stage, the producer would be unwise to go to the expense of buying the rights outright, since, as development work progresses, it may become clear that the project is unlikely to be commissioned. But the producer needs to be in a position whereby, if there is interest in the project, his or her ownership of it is protected by virtue of the producer's exclusive entitlement to acquire the underlying rights. The beauty of an option agreement is that it enables the producer to obtain this exclusive entitlement at a relatively low price.

From the owner's point of view, the rights are not being sold off for years to a producer who may prove unable to do anything with them. If the producer does not exercise the option it lapses and the owner is able to sell or option the rights elsewhere.

There can, of course, be option agreements other than those which deal with rights of copyright, for example, an exclusive option to cover a live event, such as a pop concert or exhibition. Similarly a producer may obtain an exclusive option on a presenter's services or on key cast for a sequel production. These are dealt with in *Chapter 9*.

KEY TOPICS & ISSUES

1   STRUCTURE OF AN OPTION AGREEMENT

1.1   Oral/written agreements

Option agreements must always be confirmed in writing. Even if an oral agreement has been reached with a long-standing friend or colleague that the producer can seek interest in a programme based on their work, the producer must always confirm this in writing, specifying the contractual arrangements which will apply if a financier commits to production and rights are acquired by the producer in order to produce the programme. However bureaucratic it may appear to insist on this procedure with a person with whom the producer may have a long and trusting relationship, it is a depressing reflection on human nature that if this procedure is not followed, time and again, when commitments to production are being negotiated, irreconcilable divisions of opinion emerge between the parties as to the terms of their agreement.

1.2   Rights agreements

In the case of option agreements for major copyright works, such as books, which may be intended for adaptation as a feature film or major television drama, it is best practice for the option agreement to have attached to it, as an appendix, the agreed form of rights agreement which will be entered into if and when the option is exercised. When the option agreement is attached to the form of rights agreement, it is possible to keep the option agreement itself quite short, since the key clauses in the option agreement relating to purchase price, rights and warranties can refer to the wording in the rights agreement.

Long-form rights agreements are very heavy duty and thus time-consuming and expensive to negotiate. It is particularly onerous to have to do so at an early stage of development. Producers will, therefore, often negotiate an option agreement which addresses in some detail the key terms which will apply if and when the option is exercised and contains the warranties which are needed from the owner. The option agreement goes on to provide that, in the event that the producer elects to exercise the option, the parties undertake to negotiate in good faith the provisions of the long-form agreement which shall include the provisions for the grant of rights contained within the option agreement (unless variations are mutually agreed). Until such further agreement is entered into, the terms of the option agreement are binding on the parties.

It may happen that when a financier comes on board during the development phase they will require the form of the eventual rights agreement to be settled as a condition of development finance. Provided the option agreement has addressed the key terms this should not present a problem.

2   ESSENTIAL TERMS FOR AN OPTION AGREEMENT

Whether or not the option agreement has attached to it a long-form agreement, the following provisions must be provided for within it if it is to be effective. Failure to include any one of these points can render an option agreement valueless.

2.1   Description of the work

To avoid any future arguments as to exactly what work has been optioned, the agreement should contain a preamble describing the work. In the case of a book this could read "a novel by A.N. Other published by X.Y. Publisher". In the case of a less well documented copyright work, such as a treatment, format or even screenplay it would be advisable to briefly describe it in the body of the agreement and attach it as an appendix: for example, "an original format for a television game show devised by A.N. Other attached hereto as Appendix A".

Term 2.2

Ideally, it should not be necessary to exercise the option and purchase the rights until commencement of production. Given the length of time it can take to carry out initial work on a project, elicit interest in it from financiers, carry out further development work and secure commitments to production, unless the subject is highly topical and the programme, therefore, needs to happen quickly, the producer will generally require a total option period for a minimum of two years. For major television dramas three or four years would be advisable; for feature films, options of five years or even longer would not be excessive.

While two years is the minimum option period, rights owners are likely to expect a considerable sum if their rights are going to be tied up for that length of time and it may be that after a few months the producer will have decided not to proceed further with the project. It is, therefore, usual for options to be staged so that the initial option period runs for 12 months, with the producer having the right to extend the option for further, consecutive periods of 12 months each, with each extension attracting a further option payment for the rights owner.

It is quite common for rights owners (or their agents) to be prepared to grant extensions to options only if it can be demonstrated that progress is being made towards setting up production. Unless the producer is paying a very large sum of money for the option, this is not an unreasonable line to take, particularly for a third or subsequent option period. The producer must, however, take care to ensure that the required 'demonstration of progress' is pinned to a specific action having taken place, so that there can be no subsequent argument as to whether progress has or has not been made. For example, if the rights being optioned are in a book, the commission of a screenplay based on it is a clear demonstration of progress; proof of third-party commitment to fund development can be another. If these specific demonstrations of progress can be met, the producer's right to extend the option must be irrevocable.

If the producer wants to take up an extension to the option, this must be confirmed in writing by the producer prior to the end of the existing option period. It is usual for the extension payment to be made at the same time.

Production companies must keep a diary note of option dates since, if the option has lapsed even 24 hours before the producer notifies the rights owner that he or she wants to extend it, the rights owner is entitled to require a complete renegotiation of the terms before agreeing an extension, or indeed not agreeing to extend at all.

Payments 2.3

An option agreement is a contract and, therefore, there must be consideration for it to be legally binding. Normally consideration is a payment, but a promise to do something in return for being granted an option on the rights is also consideration.

Option payments are generally equivalent to 10% of the purchase price to be paid for the rights. So, if the purchase price for the rights is to be £10,000, the payment for the first 12-month option will be £1,000. Extensions to the option usually attract further payments which may be proportionately slightly higher than the payment for the first option period.

It is customary for the purchase price for the rights to be offset by at least the first option payment and sometimes subsequent extension payments as well. The question of whether the option payment is or is not offset can be used as a negotiating tool in determining the level of option payment and/or purchase price. For example, it may be possible to settle for a lower option payment on the basis that it will not be offset against the purchase price.

Sometimes it is possible to obtain agreement for a 'peppercorn' payment for a first option on the basis that if, during the first option period, the producer is able to raise third-party development finance, the subsequent option payments may be higher than would customarily be the case.

Other types of consideration which are occasionally agreed are that the option is granted on the basis that the rights owner will, say, have a role on an eventual production or some financial interest in it. Great care needs to be taken with this type of provision, however celebrated the rights owner may be. The producer must always ensure that he or she is in a position to be able to respond to a financier's requirements for commitment to production. If, for example, an option has been granted on the basis that the rights owner will be engaged as director or scriptwriter, or be cast in a key part, this can kill or seriously endanger the project if this is not acceptable to the production financier. As a precaution against this, the option agreement must state that the engagement is subject to the financier's approval and go on to provide for a clear fallback position, say a profit share or consultancy fee on the production, if the financier's approval is not forthcoming. There must be no possibility that, if the production financier will not agree the engagement, the rights can revert to the owner since all the producer's work in developing the project and raising finance will then have come to nought.

Care should also be taken in agreeing a financial interest in the eventual production in return for an option. If the financial interest takes the form of a profit share, it must be defined as a share of the 'producer's net profits' from the production, not of 100% of net profits, since financiers will almost never agree to this and will insist, if this has been agreed, that the entitlement is met entirely out of the producer's own share. It can also be risky to agree a share of the production fee. Production fees are not usual on feature film budgets. They are in television budgets but in the first instance the producer may be required to use the production fee to meet an overspend on the production. If a share of the production fee is offered it must, therefore, be defined as being a share of the production fee actually received by the producer, not of the production fee provided for in the budget, otherwise the producer may be seriously out of pocket.

2.4   Rights

There is no point in having an option agreement if it does not specify what rights are being optioned. For books, screenplays, stage plays and other major copyright works being used as the basis for feature films, this should be exclusive worldwide film and television rights; for television drama it should be exclusive worldwide television rights. In both cases (unless the option agreement has attached to it the long-form rights agreement) it should be defined in reasonable detail. It is also important to specify whether the rights are being assigned, when the rights are sold irrevocably for the full period of copyright, or licensed, when the producer is granted an exclusive licence for a fixed period. For a more details see *Chapter 5* and *Chapter 6*.

In the case of treatments, formats and other less developed works the position is rather different. These are much less substantial works, in which copyright may or may not subsist. They will necessarily be subject to extensive further development by the producer if they are to go into production and it is really that work which is undertaken by the producer which creates the copyright in the material. In these circumstances the option agreement should provide that the rights (to the extent that they exist) will be assigned to the producer for the full period of copyright and all extensions and renewals (see *Chapter 7, Paragraphs 2.2* and *3.2*).

Purchase price for the rights   2.5

The option agreement should specify the price which is to be paid for the rights if and when the option is exercised, otherwise the owner can hold the producer to ransom at that stage. For books and other major copyright works, there is a very rough rule of thumb that the price for rights should be equivalent to 2% of budget. Obviously this is not a rigid formula: a major best-selling novel would attract much more; an obscure book with a limited term of copyright remaining, much less. However, a percentage-of-budget formula can be a useful means of establishing a fair method for determining the eventual purchase price at a stage when it is very hard to predict what the value of the production may be. For a more detailed explanation of this provision see *Chapter 5, Paragraph 5*.

For treatments and formats it would be more usual to agree a fixed fee or a royalty. Suggestions are contained in *Chapter 7, Paragraphs 2.2* and *3.2*.

If rights are being granted in return for a role on the production, the fee for that role should be expressed as being subject to financiers' approval and the agreed budget and negotiated in accordance with rates payable under the appropriate talent union agreement (if applicable) or in line with fees customarily paid within the film or television industry for such services.

Owners' warranties   2.6

It is very important that option agreements contain warranties from the owner that they own the rights which are being optioned and there are no restrictions preventing them from granting the option and, if the option is exercised, the rights to the producer. The requirement for the owner to sign off on a warranty and indemnity clause can sometimes have a galvanising effect in bringing to mind inconvenient details which the owner may have preferred to forget, such as the fact that they collaborated with someone else when creating the copyright work; or that it was originally commissioned by another producer; or that the rights are already the subject of an earlier agreement. It is very important that these things come out and are resolved (or not) before the rights are optioned. If it is left to the time when rights are being purchased, after all the development work has been done, it may prove impossible to satisfactorily resolve any imperfections in the chain of title.

Essential warranty clauses are:

i   if the owner is the original creator, that the work is original to him or her and does not infringe the rights of any third party. If the owner is not the creator, that he or she is the sole and exclusive owner of the rights. In both cases there is a warranty that the work does not contain material which is libellous or defamatory;

ii there are no agreements in respect of the rights which could derogate from the rights granted to the producer;

iii no previous film or television productions have been produced based on the work; and

iv a waiver of moral rights, or, where the owner is not the creator, a warranty that moral rights have been waived.

These are the minimum warranties required for an option agreement, but they will serve to flush out any major impediments. The warranties required for substantial copyright works for major productions may run to several pages of fine print.

2.7 Right of the producer to adapt the work

Notwithstanding the inclusion of a moral rights waiver under the warranties, it is essential that the option agreement gives the producer the right to adapt, edit, translate and otherwise change the work as required for the purposes of developing the work and proceeding to production based on it.

This clause must be included in the option agreement, since it can bring to light an owner's intention to make the grant of rights conditional on the retention of control as to how the work is adapted for production. In all normal circumstances this type of condition must be a deal breaker for a producer and it must be resolved before things go any further. In the annals of film history it is probably possible to count on one hand the number of authors whose work has been so sought after that financiers have agreed to them retaining rights of approval or other creative controls. There are a number of famous books which have never been adapted for production simply because the owners of the copyright (in some cases, the executors for the deceased author's estate, who can be much more difficult to deal with than a living author) have sought to make the grant of rights conditional on their having approval of screenplay and/or director and/or casting or budget. The bottom line is that all production financiers, be they film financiers or broadcasters, will require final creative control of all aspects of production and will not relinquish approval to someone who may or may not have the first idea what would work on screen. A compromise which is often accepted is for the owner to be consulted about these matters, but with the financiers' decision being final.

In the case of an option agreement for an existing screenplay, be sure to make provision to bring in other writer(s) (see *Chapter 6, Paragraph 2.3*).

Obviously, option agreements can contain many more provisions than those listed above, but these are the key terms which need to be negotiated and provided for within an option agreement to render it viable.

3 AGENTS' AND PUBLISHERS' OPTION AGREEMENTS

Producers should be wary of contracting for options for film and television rights on agreements issued by writers' agents or by publishers. Understandably, these tend to be drafted to afford maximum protection and benefit to the writer and the provisions are frequently at odds with the contractual arrangements the producer will require to be able to mount production. Badly drafted option agreements can cause major difficulties for a producer and it is advisable to seek advice on an option agreement from a lawyer with experience of the contractual arrangements required for film and television production.

There is a growing trend for agents to propose a form of agreement which is not an option agreement at all, but one which simply gives the producer, in return for a payment, the exclusive entitlement to negotiate for the rights for a limited period, usually about six months. This form of agreement gives the producer nothing at all except the dubious pleasure of making a payment to spend several months negotiating with an agent, with no guarantee whatever that anything will come of it. In usual circumstances such agreements should be stoutly resisted.

C5

BOOK RIGHTS AGREEMENTS Chapter 5

Deals for film and television rights in existing published books, in particular fictional novels, can be very complex to negotiate. Any book is a substantial work of copyright, and each of the different rights of copyright may have potential for separate exploitation. Further, a production based on the book has its own copyright and the secondary rights in the production may have possibilities for separate exploitation too. Leaving aside the obvious examples such as Winnie The Pooh and Harry Potter, a relatively modest example is Christopher Isherwood's slim novel, *Goodbye To Berlin*. This has been made as a feature film, as a television film and as a stage play; there have been readings on radio and a radio play; it has also been adapted, as *Cabaret*, a stage musical which was also made as a major Hollywood movie, with the soundtrack album achieving significant sales.

It is interesting to speculate the extent to which Christopher Isherwood benefited from all this. When the book was written in the 1930s, it was usual for publishers to take an assignment of the author's copyright. When film rights were sold they were frequently bought out by the Hollywood majors under contracts which made no distinction between film, television or any of the other audio-visual rights and which tied up the rights for the full period of copyright. There are still a number of important 20th century novels (and stage plays) for which the audio-visual rights languish, unexploited, in the archives of the major studios, largely forgotten until you try to negotiate for them and the studio decides they are a valuable asset not to be disposed of at any price.

All this has now changed. It is rare for publishers to acquire any rights other than the publishing rights in an author's work. Authors' agents are now, understandably, determined to protect their client's position in every possible way and negotiations can go deep into the labyrinthine realms of 'what if…'. This chapter aims to address the key terms which a producer will need to negotiate when acquiring rights.

KEY TOPICS & ISSUES

C5

STRATEGY/KEY TERMS FOR NEGOTIATION OF BOOK RIGHTS   1

Book rights deals can become tortuously complex and the producer needs to work out a clear strategy before embarking on negotiations, to keep in focus those rights it is essential to acquire, those it may be desirable to have and the purchase price. Even if a lawyer is being engaged to handle the negotiation, the producer must keep very close to the deal since only the producer really knows his or her vision for the production and thus what rights are required and what the budget is likely to sustain. Further, as negotiations can be very protracted, it may be expensive to engage a lawyer to handle them. In many cases it is the producer who handles negotiation of the key terms, engaging the lawyer when these have been settled to draw up the long-form agreement.

Initially the producer needs to make a careful assessment of the (realistic) prime objective for the production and the potential for subsequent exploitation as follows:

Type of production   1.1

Is the prime objective to adapt the book as a:

i   major, high-budget (over $15 million) theatrical feature film;

ii   low-budget (less than $15 million) theatrical feature film;

iii   single television movie with a budget of approximately £2 million; or

iv   television series?

Sequel production   1.2

Is the story finite or could it have possibilities:

i   for prequels, sequels and spin-offs; and/or

ii   is it likely that the author will write a sequel?

Secondary exploitation   1.3

Could either illustrations in the book or the production itself have possibilities:

i   for merchandising, i.e. highly distinctive sets, characters, costumes and such like which could be reproduced in computer and board games, on yogurt pots, as dolls or other children's toys; and

ii   would the release/opening of a stage production or a radio adaptation at the same time as the film or television production be of concern; and

iii   what arrangements, if any, are appropriate for the publishing rights?

Appropriate terms for different types of production   1.4

The producer's strategy should then be to work out appropriate and reasonable terms for the acquisition of those rights which are of prime interest, at the same time protecting his or her position on other rights if plans for the production change during the course of development.

An explanation of terminology and structures for the deal terms used in this paragraph are detailed in *Paragraphs 2* and *3*. The key terms to negotiate for the different types of production listed under *Paragraph 1.1* are:

High-budget theatrical feature film

i   **Primary rights** – an assignment of all audio-visual rights including, specifically, feature film rights, television rights, soundtrack rights, merchandising rights.

ii   **Sequel rights** – an assignment of prequel, sequel and spin-off rights. If for any reason the author is not prepared to grant this, the procedures to be followed should be in accordance with *Paragraph 3*.

iii **Secondary rights** – an assignment of all available secondary rights, including stage and radio rights, and the right to publish the material associated with the film in accordance with *Paragraph 4.5*.

iv **Purchase price** – a single fee which is a buyout of all forms of exploitation throughout the world against an escalator (see *Paragraph 5.1*). If remake, prequel and sequel are not bought out by the purchase price, these may attract a fee of 50% of the original purchase price. A net profit share is usually agreed about 2.5% of producer's net profits.

Low-budget feature film

i **Primary rights** – ideally an assignment of all audio-visual rights. If this is not forthcoming, a long, at least 25-year, licence.

ii **Sequel rights** – an assignment or licence of prequel, sequel and spin-off rights. If for any reason the author is not prepared to grant this the procedures should be in accordance with *Paragraph 3*.

iii **Secondary rights** – entitlement to exploit merchandising rights in the production according to *Paragraph 4.1*. Holdback on stage and radio rights. Publishing rights in the production in accordance with *Paragraph 4.5*.

iv **Purchase price** – a single fee as a buyout of worldwide exploitation rights in the film against an escalator. Remake, prequel and sequel rights for 50% of the purchase price. Share of net profits usually about 2.5% of producer's net profits.

Single television movie

i **Primary rights** – a television licence for a single production. This should provide that, though the intention is to make a single film the producer, alternatively, has the right to adapt the book as a series or miniseries. The licence should be for not less than about 12 years. Try to negotiate for the licence to cover a very limited theatrical release, for example on 'art-house' circuits of not more than ten cinemas, and for a limited number of performances. Provide a first opportunity position to acquire feature film rights according to *Paragraph 2.8*.

ii **Sequel rights** – first opportunity to negotiate for sequel and spin-off rights in accordance with *Paragraph 3*.

iii **Secondary rights** – entitlement to exercise merchandising rights in the production. Three-year holdback on exploitation of stage and radio rights (see also *Paragraphs 4.2* and *4.3*). Right to publish synopsis of the book (see *Paragraph 4.5*).

iv **Purchase price** – fixed fee to cover a single production of a certain length, say 120 minutes of material. If the production is longer (or made as a series) the fee is increased pro rata to the length of the production. A strategy for keeping the initial purchase price down is to offer additional payments for the USA, payable if and when a sale is made to that territory (see *Paragraph 5.2*).

Television series

i **Primary rights** – an exclusive worldwide television licence, which can be as short as about seven years, provided that there is provision for it to be a rolling licence, whereby the licence term is renewed on completion of each new series based on the book. It is sensible to provide for the book to, alternatively, be adapted as a single film. First opportunity to acquire feature film rights (see *Paragraph 2.8*).

ii   **Sequel rights** – licence should extend to sequel and spin-off rights.

iii   **Secondary rights** – three-year holdback on stage and radio rights and provisions of *Paragraphs 4.2* and *4.3*. Provision should be made to publish books based on producer-created sequels (see *Paragraph 3.2*).

iv   **Purchase price** – fixed fee to cover a certain number of hours of material. Each additional hour attracts the same fee pro rata. As a very rough guide an appropriate per episode fee might be about two-thirds of the script fee for the episode (excluding the scriptwriter's residuals).

PRIMARY RIGHTS   2

Assignment   2.1

Assignment is when the owner of the copyright sells to the purchaser all or certain of the rights of copyright in the work, irrevocably, worldwide, in perpetuity.

In the case of book rights deals, production financiers of very high-budget feature films require an assignment of all available rights of copyright as a condition of financing. Of the various reasons for this, the principal is that it is unwise to make a multi-million dollar investment in a film if there is any risk at all that the underlying rights could revert to the author, who could then prevent any showing of the film. As an assignment is irrevocable there is no possibility of this happening. The other reason why financiers of extremely expensive movies require all available rights is to retain 'brand exclusivity' by preventing third parties from being able to capitalise on the success of the film by exploiting other rights in the book, such as stage or merchandising.

Licence   2.2

Under a licence agreement the author grants the purchaser an exclusive licence for a fixed term in certain rights in the novel, during which time the purchaser has the exclusive right to produce production(s) based on the work. On expiry of the term the rights revert to the author. If any provisions of the licence agreement are not honoured, the licence can be terminated with the rights reverting to the author. A licence of rights in a book (provided it is properly drafted) is usually adequate for the vast majority of television productions and for low-budget feature films, so long as the licence provides that, following its expiry, the production made during the term of the licence can continue to be exploited for the full period of copyright.

Licence agreements for book rights must be sole and exclusive and worldwide. A non-exclusive licence would mean that the same rights could be licensed to another party and it would obviously be unacceptable to have the possibility of two productions based on the same work. A worldwide licence is necessary because, in order to fund major drama, it must be possible to sell it throughout the world.

Feature film rights   2.3

Feature film rights (sometimes described as cinematograph or theatrical feature rights) are generally defined as all audio-visual rights of all descriptions throughout the world including theatrical rights (i.e. the right to screen the film to paying audiences in cinemas), non-theatric and television rights (as defined in *Paragraph 2.4* below) lending and rental rights and including soundtrack and merchandising rights in the production.

2.4 Television rights

The definitions of television rights are being added to all the time, as technology finds new means of disseminating programmes. At present television rights are generally described as television of all descriptions now known or hereafter invented including, without limitation, terrestrial, non-terrestrial, satellite, broadcast, non-broadcast, basic cable, pay cable, on-line and interactive rights, video, video-on-demand, non-theatric, trapped audience rights (and lending and rental rights). It is important not to accept any exclusions, such as video rights, from this definition.

2.5 Holdback

Holdback is an agreement by the rights owner not to exercise rights for a certain period of time. On book rights deals, where rights other than film and television rights are retained by the author, there is frequently a holdback on stage and radio rights for example.

2.6 First opportunity/first option

To have first opportunity or first option to negotiate for rights means that the owner has agreed to negotiate terms for the acquisition of the rights with that individual before entering into negotiations with anyone else. This is usually accompanied by a matching rights provision (see below) if the parties cannot agree terms.

2.7 Matching rights

Means that if the owner and the purchaser cannot agree terms for the acquisition of certain rights, the purchaser has the right to acquire the rights in return for matching the same terms as those being offered by a third party.

Timescales should be attached to such matching rights provisions: a three-month negotiation period in respect of the first opportunity entitlement. If terms are not agreed and the author subsequently proposes to contract with a third party, a period of 21 days from receipt by the producer of written notification of the terms of the third-party offer in which the producer can match the offer, and thus, acquire the rights.

2.8 First opportunity/matching rights on feature film rights

There is always the possibility that during development of a production for television it may be seen to have possibilities for release as a feature film. Obviously the feature film rights would cost more than the television rights, but the producer can address this in the negotiation in the following ways:

i   for a period of, say, three or four years from acquisition of the television rights there will be a holdback (see *Paragraph 2.5*) on any exploitation of the feature film rights;

ii   during the holdback period the producer has first opportunity to negotiate for the acquisition of feature film rights; or alternatively, and preferably

iii   the producer is entitled to acquire feature film rights for a pre-agreed enhanced purchase price.

Failing agreement to any of the foregoing,

iv   during the licence period the producer has the right to match any offer the author may receive for the feature film rights (see *Paragraph 2.7*).

SEQUEL RIGHTS
3

There can be few things more galling for a producer than to find himself or herself in the position of having produced a successful programme, only to discover, when the world is clamouring for a sequel, that they have no entitlement to make one. In the first instance the author of the book obviously has the right, and may well have the intention, to write sequels to the original book. Ideally the producer needs to be in a position, not only to acquire rights in a sequel book, but if the author does not write one, to create sequels for production. Strategies for dealing with this are:

Author-originated sequels
3.1

In the case of author-originated sequels, it is usual to provide that, in the event that the author proposes to publish a sequel novel (i.e. a novel containing some or all of the characters and situations portrayed in the original novel), the producer has the first opportunity to negotiate for the rights. Sometimes a price is agreed at the stage when terms for the original book are negotiated; for example, it may be agreed that the producer can purchase the same rights in any sequel work for 10% more than the purchase price of the original work.

If the purchase price is left for negotiation at the time, it is important to provide that, in the event that the producer and the author are unable to reach agreement on terms, the producer will, nonetheless, be entitled to match any bona fide offer which the author may subsequently receive for the rights (see *Paragraph 2.7*).

Producer-originated sequels
3.2

With producer-originated sequels (or prequels), not all authors will agree to anyone else being able to write a sequel to their original work, and if they will not agree to it there is little that can be done since the underlying rights in the characters belong to them. If, however, the author will accept the principle of the producer being able to create sequels, it is usual to make the following provisions:

i   the author will either receive a fee equivalent to 50% of the purchase price (and, if applicable, 50% of the profit share) paid for the original book in respect of the sequel production or alternatively a fee for each sequel episode;

ii   the author will have the sole right to publish a novelisation of the sequel production; and

iii the author will be fully consulted about the development of the characters and storylines (with the producer's decision being final).

SECONDARY RIGHTS
4

Merchandising rights
4.1

A distinction needs to be made between the merchandising rights in the book itself, and the merchandising rights in the production – they are not always the same thing.

Merchandising rights in the book

If it is an illustrated book and it is intended that the visual illustrations will be animated in a film and television production, the negotiation of the merchandising rights is likely to be a highly sophisticated process since these types of books and animated productions, tend to be those which have greatest potential for character merchandising. Any producer lacking extensive experience in the field would be well advised to engage a specialist lawyer from the very outset of negotiations. Obviously these types of deals will vary, depending on such factors as how well known the book is, how extensively it will need to be adapted for production, the form the production is to take and so forth. Fundamentally the producer requires an assignment of the merchandising rights, along with an assignment of the film and television rights, so that there is no question that he or she has an unfettered entitlement to produce programmes and license merchandise associated with them for an indefinite period.

Merchandising rights in the production

For a general fiction work (except perhaps if it is a children's book) the merchandising rights will almost certainly be much less significant. In any event it is arguable, under copyright law, whether the author has any position on merchandising derived from a production since merchandising rarely draws on the literary material, but on visual images which have been specially created for the production. To avoid any argument, however, a book rights agreement should provide that the producer has the right to arrange for merchandising derived from the production based on the book (as distinct from merchandising derived solely from the book itself).

4.2 Stage rights

Stage rights are the rights to adapt the work for live stage performance. For feature films, if these rights have not been acquired by the producer, it is usual for there to be a lengthy holdback on the exploitation of the rights from first release of the film. For television rights there is generally a fairly limited holdback (about three years) from first transmission of the television production.

Spin-off stage productions

It is, of course, possible that a stage production might spin-off from the film or television production. While it might be difficult, under copyright law, for a producer to claim that engagement of the same cast infringed the copyright in the production, contractual provision can be made that, in the event that a stage play drew on elements originally devised for the production, such as casting, set and costume design, music, graphics and so forth, such usage would be subject to the payment to the producer of a share of net profits from the production, to be negotiated in good faith at the time.

4.3 Radio rights

There are two forms of radio rights: the dramatic radio rights, i.e. adaptation of the work as a play for radio; and straight reading rights (for *Book at Bedtime* type programmes). It is quite usual for there to be a holdback on the exploitation of the dramatic radio rights (three years is the norm), but it is not usual for there to be any restriction on the straight reading rights: exploitation of these rights might well serve as good publicity for the production.

4.4 Single voice reading rights

These are the rights to release a recording of the reading of the book. As with the straight reading rights, exploitation of these rights is not generally regarded as detracting from the production, and the rights are, therefore, unconditionally reserved to the author.

4.5 Publishing rights

The publishing rights will, of course, be reserved to the author, who in turn will almost certainly have assigned or licensed all the print publishing rights to the publisher.

However, it is usual for the rights agreement to entitle the producer to arrange the following forms of publication associated with the production:

i   synopses of the book, to a length of approximately 5,000 words, for publicity and promotional purposes;

ii   the screenplay for the production; and

iii a 'making of' book of the production.

Tie-in editions

It is not generally possible for the producer to be able to obtain any financial benefit from the enhanced sales of the book which may be generated by the production. The publisher is entitled to promote the book as being the book of the production since that is a statement of fact. It is not difficult for a publisher to devise ways of designing a cover and promotional material which associates the book with the production without infringing copyright. So far as television productions are concerned, in the UK current rules do not allow on-screen promotions for books which have been published prior to the transmission of television programmes.

One positive way to proceed is to obtain an undertaking in the contract that the author will endeavour to ensure that the publisher will liaise with the producer over the arrangements for any tie-in edition of the work, so that the book will promote the production in the style in which the producer wants.

PURCHASE PRICE   5

Buyouts   5.1

On all book rights deals a fixed purchase price should be agreed which is a buyout, that is to say, it should be in "full and final consideration" of all exploitation of a production based on the work with no further payments falling due except, perhaps, for a share of producer's net profits from sales of the production. Agents will frequently try to negotiate for authors to receive residuals/additional use payments on sales of the production in accordance with the Writers' Guild agreement provisions. This is not appropriate. The Writers' Guild agreements are designed to cover new script commissions and not the acquisition of rights in existing books. More importantly, producers should resist any claims for residual payments since these are always unacceptable to feature film financiers and very unlikely to be acceptable to broadcasters.

A rough rule of thumb for arriving at an appropriate purchase price is to calculate it as 2% of the projected budget. Usually, if an option has been taken out before the rights are purchased, the purchase price is usually offset by one or more of the option fees.

Escalator   5.2

Notwithstanding the provision for the fixed fee to be a buyout, on feature films the author needs some protection if he or she has accepted a low purchase price and the film turns into a huge movie. The usual procedure is to provide for a fixed minimum purchase price, the 'floor', which is against a percentage, frequently 2% or 2.5% of the budget for the film (the escalator), rising to a 'ceiling', generally calculated as three times the 'floor' price. Producers should be wary of agreeing any higher escalator than 2–2.5% since this has the effect of making the underlying rights payments too expensive in relation to other budget provisions, particularly when account is taken of the fee to be paid to the writer of the screenplay.

If there is a problem agreeing a reasonable ceiling, it is sometimes possible to resolve it by providing that, after the author has received a certain level of fee, say £100,000, the percentage applied to the budget for the purpose of arriving at the fee is reduced to 1%.

The definition of budget for the purposes of calculating an escalator is the final approved budget for the film less, as a general rule, contingency, completion guarantee charges, financing costs and fees paid in respect of the rights. The deduction of these charges brings about a significant reduction in the budget figure and financiers will expect to see this type of provision in the agreement.

The escalator structure is rarely used on television deals since the parameters of television budgets are generally well known. If there is a problem on settling a reasonable price for television rights, and notwithstanding the fact that the prime objective should be to have a buyout deal, a reasonable way round it is to provide that extra payments may fall due on a sale to the USA. For example a sale to a US network might attract 50% of the purchase price, to PBS or a cable station, 20% of the purchase price. These additional payments only fall due if and when the sale is made.

5.3 Remake, sequel and prequel payments

Where the producer is acquiring an assignment of rights for a high-budget feature the purchase price may be so high that it buys out any number of productions based on the work. However, except in this type of case, it is usual for the purchase price to be a buyout price for exploitation of a single production (or series) based on the book. If the producer makes a remake, sequel or prequel production this usually attracts a fee equivalent to 50% of the original purchase price.

In the case of spin-off series, if the rights were originally acquired for production of a series it is usual for the deal to be structured so that the price covers a certain number of hours of produced material, and for the agreement to provide that the author will receive payments pro rata for each additional hour of material not covered by the original purchase price.

On spin-off series which only draw on the characters, and not the author's own story, it is fairly usual to arrange for the author to receive a payment equivalent to 10% of the scriptwriter's fee for each episode.

5.4 Net profits

Agents will frequently ask for a share of net profits from sales of the production. This is generally agreed since the entitlement to a share of net profits, should they ever be earned, can be a good means of ensuring, if the production is a huge success, that the author does not feel cheated having earned nothing beyond the original purchase price.

It is, however, very important when agreeing a share of net profits to define it as being of 'producer's net profits', not of 100% of net profits (however hard the agents try to insist on this). Production financiers will not accept a third-party entitlement to net profits being paid out of their share, and if the producer has agreed this, the financier will require that the amount due to the author from his or her share is met entirely out of the producer's own net profit entitlement. This can be painful, particularly when any shares agreed for other talent also have to be paid from producer's net profits.

As it is extremely unlikely that the producer will control distribution rights in the feature film or be responsible for disbursement of net profits from sales, the book rights agreement should provide that producer's net profits will be as defined in the principal financing and production agreement for the film. The producer will account to the rights owner for such net profit shares and pay any sums due within 28 days of receipt by the producer from third parties of accounting statements/shares of producer's net profits.

The definition of net profits on films will include revenues received from secondary exploitation of the film, such as merchandising and soundtrack rights, so avoid negotiating any separate entitlement to shares of net profits from these activities.

Profit shares from sales of television productions are less usual, but they are sometimes agreed. Again, any entitlement must be to a share of net profits received by the producer from sales of the production, not of 100% of net profits.

Expenses 5.5

It is quite common for agents to request return first class air travel and accommodation for two people at film premieres and major award ceremonies. This can prove expensive so the producer's liability should be limited to reasonable endeavours to arrange for the film's distributor to meet the cost.

The above are the key commercial terms. The following are other negotiable points on which the producer, as distinct from the lawyer, will need to be involved.

CREDITS 6

Contracts for book rights sometimes specify that the production must bear the same title as the book, unless the author is unhappy with the production, in which case he or she is entitled to require that the production bear a different title and no reference be made to the fact that it is based on the book. The important point to bear in mind when negotiating such requirements is the extent to which the general public knows the book and its existence, therefore, serves to promote the production. There is no point in paying a lot of money for book rights, only to run the risk of not being able to gain the promotional benefits for the production of association with the book.

If this type of provision has to be accepted, it must be conditional on the author notifying the producer of his or her requirements before the credits are completed, since to redo credit sequences can be hugely expensive.

Leaving aside these considerations, which don't always arise, it is usual to provide that:

i   the producer is entitled, but not obliged, to give the production the same title as the book;

ii   if the production bears the same title as the book, the credit is "based on the book by..."; and

iii   if it does not have the same title the credit is "based on the book [title] by [author's name]".

ENTITLEMENT TO ADAPT THE BOOK 7

The rights agreement must provide that the producer is entitled to alter, adapt, edit, translate and otherwise vary the book as may be required for the purposes of production. As explained in *Chapter 4, Paragraph 2.7* the producer must not allow the author to retain any creative or other control over the production since this would be unacceptable to any production financier.

C5

8 WARRANTIES, INDEMNITIES AND PUBLISHER'S RELEASE

A clean 'chain of title', meaning watertight agreements for underlying rights of copyright in a film, are a pre-condition of a production deal for production financiers, completion bond companies, sales agents and distributors for the film. The book rights agreement must, therefore, contain extensive warranties and indemnities from the author as to the ownership of the rights. The warranties and indemnities must also contain a full waiver of the author's moral rights. There are standard, if lengthy, forms for these warranties and the producer must ensure that they are contained within any rights agreement to make it effective.

9 TURNAROUND

It is fairly usual for the author to be entitled to reacquire rights in the novel if the producer has not entered into production within a certain period of time. This is known as turnaround.

Care needs to be taken with these provisions since agreements the producer may have entered into with third-party financiers for the development of the production generally provide that, in the event that the producer relinquishes the rights, the financier has to be repaid sums paid to the producer, plus interest. If the author wants to take the rights into turnaround this should be subject to him or her accepting an obligation to meet any such repayments. These payments generally only fall due on first day of principal photography of a production and the cost is customarily included in the production budget. The author will not have to pay it out of his or her own pocket.

Turnaround provisions generally come into effect after approximately seven years. Where there is no obligation to repay development financiers, it is fairly common to provide that the author can acquire rights in turnaround after five years, subject to repayment of the purchase price; after seven years the rights may revert without repayment.

C6

SCRIPT, SCREENPLAY AND TREATMENT AGREEMENTS

Chapter 6

It is essential to enter into properly drafted agreements for scripts and screenplays, since these are major works of copyright on which a production is based and failure to address issues of rights and ownership correctly can jeopardise the exploitation of the production and the secondary rights in it. Broadcasters and feature film financiers make approval of the writer's contract a pre-condition of any agreement to finance production so it is extremely important to ensure, when negotiating terms for a writer's contract, that the arrangements are acceptable to potential financiers.

It is relatively unusual for a producer to be acquiring rights in an existing screenplay or script, as distinct from commissioning one to be created, but it does occasionally happen. When it does, the first stage is usually for the producer to take an option on the work, but thereafter the terms should be in accordance with industry practice for commissioned scripts and screenplays. It is quite common for writers to write treatments speculatively before approaching producers and the key issues are addressed here.

This chapter sets out customary arrangements for commissioning scripts and screenplays and for acquiring rights in existing treatments. (In industry terminology it is usual to refer to a 'script' if it is for a television production and to a 'screenplay' if it is for a feature film.) In many respects the terms are similar to those for acquiring rights in existing books, so a number of matters are cross-referenced to *Chapter 5*.

KEY TOPICS & ISSUES

C6

TELEVISION SCRIPTS   1
Writers' Guild agreements   1.1

Television scripts should be commissioned in accordance with the terms of agreement between the Writers' Guild of Great Britain and, for the independent production sector, PACT, Producers Alliance for Cinema and Television. The BBC and ITV have their own agreements with the Writers' Guild for in-house productions. There are some variations between the different agreements, but fundamentally they all provide similar arrangements for the following:

i   minimum rates of payment for different forms of commissions;

ii   residual or royalty payments in respect of repeats and/or overseas sales;

iii   assignment of copyright in the script to the party commissioning it;

iv   entitlement of the commissioning party to engage other writers on the script; and

v   'turnaround' of rights to the writer when it is an original script written solely by the writer and production has not commenced within a certain period.

The agreements cover many other detailed matters: the entitlement to payment of expenses; credit provisions; arbitration procedures in the event of dispute and so forth.

The terms of the agreements with the Writers' Guild are formally approved and recognised by all broadcasters and they will expect to see writers contracted in accordance with the agreed arrangements. It is, therefore, important when negotiating with writers' agents to maintain that the terms of the contract must be in accordance with the provisions of the applicable Writers' Guild agreement (and of only one specific Writers' Guild agreement; don't allow agents to 'cherry pick' the most favourable provisions from different Writers' Guild agreements).

Fee   1.2

Writers' fees are negotiable. The scales in the Writers' Guild agreement are minimum rates usually only agreed when the writer has little or no track record. Rates for established writers are generally significantly higher than the minimums.

Net profits   1.3

It is not usual to agree shares of net profits for writers on television deals since, unlike feature film deals, the writer has entitlements to additional royalty or residual payments in respect of sales of the production.

Formats   1.4

Where the writer has speculatively written the format for the script and brought it to the producer, rather than being commissioned to devise the format or having one suggested by the producer, it is usual to agree entitlements for the writer in respect of any exploitation of the format rights. Arrangements for this type of deal are explained in *Chapter 7*. It is normal to negotiate a licence agreement for the format, with individual scripts being separately contracted under the standard form Writers' Guild contract.

FEATURE FILM SCREENPLAYS   2
Writers' Guild agreement   2.1

At the time of writing the Writers' Guild/PACT agreement is being renegotiated and it is hoped that the new agreement will come into effect during 2002. The provisions for feature films and single television films in the current Writers' Guild/PACT agreement, which dates back to 1992, are widely recognised as being unworkable in relation to the current requirements of film financiers. It is, therefore, not usual to use the Writers' Guild standard agreement for single films and screenplays but to draw up an agreement which contains the following terms and conditions.

2.2   Rights

On all screenplays there should be a full assignment of copyright in the screenplay to the producer. Notwithstanding this assignment of copyright, it is customary, when the writer has originated the screenplay and is the sole writer of it, for the writer to have the following entitlements in respect of the secondary rights in the screenplay:

Remake, prequel, sequel and spin-off rights

Subject to financiers' approval, reasonable availability and to good faith negotiation of fees, the writer may be accorded first opportunity to write any remake, prequel, sequel or spin-off production. If the writer does not write it, he or she is customarily entitled to receive the following additional payments:

i   remake, prequel, sequel – 50% of the original fee, payable on commencement of photography; and

ii   television spin-offs – a royalty of 10% of the script fee paid on any episode not written by the writer, payable on recording of each applicable episode.

Publishing rights

The first opportunity to write any novel based on the screenplay. The writer will be entitled to a fee in respect of the novelisation and remaining revenues from exploitation of the publication may be shared in percentage proportions between the producer and the writer. The percentage shares offered vary considerably; generally from 50:50 to 25:75 in favour of the producer.

Screenplay publication

It is usual to provide that revenues from any publication of the actual screenplay will be shared 50:50 between producer and writer.

Changed format rights

It is usual to agree a 50:50 share between producer and writer on any net revenues received from a licence of the changed format rights.

Merchandising rights

An entitlement for the writer of 25% of net profits from exploitation of merchandising rights in the film is not uncommon.

Stage and radio rights

It is usual to provide that, subject to good faith negotiation of fees, the writer will be accorded first opportunity to write any stage or radio version of the screenplay. In addition, the writer will generally be entitled to receive 25% of net profits received by the producer from exploitation of the rights.

For major feature films the producer must retain stage and radio rights. For lower budget films the rights may sometimes be retained by the writer but it is usual to provide that there will, nonetheless, be a holdback on any exploitation of the rights for a period of three to five years from first release of the production. It is also sensible to provide that, if the stage production were to draw on elements devised for the film, any usage of these is subject to the producer's agreement and to good faith negotiation of a share of net profits.

Structure of the commission   2.3

Generally, the structure of screenplay agreements is such that, after commission of a treatment, a first draft is commissioned. Following delivery of the first draft there is a provision for a revision and then a 'polish' of the first draft. Thereafter the second draft may be commissioned, after which a revision and sometimes several polishes may be commissioned, before the screenplay reaches the stage of being the 'principal photography' screenplay. There is no binding contractual obligation on the producer to commission further drafts; it is at the producer's absolute discretion.

The agreement provides that the copyright in all material completed at each stage is assigned to the producer. This is important, because another central condition of all agreements for screenplays is that the producer is entitled to 'cut-off' the writer at each stage, that is, to terminate the commission and to bring in one or more writers to work on the subsequent drafts.

Sometimes timescales are inserted in the agreement under which the writer must be notified of the required revisions/polishes within a certain period of delivery of the applicable draft/revision and, provided the timescale for such notification is met, the writer must undertake to be available to carry out the revisions and polishes for delivery by a certain date. This ensures (or endeavours to ensure) that the writing period will not be unduly protracted.

Fee   2.4

On screenplays the fee is a 'buyout', a once-and-for-all payment in respect of the assignment of rights. Feature film financiers will not accept an obligation to pay any residual or royalty payments in respect of exploitation of the film.

It is fairly usual practice to negotiate the fee on the basis of a 'floor' and a 'ceiling' and an 'escalator' based on approximately 2% of budget. The arrangements and percentages are generally similar to the arrangements for negotiating a purchase price for an existing book (see *Chapter 5, Paragraph 5.1* for details).

The overall fee is paid in instalments, linked to the stages of commissioning material. The percentage proportion to be paid at each stage is subject to negotiation depending on the status of the writer and the extent to which the early development of the script may be being funded out of the producer's own resources. As a very general indication, the fee for the treatment may be between 10% and 20%: for the first draft script, between 40% and 50%; for the second draft, about 15-20%; with the principal photography payment being about 25-30%. Any additional amount in respect of the escalator is paid on commencement of principal photography.

When other writers are brought in they receive the instalment of the overall fee for the applicable draft/revision they are contracted to write. The principal photography payment is divided between all the writers of the screenplay who are entitled, under the Screenwriting Credits Agreement 1974, to receive credit on the film. The shares are subject to negotiation, in accordance with each writer's respective contribution to the final screenplay, although there is some custom and practice for the writer of the first draft having an entitlement to not less than 50% of the principal photography payment. Negotiation of these shares can be tricky, but Writers' Guild arbitration procedures can be used as a last resort to resolve matters, if agreement cannot be reached.

2.5   Net profits

Although the fee is in 'full and final consideration' of the exploitation of the film by all means and in all media, it is customary for writers to receive a small share of producer's net profits from the production (see definition in *Chapter 5, Paragraph 5.4*). The usual share is 2.5%. If other writers are engaged on the production, the share may be split in the same proportions as the principal photography payment is split between the writers.

2.6   Credits

The size, wording and placing of the writer's credit is subject to individual negotiation (before the title/in the closing credits; same size/larger/smaller than the director's; before/after the producer credit and so forth). Other general matters relating to credits are customarily governed by the Screenwriting Credits Agreement of 1974, which addresses writers' entitlement to receive credits or shared credit and the circumstances in which credit does not have to be accorded.

2.7   Rights of cut-off

As explained in *Paragraph 2.3*, it is very important that in agreements for a screenplay there is always provision for 'cut-off' at each stage of delivery/payment to allow other writers to be brought in to do further drafts or polishes. Even the most reliable writers sometimes have blocks, and a producer cannot risk being placed in a position where the screenplay cannot be worked into an acceptable shape because the writer will not allow anyone else to work on it.

Whereas for a commissioned screenplay the producer does not have to pay the full fee to the first writer if another writer(s) is brought in, this can be more difficult to negotiate in circumstances when the screenplay is the writer's original screenplay, particularly when they have developed it at their own risk. It may be that the only compromise is to agree that the writer will receive the full screenplay fee, but the producer nonetheless has the right to bring in another writer for an additional fee. The credit provisions also need to allow the possibility of a shared credit for the writers.

2.8   Warranties

As with all agreements for copyright works, the screenplay agreement must contain warranties from the writer as to originality, ownership and moral rights waivers. In this connection it is important that the agreement expressly provides that the producer is entitled to adapt the screenplay as required for the purposes of production. The writer must also warrant that the material is not libellous or defamatory.

2.9   Turnaround

It is usual in most screenplay agreements to provide that, if the work is original and it turns out to have been written by only one writer, that writer is entitled to take the screenplay into turnaround (to reacquire the rights in it) if it has not been produced within a certain period of time. Details of how to negotiate turnaround to ensure the producer's position is properly protected are contained in *Chapter 5, Paragraph 9*.

3   TREATMENTS

The expression 'treatment' is not, as lawyers say, a 'term of art': that is to say, there is no precise definition as to what constitutes a treatment. Particularly in the USA, for feature films, it is common for the treatment to be a lengthy document (about 50 pages) which sets out the entire structure and narrative of the screenplay. In the UK a treatment is often a fairly brief (eight- to ten-page) outline of the narrative and characters. If the treatment is for a multi-episodic drama series usual practice would be to enter into a format deal with the originator, and terms for this are described in *Chapter 7*.

When a producer commissions a treatment the terms and conditions for it are contained in the contract for the commission of the screenplay. In circumstances where the writer has originated the treatment prior to approaching the producer the following matters need to be addressed:

Option   3.1

For a pre-existing treatment it would be usual for the producer to acquire an option on the treatment, with the rights in the treatment being acquired by the producer on commission of a screenplay based on the treatment, in accordance with the terms of the screenplay agreement. Where the treatment has been developed by an established writer, the writer's agreement to grant rights will, of course, generally be conditional on that writer being commissioned to write the screenplay based on the treatment.

The producer must nonetheless ensure that he or she has the ability to bring in other writers. The type of arrangements which can be agreed are that the producer must guarantee that the writer will be commissioned to write not less than the first draft and revisions; the choice of other writers may be subject to the approval of the original writer (with the producer's decision being final), and the producer may be placed under an obligation to consult fully with the original writer about the development of the screenplay.

In circumstances where a treatment has not been written by an established writer and the producer does not intend to engage the writer to write the script or screenplay, before proceeding further the producer should enter into an agreement under which there is a complete, unconditional assignment of the writer's copyright in the treatment. During the course of production the original treatment will be so fleshed out by other copyright materials created by other writer(s) that any attempt to share ownership of the copyright in the original treatment would be impractical.

This is not to say that the original writer should not have some continuing entitlement to participation in net profits from exploitation of productions based on the treatment. But in agreeing this, account needs to be taken of the fact that other writer(s) subsequently engaged to work on the treatment and screenplay are also likely to want entitlements to a net profit participation.

Fee   3.2

As there is no precise definition of what constitutes a treatment the fees paid for them need to be negotiated case by case. For lengthy treatments which set out the complete structure and narrative of the screenplay it might be as much as 25% of the screenplay fee; a treatment which is little more than an outline rarely attracts a payment of more than about 10% of the screenplay fee. In both cases the treatment fee would generally form part of the overall screenplay fee, although this is negotiable.

Net profits   3.3

It would be reasonable for the originator of the treatment to receive a small share, 1-2%, of producer's net profits from exploitation of the production.

3.4 Credits

Credits in respect of treatments can be a delicate matter when other writers are brought in to write the screenplays. The other writers may be reasonably entitled to consider that they have contributed so much to the original treatment to make it viable for production that they are entitled to a "devised by" or similar credit. "Based on an idea suggested by…" or "Concept by…" are fairly usual credits for the originator of a treatment who does not write the screenplay. However, any agreement to accord this credit should be expressed as being subject to financiers' approval and to the credit requirements of writers engaged on the production.

3.5 Warranties

As with agreements for existing screenplays, the rights agreement must also contain all customary provisions for warranties and indemnities from the originator of the treatment. It must also include a moral rights waiver and specific provision for the producer to be able to adapt the treatment as required for the purposes of production.

FORMAT AGREEMENTS   Chapter 7

There are various definitions of format, but generally a format is defined as "the characteristics including any or all of the idea, concept, structure, setting, characters, character relationships, themes and other material factors which together comprise the original and distinctive elements for a programme or series of programmes".

Rights in formats are a difficult and ongoing issue. Legally, formats are regarded as being ideas, albeit well-developed ideas, and as such do not attract protection under copyright law.

Some years ago a test case was brought by the late Hughie Green claiming that a New Zealand production of a talent contest entitled *Opportunity Knocks* infringed the copyright of the popular talent show of the same title which he originated and hosted in the 1960s. This test case was pursued through to the Privy Council, the highest court of appeal for New Zealand and whose decisions are followed in UK law, and it was unsuccessful. Since then there have been continuing attempts to have provision made for the protection of formats in the Broadcasting Act and in the Copyright, Designs and Patents Act 1988, but at the time of writing no way has been found of securing legislative protection for television formats.

Notwithstanding this lack of legal protection for formats, it has become the custom and practice of the television industry in both the UK and overseas (where the legal position as regards lack of copyright protection for formats is generally very similar to that in the UK) to contract for rights in a proven format in much the same way as contracts are entered into for the use of copyright material. These format contracts are legally binding on both parties, even though neither party may have statutory protection against third-party infringement, and are the industry's method of protecting ownership and ensuring a commercial return from the work required to develop a successful format. An explanation of the ways in which formats are treated and the various types of contract which a producer may enter into in respect of rights in a format are addressed in this chapter.

KEY TOPICS & ISSUES

C7

DIFFERENT TYPES OF FORMAT   1
High-concept and low-concept   1.1

There is much loose talk about the huge value of formats and protecting rights in formats, but it is important for producers, when approaching format negotiations, to distinguish between 'high-concept' and 'low-concept' formats. Nearly all television programmes, with the possible exception of sports, news and outside broadcasts, have a format. However, a low-concept format is unlikely to have any intrinsic value. These are, for example, chat shows and other factual entertainment programmes such as cookery, gardening and other lifestyle shows. They can be said to have a format but are much more likely to be presenter driven, with the format being little more than a variation on extremely well-worked themes already being produced in many different forms all round the world.

Most documentaries fall into the same category, albeit they are subject rather than presenter driven. In these cases the format itself has no real value and it is unnecessary, and possibly even inadvisable, to try and contract for it as if it did. Inadvisable because the producer may then find himself or herself in a position of having to pay format royalties to the originator of the idea if they go on to produce similar programmes in the same genre in future.

High-concept formats are those for drama and situation comedy series and game shows, where the format and scripts, or the game, can be taken and adapted successfully for other productions in other territories. The packaging and licensing of these types of formats is now a sophisticated commercial activity and several major production companies have created substantial businesses out of devising and marketing formats, particularly for game shows.

Notwithstanding the current lack of protection for formats under copyright law, it is important for producers to enter into a contractual agreement with any individual who might have claim to have originated the format, to protect themselves against future claims that they have plagiarised an original work. While such claims may not ultimately stand up in a court of law, the process can, nonetheless, cause such problems that the production can be jeopardised.

Procedures for packaging and contracting for formats are as follows:

GAME SHOW FORMATS   2
Preliminaries/packaging   2.1

It is generally recognised that game shows are the most commercial type of format. The programmes are generally inexpensive to produce and, thus, the financing is not conditional on them having overseas sales potential. The format can, therefore, be licensed for domestic production territory by territory. Also, game shows, generally, travel better than drama or comedy: what works well in one territory is likely to work equally well in another.

Given the lack of protection under copyright laws for formats and titles, one of the first things to do, when a promising format has been created, is to take out trade mark protection for the title of the show in the audio-visual category and in categories covering the kinds of products which could be merchandised as spin-offs from the show (see *Chapter 1, Paragraph 6.4*). Since game shows can easily have a separate life on a website, it is also advisable to register the title as a domain name (see *Chapter 11, Paragraph 2*).

Having thus protected against unauthorised use of the title, it is becoming increasingly common practice to devise a complete bible, or specification, for the programme which sets out in considerable precise detail all aspects of the production, not only the actual game play, timings, number and role of contestants, role of the presenter and questions, but also set design, graphics, lighting rig and music stings. When licensing the format for production, it is a contractual requirement that the production has to adhere to these specifications, in much the same way as McDonald's franchises its restaurants on the basis that the franchisee must conform to the last detail of its specification for everything from the design and seating plan for the restaurant to the exact size of the chips and temperature at which they are cooked.

Not only does this requirement ensure a level of quality control for the format 'brand', but it is also possible, if another test case were to be brought on the issue, that the bible may contain sufficient written detail for the format to attract a measure of protection under copyright laws.

2.2   Agreement with the originator

Where a producer is acquiring rights in a format which might form the basis of a game show, it should be borne in mind that the ideas for this type of show are very rarely original. They are generally derivative of some kind of 'parlour game', school or newspaper quiz, talent contest, 'end-of-pier' entertainment or radio shows which have been played for generations. It is the professional development work, required to work the idea into a successful television programme, rather than the idea itself, which is of any value. Without this development, the format is no more than an idea and if its originator insists on rights of control and on large fees and generous participations in return for the idea alone, it would be advisable for the producer to walk away and find another idea on which to devote time, effort and money. It is essential, from the producer's point of view, to retain ownership and control of all rights of copyright in the developed format, since these kind of formats undoubtedly have the greatest potential for exploitation.

Rights

Notwithstanding the fact that it is unlikely that any rights subsist in the idea for a game show, to avoid subsequent claims a producer must always enter into an agreement in respect of rights, if any, in the idea. A letter of agreement between the producer and the originator covering the assignment to the producer of all rights (if any) of all descriptions in and to the format worldwide for the full period of copyright, coupled with moral rights waivers and customary warranties, and some form of 'consideration' will be sufficient.

Payments

There must, of course, be some 'consideration' in respect of the grant of rights. A one-off payment to the originator in respect of the contractual grant of rights (if any), and an entitlement to a small, single figure share of net profits from any exploitation of the format, is probably the best way forward.

If the originator of the idea also works on the development it may be appropriate to agree a small royalty in respect of each programme based on the format. This can be agreed as a fixed fee per programme, with a percentage escalator after production of a certain number of programmes based on the format. Alternatively, it can be expressed as a royalty based on a percentage – possibly 1% or 2% – of the budget for the programme.

Credits

Credits can be tricky, since it is those who are carrying out the development work who are effectively creating the format. "From an idea by…" may be a possibility.

Agreement with first commissioning broadcaster 2.3

Very different considerations apply to the agreements with broadcasters for game show programmes to those which apply to drama and situation comedy, largely because the programmes are generally inexpensive and the completed programmes rarely have any potential for sale outside the domestic territory. As such, it is reasonable to expect the commissioning broadcaster to be prepared to agree a deal whereby they acquire an exclusive licence in the programme in their territory only, leaving all the overseas rights to the producer. The broadcaster may jib at this if they have expended considerable sums on producing pilot programmes based on the format, but in such circumstances this can generally be resolved by the producer offering an entitlement to shares of net profits from subsequent exploitation of the format rights.

Negotiations with the original broadcaster may need to address specifically the financial contribution the broadcaster has made to development of the format, particularly if the broadcaster has funded a pilot programme. Structure of the licence agreement, however, can be broadly the same as when the producer is licensing rights for production of a changed format version in other territories, as described in *Paragraph 4*.

DRAMA AND SITUATION COMEDY FORMATS 3
Preliminaries/packaging 3.1

The treatment of drama and situation comedy formats is very different to that for game shows. Essentially what the purchaser of the format rights in a drama/situation comedy wishes to acquire is not just the format but, more importantly, the scripts which have successfully developed the dramatic dynamics of the storyline and plots, pacing, the realisation of the characters and so forth, all of which can then be adapted for production in the licensees' home territory using local actors, speaking in their own language. In practice it is highly unlikely that there would ever be a sale of format rights in a drama or situation comedy unless the series had been fully scripted and successfully produced.

Any potential licensee will want a format 'package' which includes the right to adapt and produce the scripts as well as the right to create further sequels and spin-offs. The UK is still regarded as a major stable of television writing talent and in English language territories as well as in the rest of Europe there is a market for successful British television scripts, although it may be more limited than is often imagined.

Agreement with the originator 3.2

It is customary, when a writer has devised an original format, to enter into a separate agreement in respect of the format rights. However, copyright in the scripts and programmes will not be vested with the writer but the producer and/or commissioning broadcaster. As it is virtually impossible to exploit the format rights without also owning the rights in the scripts and programmes, the most workable arrangement is to provide that rights in the format are vested with the producer, with the format agreement containing various entitlements for the writer in respect of any exploitation of the format rights.

The same thing applies to the exploitation of secondary rights in the format. Anyone proposing to publish a book based on the format, or a stage or radio play, or even a theatrical feature, will almost certainly need to be able to draw on the material contained in the scripts. Also there may be other aspects of the production, not originated by the creator of the format, which those acquiring rights in the format would also want to have the right to use, such as set design, graphics and music.

This fact of life in relation to the exploitation of format rights is now generally recognised and accepted by writers' agents experienced in format deals. Customary arrangements are outlined below.

Rights

i   **Assignment or licence** – If the producer commissions a format to be created, copyright in it should be assigned to the producer. Where the format has been created by an established writer prior to any approach to the producer, although an assignment of copyright is always ideal, it may not be possible for the producer to get the writer's agreement to a complete assignment. The producer must instead settle for an exclusive worldwide licence in the format which should initially run for a minimum period of about five years, and be a rolling licence which is automatically extended on commission of each new series. As explained, this licence should be for all rights in the format, not just television rights.

ii   **Originator's entitlement to write** – It is fairly usual, if the originator of the format is an established writer, for the assignment or licensing of rights to the producer to be made conditional on the originator having the opportunity to write scripts based on it. If the originator has a proven track record of writing scripts which have been produced for television, it would be churlish not to agree this. However, to safeguard the producer's position, the agreement should be made subject to: the agreement of production financiers; the writer's reasonable availability in relation to the proposed production schedule; and good faith negotiation of fees. In this connection, it is sensible to agree the fee which will be paid for scripts commissioned within about the first 18 months after signature of the agreement.

iii   **Secondary rights** – If there has been an assignment of rights, the secondary rights will have automatically been granted to the producer. In the case of an exclusive licence, the most workable arrangement is to provide that, during the term of the licence, the producer will own and control all the secondary rights in the format, scripts and programmes subject to payment to the originator of shares of profits and other entitlements. If the format originator is the principal scriptwriter, it would be usual for them to be accorded first opportunity, subject to financiers' approval, to write any book, stage or radio play or theatrical feature which the producer proposed to license.

Payments

The usual method of payment for a drama or situation comedy format is a royalty calculated as a percentage of the script fee, usually defined as the highest script fee paid on the series, with royalties being payable on recording of each episode.

For the original series based on the format a royalty of 10% of the script fee is the norm. Occasionally an 'escalator' is agreed, for example, the royalty rises to 12.5% after 13 episodes, and to 15% after 26 episodes. Producers should, however, be aware that over recent years all the UK broadcasters have been adopting a similarly firm stance on format royalties and may well refuse to pay a royalty higher than the 10% norm.

The originator does not receive a royalty on episodes for which he or she writes the script.

In cases where a writer has not originated a format, but has been commissioned to create one by the producer, it is fairly usual practice to agree a royalty, but this is generally set at about half the usual royalty rate, i.e. 5% of the script fee, and for it to be conditional on the writer creating not only the format but the first scripts based on it which are accepted for production.

i **Changed format payments** – The format originator will generally have an entitlement to a negotiated share of net profits received by the producer from any licence of the changed format rights. Frequently the deal for the sale of the changed format rights will be a package deal, which includes the right to adapt the scripts for production. The originator's share of net profits from the sale will be negotiated case by case and is likely to include payment in respect of the scripts. If the scripts are sold separately some companies take the view that the additional use payments made to the writer in respect of the original script cover this usage as well. In other cases it may be agreed that the writer should receive part of the fee. It is very much a matter for individual negotiation.

ii **Payments for secondary rights** – Entitlements to shares of revenue from exploitation of secondary rights are obviously for separate negotiation in each case, depending on the writer's contribution to the format and the series, and to their track record in creating successful television series. However, as a very general indication, it is usual to agree a 50:50 share of net receipts between producer and originator from licences for changed format rights and 75:25 in favour of the producer in respect of publishing, merchandising, stage, radio and theatrical feature rights. In all cases the definition of net receipts should be gross receipts received by the producer from licensing format rights less customary commissions, costs and copyright fees and payments due to third parties. Where the writer is commissioned to write material for the exploitation of secondary rights, the fees would be subject to good faith negotiation at the time. They would be additional to any entitlement to a share of net receipts.

Credits

It is usual to agree a separate credit for the creator of the format of "Format created by…" which appears on-screen for every episode. This is separate and additional to any credit the format creator might receive for services in writing scripts for the series.

Agreements with first commissioning broadcaster   3.3

Drama and situation comedy series are generally amongst the most expensive types of programming. Commissioning broadcasters who are funding the whole, or the majority, of the cost of production will generally require ownership of all rights in the completed programme worldwide and the right to sell the series in all territories and markets.

This requirement does not preclude the producer retaining some ownership and control of the format rights. In particular, it can usually be agreed that the broadcaster has first opportunity to commission second or subsequent series based on the format, but if they do not do so within two years of commission of the last programme based on the format, the format rights revert to the producer who is then entitled to approach third parties.

For exploitation of changed format rights, where the format and scripts are adapted for production in another territory, while the producer may negotiate to control the changed format rights, in order to enter into agreements with third parties for the exploitation of the rights, it will generally be necessary to obtain the broadcaster's agreement to the use of the scripts and other elements of the original production in the changed format version. The broadcaster's agreement is likely to be conditional on receiving a significant share of the net receipts. It may also be necessary to secure the broadcaster's agreement not to sell the original series in the territory where the changed format series is going to be produced. Given these practical obstacles, although it may not be the most entrepreneurial approach from the producer's point of view, there may be advantages in allowing the broadcaster to control the changed format rights, provided that the producer receives a significant, not less than 50%, share of revenues from any exploitation of the rights.

With secondary rights exploitation may require the broadcaster's agreement to use material from the original series and a share of revenues may be required in return for this. If the broadcaster's distribution arm is set up to handle exploitation of secondary rights, such as publishing and merchandising, there may be advantages in allowing them to control the rights. They may then be prepared to give the exploitation the maximum levels of promotion, along with promotion for the television programmes themselves, provided always that the producer has an entitlement to a share of the revenues. If the producer retains control of the rights, this is likely to be conditional on the broadcaster having an entitlement to a share of the net profits from exploitation of the rights.

4   **AGREEMENTS FOR LICENSING CHANGED FORMAT PRODUCTION**

As a general rule the agreement is structured in such a way that the producer (the licensor) grants the potential licensee the opportunity to produce a pilot programme before committing to a series. If commitment is then made the licensee is granted an exclusive licence in the format in their territory. It is usual to provide that the original producer is engaged as consultant on the production of the pilot programme and possibly the first series too. Key terms are as follows:

4.1   Option

The usual arrangement is to provide that the licensee acquires an initial option for between six and 12 months. The level of option payment is a matter for negotiation, but a starting point for calculation could be 10% of the licence fees payable in respect of the first series. If a series is not commissioned during the option period, the option terminates and the rights revert to the producer.

4.2   Rights

The licensee will require exclusive television rights in the format for the purposes of production of a series. The licence agreement must specify what form of television:

it could be for all forms of television in the territory, or limited to only certain types, e.g. standard terrestrial or pay television. If it is limited to one form of television it would be usual to provide that there is a holdback on the exploitation of the format on other forms of television in the territory during the term.

It would be advisable to expressly exclude any form of Internet screening from the licensee's territory since, as Internet screenings cannot (as yet) be limited territorially, such showings could infringe rights granted to licensees in other territories. Further, and particularly in the case of game shows, the producer may well propose to set up a website where the game can be played interactively.

Territory   4.3

The territory should be limited to production in the licensee's home territory and as a general rule the licensee should not be entitled to sell the programmes outside their territory, unless special terms are agreed for this.

If the licensee does require the right to sell the programmes worldwide, this requires careful negotiation in relation to the extent that this might jeopardise the likelihood of sales of the format rights to other territories, and sales of the original UK production. If the commissioning broadcaster acquired worldwide rights in the original series, any such arrangement would be subject to their agreement, which is likely to be conditional upon entitlement to receive a share of the proceeds. In any event the producer should negotiate to receive a share of net profits from overseas sales of the changed format series.

Secondary rights   4.4

Ideally the producer (licensor) should retain control of the secondary rights in the territory with the licensee being entitled to share in the revenues from any exploitation during the term of their exclusive licence. If the licensee is granted secondary rights, the contract must provide that the rights can only be exploited during the term of the television licence, and be subject to the producer (licensor) having right of approval of any merchandise and an entitlement to a share of revenues from exploitation.

Term   4.5

In the case of game shows, the term should be short, probably not more than two or three years. For drama or situation comedy series, five years would be more appropriate. In either case the usual arrangement would be to provide that it is a rolling licence which, provided an agreed number of programmes is produced during each calendar year, is automatically extended to run from date of production of the last programme in the first, or any subsequent, series.

Payments   4.6

There are obviously a number of ways of structuring the payment depending on the material and services being made available. Sometimes, for example, the overall payment will include the right to use the scripts; in other cases this may be negotiated separately. The usual arrangement would be to provide for a fee to be payable on grant of the licence. This may be additional to subsequent royalties, or an advance against them. In any event a royalty should be payable for each programme. This may be negotiated as a fixed price for the first series, with fixed percentage increases after a certain time period and/or production of a certain number of programmes.

Alternatively, as it may be difficult to determine at the stage of licensing the rights what a reasonable royalty might be, a good solution is to provide that the royalty will be based on a percentage of budget. Budgets will be a very accurate barometer of production values, slot time and frequency, and will increase over the years through inflation and other factors as the licence continues to run. By this method the royalty should always be appropriate to the value of the production. The percentage is obviously subject to negotiation, but anything between about 4% and 10% is frequently agreed.

4.7 Producer consultancy

Whatever deal is being negotiated, it is usual for the producer of the original series to supply consultancy services on the production of the series (whether the licensee wants this or not!). This may be confined to a single visit to the territory, or more extensive involvement may be necessary. In either case, the licensee is required to pay a consultancy fee plus expenses.

5 DEALS WITH FORMAT AGENTS

There are some agents, often attached to distributors, who specialise in selling changed format rights and obviously, where a producer has little experience of this type of activity, it may well be advantageous to engage them. The deal should be on a commission basis, like a distributor, with the format agent receiving a percentage of gross receipts as commission from which he or she recovers a fee and all costs incurred in making the sale.

It is always important to enter into a written agreement with any third party who is being granted rights to represent a property. The deal entered into with a format agent should be similar to the deal for a 'finder', as described in *Chapter 19*.

In the case of sales of game show formats to the USA, the usual practice, as with all approaches to broadcasters in the USA, is through an agent. Over the last year or two a number of UK-originated game shows, most notably *Who Wants To Be A Millionaire?* and *The Weakest Link*, have been adapted for US network production and been spectacularly successful. The William Morris Agency in London has recently led the field in brokering deals for game show formats with US broadcasters.

PUBLIC DOMAIN MATERIAL Chapter 8

There is a great deal of angst among producers working in factual programming as to how to protect ideas for programmes when the subject matter is in the public domain, that is to say, about real life events, people or happenings and as such not an original work protected by copyright. This is, of course, a very difficult area. Anyone who has worked on the receiving end of programme submissions within a broadcasting organisation will, from time to time, have experienced the 'in the ether' syndrome when, over a short period of time, several very similar proposals for a programme on a particular subject land on their desks.

In these circumstances it is completely understandable that those who have unsuccessfully submitted a proposal will be convinced, if they subsequently see the programme on screen, that their idea has been ripped off and letters from a broadcaster assuring them that theirs was just one of a number of similar unsolicited proposals is unlikely to assuage their concerns.

It must also be said that there is frequently considerable circumstantial evidence that the producer's idea has been hijacked by a broadcaster but, because it is based on public domain material, there is no obvious course of legal action available to the producer.

Drama producers frequently plan to base programmes on the life and experience of living individuals. Individuals' life stories are in the public domain and in the vast majority of these cases the individual's story will be drawn from newspaper and magazine articles.

This chapter deals with the steps the producer can take to safeguard his or her position when using public domain material.

KEY TOPICS & ISSUES

C8

**1 AGREEMENTS WITH KEY PARTICIPANTS
AND ORGANISATIONS FOR DOCUMENTARY PROGRAMMES**

Very many documentaries about subjects in the public domain will require the collaboration of key individuals or organisations whose agreement to be filmed and to participate in the documentary may be central to any telling of the story. In the first instance, before approaching a broadcaster with a proposal for a factual programme, it is good practice to obtain a letter confirming the individual's or organisation's agreement to collaborate in the production of the programme. Not only does this add credibility to the proposal, but it also provides a means of enabling the producer to discover whether anybody else is pursuing the same story or whether anyone else subsequently starts to pursue it.

1.1 Exclusivity

Having established contact, a wise move is then to attempt to obtain some kind of exclusivity. The type of agreement required need not be particularly complicated or expensive, but simply provide that for a certain length of time, perhaps six months to a year for topical subjects, the individual and/or organisation agrees to collaborate exclusively with the producer on the preparation and submission of a documentary proposal based on the subject. During this period they also agree not to collaborate with any other person or broadcasting organisation in plans for a programme on the same subject. The agreement may also go on to request that during the exclusivity period the producer is informed if other approaches for production are received.

1.2 Payment

In order to be legally binding (and fair) there will need to be some 'consideration' for the agreement. This can generally be addressed by providing that the exclusivity is granted on condition that, if the producer is successful in mounting production, a fixed fee will be paid. In the case of an individual it might be appropriate to provide that they will be engaged as a consultant, at a fee "commensurate with industry rates for such services current at the time", or "in accordance with the provisions of the final production budget". That is to say it must not be left entirely open for negotiation as and when production is committed since that can prove highly problematic for the producer if reasonable terms cannot be agreed.

If, of course, the subject is about a criminal or about behaviour which is seriously antisocial, under the ITC Programme Code, payments should not be made in respect of the individual's participation in the project unless an important public interest is served.

1.3 Warranties

It is helpful to add a warranty confirming that the individual and/or organisation is in a position to enter into the agreement and that there is no prevailing legal or other reason which limits their ability to do so. It is surprising how often the inclusion of this kind of wording flushes out potential problems.

1.4 Venues

If a venue is key to the telling of the story, agreement needs to be reached with those legally entitled to enter into agreements in respect of filming on the property allowing exclusive access to the producer. Obviously there needs to be a timescale on this exclusivity, say, subject to confirmation of filming dates, within 12 months of the date of agreement, the owner will not allow any other party access for the purpose of filming a documentary on the particular subject. The 'consideration' for this might be a location fee if and when production is mounted.

Details on means of safeguarding programme proposals submitted to broadcasters are contained in *Chapter 12*.

DRAMA PROGRAMMES BASED ON LIVING PERSONS   2

Drama producers frequently wish to base drama productions on the life and/or experiences of a living person. It is a fairly common assumption that to do so it is necessary to obtain the person's prior consent. Under UK law this is not the case, although it seems that in due course privacy laws may be introduced which could change this position, as might the protection afforded to individuals by the Human Rights Act. There is also a possibility that if the programme is shown in other countries the privacy laws of that country could be invoked.

Whether or not to enter into an agreement with the individual is currently a matter of individual judgement. If the person is going to be identified in the programme then this would seem to be the best way of ensuring that the portrayal will be accurate. It is, however, important that such an agreement should not allow the individual any rights of editorial control or approval. However enthusiastic they may be at the outset, there are a great many examples of individuals becoming seriously, and publicly, unhappy as production proceeds as to the manner in which they are being portrayed. If they have any entitlement to withhold approval of editorial matters, the production could be jeopardised.

Further, an agreement does not afford any protection to the producer against subsequent claims by the individual that the programme had libelled them since if the individual could demonstrate that aspects of the portrayal were libellous (meaning that they were both defamatory and untrue) a claim for libel could be upheld. Notwithstanding the existence of an agreement, the producer would be well advised to check out the completed screenplay with a libel lawyer before filming commences.

If it is not proposed to identify the individual in the programme but to base the drama on public domain material about his or her life, whether or not the producer has reached an agreement with the individual, the producer would be well advised to consult with a lawyer specialising in libel as to the development of the storyline. The lawyer will be able to advise on the steps to be taken to ensure that the individual will not be able to claim that he or she can be readily identified in the story and that the narrative does not contain material which could be construed as being libellous.

If the programme is about a deceased person the laws of libel do not apply to the portrayal of that person. If relatives and contemporaries who are still alive are also portrayed libel laws do apply to them even though they may not be central to the story.

AGREEMENTS FOR PRODUCTION SERVICES AND MATERIALS

CHAPTER 9

This chapter is concerned with rights the producer needs to acquire in respect of engagement of individuals to render services on a production and agreements for the use of existing copyright material, such as stills and library footage, generally described as 'limited rights materials'. (Writers' agreements are dealt with separately in *Chapter 6* and composers' agreements in *Chapter 10*.)

During the course of a major production there are any number of contracts which the production company has to enter into in respect of services, materials and facilities of various kinds but there is not scope within this book to deal with them all. This chapter is confined to those services and materials which entail a grant of rights, be they of copyright or in the form of consents, from an individual or organisation and without which the producer's ability to fully exploit the production might be jeopardised.

It is, of course, a condition of all agreements for production finance that a producer must acquire copyright in all materials specially commissioned for the programme and it is best practice to do so. This extends to acquiring the copyright in the products of the services of all the individuals engaged on the production team, from the director to the runner. In very many cases there may be no copyright at all in the product of an individual's services, but productions involve teamwork, and it can always happen that someone who may not be engaged in a creative role on the production may nonetheless suggest, for example, an image or some lines of dialogue, in which copyright could be deemed to exist, hence the need for the assignment.

In practice, in the vast majority of cases this necessity to get assignments of copyright is not as daunting as it may sound. All the standard form Equity, Writers' Guild, BECTU, Musicians' Union and FAA contracts for talent and technical personnel, and the industrial relations agreements which govern them, provide for an assignment of copyright and give necessary consents to the producer. Further, the PACT standard form contracts which PACT members can use for most types of engagement on production – director, producer, consultant, technical adviser, special researcher, presenter, composers, location consent and interview release forms – also provide for the necessary assignment of rights in the material.

This chapter gives background to the key terms for those agreements.

KEY TOPICS & ISSUES

SERVICE AGREEMENTS

1

Directors

1.1

Until recently, agreements for directors in the UK were customarily relatively straightforward hire contracts, routinely providing for the fee to be a buyout in respect both of the assignment of all the directors' rights and of all worldwide exploitation of the production. However, a recent European Union copyright directive which has been adopted by the member states provides that, in the first instance, the ownership of the copyright in a film or sound recording is now shared between the principal director and the person by whom the arrangements necessary for the making of the film or sound recording are undertaken (see *Chapter 1, Paragraph 3.2*).

When this grant of shared ownership for the director of copyright in the production was introduced, the Directors' and Producers' Rights Society (DPRS), the Directors' Guild and BECTU pressed for a change to the customary buyout provisions of television directors' agreements which they had long argued were unfair. Directors collectively withheld assignment of copyright in their television work until agreement was reached with the broadcasters for additional payments in respect of overseas sales of productions. This was resolved by the broadcasters setting aside a pool of revenues, representing a percentage proportion of each of their overall production spend which is paid to the DPRS for disbursement among individual directors in accordance with the volume of sales achieved by their individual productions, in rather a similar way to that in which the Performing Rights Society distributes revenues from exploitation of music rights to composers. Independent productions for the broadcasters fall within the ambit of this arrangement.

With this mechanism in place the directors agreed to resume the customary full assignment of copyright to the producer, coupled with a moral rights waiver. In practical terms this assignment of copyright is required by all production financiers, be they broadcasters or film financiers, not least because their ability to raise sale and leaseback and other forms of production finance is contingent on their holding the entire copyright in the completed production (see *Chapter 18*).

So far as directors' fees are concerned, whereas on most television productions it is usual to agree a weekly rate, on major television drama productions and on feature films, the normal practice is to agree a 'picture deal', whereby the director's fee is expressed as being a fixed amount for his or her services on the production, which applies even if the production schedule, and consequently the director's engagement, is extended far beyond the length originally envisaged.

On television productions it is very rare for a director to have an entitlement to a share of net profits. In the case of feature films, as relatively few directors are acceptable to film financiers, those who are are clearly in a strong bargaining position to demand a share of net profits in addition to their fee. If net profits are agreed it is usual for them to be in the region of 2.5-5% of producer's net profits. See *Chapter 5, Paragraph 5.4* for definition. Because of the dismal return from any entitlement to shares of net profits, it is becoming relatively common for feature film directors to also negotiate an entitlement to a bonus when a film's gross box office takings reach a certain level. These types of provision are obviously for individual negotiation in each case, in relation to the director's reputation, the size of the budget and the nature of the production.

C9

1.2 Actors

Actors, as well as singers, stuntmen and women, walk-ons, voice-over artists and some television presenters are generally members of the actors' union Equity and actors' contracts, even those for the most celebrated actors, are dealt with under the standard form agreements issued by Equity. In comparison to contracts for underlying rights material they are generally relatively straightforward once the schedule of rehearsal and recording days has been finalised and the engagement fee agreed, although key cast issues such as size and placing of credits and provision of transport and make-up/wardrobe facilities can require careful and tactful negotiation, particularly in relation to what might be being accorded to other actors on the production.

So far as issues relating to copyright in performances are concerned, these are now provided for under the Copyright, Design and Patents Act 1988. (Previously performers' rights were protected by the Performers' Protection Acts, which have been repealed.) Under the CDPA it is a criminal offence and an infringement of the performer's rights, to record his/her performance (other than for private or domestic use), televise the live or recorded performance or show it to the public without the performer's consent. In practice, this consent forms part of the standard Equity contract.

Further, under the EU directive on lending and rental rights, performers are regarded as 'authors' of a programme, and as such the rights granted to the producer must also specifically include the assignment of the lending and rental right. The payment provisions of an actor's agreement must specify that the fee represents equitable remuneration in respect of the revenues from the exercise of lending and rental rights.

EU copyright directives currently being finalised are likely to provide for moral rights for performers in much the same way as those granted to the creators of original literary works (see *Chapter 1, Paragraph 5.10*). These provisions are likely to be drafted to address, in particular, the digital manipulation of performances which new technology is bringing about. It is likely that when these moral rights provisions are introduced the standard form actors' agreements will be amended to provide for a moral rights waiver.

Cast options

Whereas actors' engagement contracts are relatively straightforward, they become more complex when an actor is being engaged for a role in a production which, if the production proves successful, may be recommissioned for a number of subsequent series. At the time of the initial engagement no-one can predict whether the production will be a success or whether the actor will prove so popular in the role that the part could not be dispensed with in the event that future productions are commissioned.

At this initial stage no production financier is going to be prepared to fund option fees, or give 'pay or play' guarantees in respect of engagements of future productions: statistically the success rate on television productions makes the risk too great. At the same time a producer cannot run the risk of not being able to engage the actor on future productions or having the actor's agreement to appear in future productions being conditional on the payment of huge fees.

The usual method of dealing with this is to establish at the very outset of the negotiation of terms for the actor's engagement on the initial production that the actor will be prepared, in principle, to accept an engagement to play the same role on future productions. Sometimes actors are not prepared to give such a commitment: they do not want to run the risk of becoming too closely identified with one role. If the storyline for the first production has definite potential for future productions, it would obviously be extremely unwise to engage an actor who is not prepared to give any commitment on future series.

If the actor is prepared to agree, in principle, to be involved in future productions, the usual arrangement is to provide that either the engagement fee for the first series (or a nominal fee of £1) is the 'consideration' for the actor agreeing to be available on future series, subject to the following conditions:

i   that he or she is notified as to whether or not the production is to be recommissioned within a certain period of completion of recording/transmissions of the first production (e.g. nine months from completion of recording of the first production or three months from first transmission of the production whichever is the earlier date);

ii   that, if the production is recommissioned, the actor's engagement will be on dates to be confirmed between month A and month B; the exact dates of the engagement will be confirmed no later than, say, four weeks prior to commencement of the engagement. (If the actor has been given notification under (i) that the production is to be recommissioned, if the production did not, in the event go ahead, the actor would nonetheless be entitled to receive the fee he or she would have received on production since, once notification has been given, the actor is under an obligation to keep him or herself available over the period in (ii).); and

iii   that the actor's engagement day fee for the first production will be increased by X% for the second series.

There may be added refinements on this structure: for example, the actor may be required, or may require, to be in all the episodes or only some episodes. The option should be a rolling one so that, if having produced a second series, the producer wants the actor to be available for third, fourth and subsequent series, the notification period, the engagement period and the increase in fee can all be specified in the original contract.

An added complexity in all this is that it is likely to be necessary to secure commitments to this type of arrangement from at least three or four lead actors in the original production: try to allow at least two or three weeks' negotiation period prior to commencement of the engagements in order to get it sorted out, since once recording has started the actor is in a very strong position and it may be too late to get a satisfactory deal.

Children

Performances by children are governed by the Children and Young Persons Acts 1933 and 1963 and the Children (Performances) Regulations 1968. Publications explaining these acts can be obtained from Her Majesty's Stationery Office (HMSO). If a child is to be engaged on a production the production company has to provide a chaperone and a tutor if filming takes place during the school term. The chaperone and tutor may be the same person and may take care of several children. Hours of work for children are restricted. A licence must be obtained from the education authority where the child lives. The local council education officer can supply the relevant application form.

C9

1.3 Musicians

As with actors, musicians are 'performers' under the meaning of the CDPA and thus rights and consents have to be obtained in their performances for a production. Musicians should be contracted under the relevant Musicians' Union agreement which specifically grants to the producer, among other things, the right to synchronise the musician's performance with the production. It also provides for the necessary consent for the use of the performance.

Singers are contracted under Equity agreements.

For further information on music copyright and on composers' agreements see *Chapter 10*.

1.4 Presenters

Some presenters may be 'performing' and be members of Equity, contracted under Equity contracts. In most cases, however, presenters are contracted by individual negotiation, with fees varying according to the type of production, the time involved and the reputation of the presenter. Issues such as exclusivity for television of the presenter's services, options to present future series (for which the proposals contained in *Paragraph 1.2* above might be adapted) and, in a number of cases, the right to publish a book featuring the presenter of the series will also require negotiation. Broadcasters often have strong views on appropriate terms for presenters' engagements, being reluctant to accept arrangements which might create difficult precedents with their other presenters. The producer may find it advantageous to consult with the broadcasters' own in-house negotiators when negotiating a deal for a presenter.

1.5 Interviewees/contributors

Now that recorded speech comes under the definition of a literary work attracting copyright, it is necessary to get a written grant of the right to use the copyright material from interviewees featured in a production. This is commonly known as a 'blood chit'. It is also necessary to obtain a consent form from an individual making some other 'real-life' contribution to a production, for example, giving a demonstration. The usual method of doing this is to get the interviewee or contributor to sign an interviewee or contributor release form, confirming their formal consent to the use of the interview or contribution within the production.

It is necessary to obtain release forms from everyone interviewed for a production irrespective of location or nationality. It is sensible, if filming overseas, to have release forms translated into the language of the country in which filming is to take place.

1.6 Stills photographers

If a stills photographer is to be engaged to take photographs for inclusion in the programme or for publicity material, it is important to note that under the CDPA the first owner of the copyright is the person who takes the photographs, notwithstanding the fact that the photographer may be being paid to do so and/or supplied with the film and other materials. It is, therefore, necessary to ensure that the agreement with the stills photographer expressly provides for an assignment of copyright to the producer. For use of existing material see *Paragraph 2.2* below.

1.7 Original research

There are standard form contracts for researchers which provide for the necessary assignment of rights in a researcher's services. However, on occasion a producer may be approached by, or discover, individuals who have carried out substantial research on a particular subject which could form the basis for a production. Such research cannot, strictly speaking, be said to constitute 'original copyright material' since if one individual can research it, so, presumably, can another. However, the researcher may have had particular rights of access to the material not available to others. Also, the expertise and resources required to research the subject may be extremely hard to come by.

In these circumstances the usual arrangement is for the producer to acquire exclusive rights of access to the research material for the purposes of production. Generally research material would be intended to form the basis for a documentary production, and in such case it would be sufficient for the producer to obtain exclusive access to the material for the purpose of producing only factual documentary programmes on the subject.

An 'end date' should be agreed for the producer's exclusive right of access: anything shorter than about two years from date of entering into the agreement would probably be cutting things rather fine. However, this type of material, by its nature, will often be topical, so, unless a high price is being paid for it, it may not be reasonable to expect exclusivity for too long a period.

The researcher may want to reserve publishing rights and may have sold the rights prior to approaching the producer. The producer should, however, try to ensure that the issue of any publication coincides with the release of the television programme. Any use of material from the production within the publication would be subject to negotiation.

There are two main possibilities for assessing the level of payment:

i   the 2% of budget formula, but expressed as a fixed price, e.g. if it is anticipated that the budget may be around £150,000, agree a fixed price of £3,000; or

ii   an estimate of the cost of employing an experienced researcher to carry out similar research.

In many cases the researcher will want to be engaged on the production in some capacity, usually as a consultant, and the producer may need to have continuing access to him or her. In this case a fee, or a formula for arriving at a fee, should be included in the research agreement. As a very general rule, no consultancy fee should be in excess of the fee payable under Writers' Guild agreements for a script for a fictional programme of the same length: in many instances it would be appropriate for it to be much less.

When research material will form the basis for a drama production, a more appropriate form of agreement would be that described for treatments (see *Chapter 6, Paragraph 3*).

Employees   1.8

Under the CDPA the employer is the first owner of the copyright in the services of an employee. There is, however, no precise legal definition as to what constitutes 'an employee': it is not as simple as whether or not PAYE is deducted from income at source. Other considerations are, for example, whether or not the services are to be carried out on the employer's premises, using the employer's equipment, working under the direction and control of the employer.

Given that ownership of copyright is essential for production and exploitation of programmes, the producer would be wise to ensure that all contracts for permanent staff, as well as those for freelance staff, who are working on a production provide that copyright (if any) in the products of their services is assigned to the producer.

C9

2   AGREEMENTS FOR MATERIALS

2.1   Location agreements

To film on private property, the producer requires the consent of the owner. It is always essential to enter into a written agreement with the owner of the property. This should confirm not only practical matters such as dates and length of filming period, payment, alterations which may be required to the property, insurance and so forth; but also specifically grant the producer the right to feature the premises in the production, exploit the production throughout the world and use images of the premises in press and publicity material – all without any further payments being due to the owner in respect of such usage. The producer must also be specifically entitled to portray the premises as being another, fictional or non-fictional, venue.

It is important to establish that the party entering into the agreement is the owner of the property or, if they are not the owner, that they have an agreement with the owner which entitles them to enter into the contract on behalf of the owner.

The PACT standard form contracts include a location agreement and producers need to be extremely careful to ensure that a signed agreement is in place before production arrangements are too far advanced. Too many productions have been held to ransom, quite literally, by the owners of property who are fully aware that, once filming is about to start (or has begun), it would be extremely expensive and difficult for the producer to change the location if the owner then objects to any aspect of the arrangements.

When a producer proposes to film in the street, if the cast, crew and attendant equipment are such that their presence is likely disrupt the normal use of the street by the general public, a permit must be obtained from the applicable local authority, as well as from the police.

2.2   Limited rights materials

Limited rights material is existing copyright material which the producer may wish to include within the production but which is not integral to the programme. If the producer is unable to obtain the necessary rights or licence in such material, it can be excluded from the production and other material, in which the necessary rights can be obtained, used instead.

Limited rights material may take many forms, but the principal types of existing material which may be required for production are archive film, still photographs and library material. Existing music and sound recordings of existing music which also fall within this category are dealt with in *Chapter 10*.

While contracts with broadcasters and other financiers will generally specify that the producer must obtain copyright and rights of all descriptions throughout the world in material included within the production, with existing copyright material the contract will recognise the producer may not be able to obtain such rights. In such circumstances, the contract (and the production budget) will specify the uses (clearances) for which the producer must obtain a licence and pay (clear) from the production budget – for example, three UK transmissions over three years.

Notwithstanding the fact that, initially, only three UK transmissions are being cleared, the producer will be placed under an obligation to ensure that the copyright material is 'clearable', that is to say that a worldwide licence can be obtained, if required, and pre-agree with the rights holders a price which will clear the rights for such worldwide usage.

If the rights owners will not confirm that the material can be cleared for worldwide use and/or pre-agree terms for such usage, it would be very unwise to use the material since, if it were proposed to sell the programme overseas, it might not be possible to obtain retrospective clearance for the material, or at least not at a reasonable price. Production agreements provide that the producer is not permitted to include such material within the production without the express prior consent of the production financier.

It is important when negotiating clearances to clarify that the library owns not only rights to the physical material but the copyright as well, since a producer might otherwise find that two licence fees need to be paid: one to the owner of the physical materials; the other to the copyright owner.

Usually clearance costs are charged on a per minute basis, so take care to ensure that, for example, the clip does not run to one minute three seconds, or the extra three seconds will cost the rate for an additional minute. Rates will, of course, depend on the nature and scarcity of the material being used.

In the case of material featuring performers, it needs to be established that the licensee has obtained the necessary permissions and clearances from those featured. Sometimes actors withhold permission for the use of material featuring performances they would prefer the public to forget!

For more detailed information on clearances, refer to *Rights Clearances For Film And Television Productions* by Stephen Edwards, published by PACT.

C10

MUSIC COPYRIGHT AND Chapter 10
COMPOSERS' AGREEMENTS

The music business is the most highly organised of any creative business in ensuring a financial return and otherwise protecting the interests of those who work in it – composers, performers and/or producers of all kinds of sound recordings. It is not surprising then that the highest earners in the world are composers and recording artists. Further, it is no exaggeration to describe music as the bogeyman of production procedures. It has been said that to understand music copyright fully takes the lifetime of the composer and 70 years thereafter! Those who do not deal with music copyright day in, day out are unlikely to have a sure grasp of what it entails, since the procedures are somewhat intricate.

Copyright in musical compositions is a bundle of different rights and, further, sound recordings of music attract a separate copyright. This chapter contains a brief explanation of copyright as it relates to film and television production and to the key terms and arrangements for composers' agreements.

KEY TOPICS & ISSUES

C10

1 NEW MUSICAL COMPOSITIONS

1.1 Owner of the copyright

The first owner of the copyright in a musical composition is the composer. With songs the copyright is shared equally by the composer and the lyricist (if they are not the same person) and the revenues are shared equally between them.

1.2 Music publishing rights

Many composers, even when being commissioned to write a piece of music, are not prepared to agree an assignment of the copyright to the commissioning party. This is because the copyright in their compositions is generally handled by their music publishing company.

Most established composers will have an exclusive agreement with a music publishing company, under which the composer grants rights in all his or her compositions to the music publishing company, which is charged with the commercial exploitation of the rights and with receiving, on behalf of the composer, all revenues from exploitation of the rights through the Performing Rights Society (PRS) and other sources. The music publishing company generally takes a commission of 20-25% of revenues earned from exploitation of the rights, with the balance being paid to the composer.

Broadcasters, and a number of production companies regularly commissioning music for production, have their own music publishing companies and when music is being commissioned for productions, the broadcaster or the production company will aim to acquire the copyright in the music and grant the rights to its music publishing company to handle on its behalf.

Not withstanding the fact that most composers have their own music publishers, it is a standard condition of most broadcasters' agreements for independent productions that, in the first instance, the producer obtains music publishing rights in any music commissioned for the production and that these rights are in turn assigned to the broadcaster's music publishing company, unless the broadcaster has expressly agreed other arrangements. More details of how this is dealt with in practice are contained in *Paragraph 4* below.

Having resolved the question of music publishing rights, the performing right and the synchronisation right now concern the producer.

1.3 The performing right

The performing right is the right to perform the music in public, broadcast it and include it in a cable programme service.

Almost without exception all established composers or, if applicable, their music publishing company, will be members of the Performing Rights Society (PRS) which is a non-profit making collecting society for composers, authors and publishers of music works. The PRS is set up to administer the performing right and to collect royalties worldwide on behalf of its members from the exercise of the performing rights. In order to do this, the PRS is affiliated to other such collecting societies throughout the world, with which it has reciprocal arrangements.

How this works in practice is that the composers (or their music publishing companies) who are members of the PRS assign to the PRS the performing rights in the music. The PRS in turn licenses the performing rights in the music to those wishing to perform it. The person who requires a licence in the performing right is not actually the producer, but the person exercising the right, i.e. the broadcaster, cinema owner, and those who own or are responsible for the premises where the public performance is taking place. These premises may range from restaurants with piped music to concert halls, to the premises of the broadcasting service or the cinema at which the film is being screened.

Blanket licences

All the terrestrial broadcasters in the UK have a blanket licence agreement with the PRS, under which they make a periodic return to the PRS in respect of all the music performed over the period and pay a licence fee to them in respect of the performance. Blanket licences are also currently being negotiated for the digital channels. (No blanket licence has yet been negotiated for Internet usage.)

Music cue sheets

To make the return to the PRS, the broadcaster requires producers to complete music cue sheets which give all necessary information about the composer, the length and type of music. With this information the PRS can then apportion the licence fee revenues between those composers/music publishers whose work has been performed.

The synchronisation right   1.4

This is the right to record the music and synchronise the recording with the visual images of the production and thus, is a separate right to the music publishing rights and the performing rights in the composition.

For music which is specially commissioned for a production the performing rights are handled through the PRS arrangements outlined above (the contract will specify that the performing rights in the music will be granted to the PRS), but the contract with the composer must specifically provide that the producer is granted a worldwide synchronisation licence in the music for the full period of copyright (see *Paragraph 4* below).

RE-RECORDING EXISTING MUSIC   2

If it is proposed to re-record existing music in a programme – and be aware that re-recording means anything from recording someone humming or whistling the tune through to a full orchestral performance of the existing music – it is necessary to acquire the following rights in the music:

Synchronisation rights   2.1

A licence in the synchronisation rights is required when a producer wishes to re-record any existing music for use in the production. The great majority of composers/ music publishing companies are members of the Mechanical Copyright Protection Society (MCPS) which acts as a central licensing organisation for all forms of music recording. The MCPS negotiates synchronisation licences on behalf of its members. It too has blanket agreements with the broadcasters in the UK under which the broadcasters are entitled to record all works in which the synchronisation rights are controlled by the MCPS, in return for the payment of a blanket licence fee and subject to the broadcasters making returns in respect of the uses.

It is important for producers to be aware that if the copyright in the production is not vested with the broadcaster, the blanket licence will not cover the use of the existing music in the production and the producer will have to reach separate agreement with the MCPS (or the rights holder if the synchronisation rights are not administered by the MCPS).

In all cases the producer should check with the MCPS whether it controls the synchronisation rights in the particular piece of music which the producer wishes to re-record and, if it is a production for a UK broadcaster, whether the usage will come under the broadcaster's blanket licence agreement.

In some cases the MCPS will not control the synchronisation rights or, if it does control the rights, will not be entitled to license them for the proposed usage. In such circumstances the producer will have to negotiate direct with the music publisher/ copyright owner. Sometimes the rights owners will simply not be prepared to grant a synchronisation licence, in which case the music cannot be used at all. In others, such an extortionate fee may be required that it cannot possibly be met from the production budget.

Whilst the MCPS controls synchronisation rights in approximately 95% of compositions, the 5% which it does not control are generally the well-known songs by very famous artists – the Beatles, Michael Jackson, Rogers and Hammerstein, Frank Sinatra, to name but a few. In very many such cases it will not be possible to obtain a licence to re-record the music (or to use the existing recordings).

2.2 Dramatic/musical works and ballets: grand rights

The rights in dramatic/musical works – operas, operettas and music plays, revues and pantomimes if the music has been written specially for them, and in ballets (as distinct from country or folk dancing, precision dance sequences or tap dancing) – are known as 'grand rights'. They are not administered by either the PRS or the MCPS but are controlled by the copyright owner. If it is planned to make a programme featuring either the whole or extracts from these works, the grand right broadcasting fee plus the fee in respect of a licence in the synchronisation rights will have to be negotiated. Rates for these are set out by the Music Publishers' Association. The fees tend to be very high and come with a number of extras, such as hire fees for the scores and parts that the orchestra will use, plus Equity rates for the singers.

2.3 Lyrics and parodies

The lyrics of a song form part of the copyright in the music and, as such, are treated in exactly the same way as rights in the musical notation.

If it is intended to change the wording of the lyrics to accompany the original tune, if the composition is still in copyright it is necessary to obtain the prior permission of the copyright owner. In the case of many well-known songs, this permission may not be forthcoming – although it is sometimes easier to obtain permission if it is for humorous purposes. If permission is obtained, it is customary for the copyright in the parodied lyrics to be assigned to the owner of the copyright in the original lyrics.

3 USE OF EXISTING SOUND RECORDINGS

In a number of cases existing sound recordings may be used, either as incidental music or as feature music within the production. In either case the issues which the producer needs to deal with are as follows:

3.1 Ownership of copyright in sound recordings

Notwithstanding the composer's (or his or her assignees') ownership of copyright in the musical composition, the separate copyright in the sound recordings of the composition is, in the first instance, vested with the person responsible for making the arrangements for the recording, generally a record company.

Performing right   3.2

The performing right is the right to perform a sound recording publicly, broadcast it or include it in a cable programme service. As a general rule, the performing rights will be controlled by Phonographic Performance Ltd (PPL) which administers the performing right in the copyright in original sound recordings in a similar way to that in which the PRS administers the performing right in the original music. Its membership is made up of record companies and other owners of sound recordings who have assigned the performing rights in the sound recordings to the PPL, which in turn enters into licence agreements with those actually performing the recordings on their premises. PPL also disburses the revenues from such licences, primarily to its record company members, but also to the performers credited on the label and to the Musicians' Union in recognition of the work of background musicians.

Dubbing right   3.3

This is the right to copy a sound recording onto film or video tape. In order to include the recording in the production, the producer needs to acquire a licence in the sound recording for the purpose of dubbing it onto the production. Unless the use of the recordings comes within the British Phonographic Industry (BPI) blanket licence, as outlined below, the usage will need to be negotiated with the copyright owner of the recording, generally the record company.

Notwithstanding the grant of a licence in the dubbing rights by the owner of the sound recordings, if the original music is still in copyright the producer will also need to negotiate a synchronisation licence in the original music (see *Paragraph 2.1* above).

The BPI represents manufacturers, producers and sellers of records, tapes and CDs. Its main function is not the administration of rights but it may, in some instances, have the right to grant dubbing licences on behalf of some of its members.

The BPI has blanket dubbing agreements with the major UK broadcasters, under which the broadcaster is entitled to dub BPI members' records onto films and broadcasts in return for an annual fee. The terms of these agreements vary from broadcaster to broadcaster: the blanket licence may only cover the right to use the sound recording on the broadcast in the UK; it may not necessarily extend to independent productions and it may not cover the recordings which the producer wishes to use. A producer must, therefore, check the proposed use of the sound recordings with the commissioning broadcasters to establish whether they will come within the provisions of the blanket licence and the extent to which the producer will require a wider licence than that provided by the 'blanket' for the purposes of worldwide exploitation of the production.

Musicians' Union clearances   3.4

Although the company responsible for making the sound recordings will generally have cleared all rights in the performances of Musicians' Union members used on the recording, the Musicians' Union requires producers to make payments for the right to use the performances on the existing sound recording on the production. PACT has negotiated terms for such payments and producers should consult with the Producers Rights Agency formerly Producers Industrial Relations Service or the Musicians' Union to check the level of payment prior to including the recordings on the production.

These are known as the 'combined use fee' and currently cover use of the music on the Internet.

4   COMPOSERS' AGREEMENTS

When commissioning original music for a production, the following issues need to be addressed. (PACT has standard term agreements for composers which provide for alternative wording depending on whether or not music publishing rights are being acquired.)

4.1   Ownership, control and shares of revenue

As explained in *Paragraph 1* above, many composers have an arrangement with their own music publishing company, which handles the copyright in their music. They may not, therefore, be prepared to accept a commission which carries with it the obligation to assign the music publishing rights or will only do so if they receive an exceptionally high fee in compensation for the loss of revenues from music publishing income. Some may be contractually bound by their agreements with their own music publishing companies not to grant the music publishing rights to a third party.

A compromise proposal can be negotiated whereby it is agreed that the rights are vested either with the composer, his or her music publishing company or with the commissioning production company's music publisher, with the revenues from music publishing, after the deduction of the music publisher's commission, being shared between the composer and the production company. The shares are subject to negotiation, but there is considerable custom and practice for a 50:50 split.

In the case of signature music for potentially long-running series it would obviously be sensible for the producer to go to considerable lengths, either to obtain the music publishing rights in the music outright, or to negotiate for a significant share of the music publishing revenues, since the revenues from PRS earnings on a long-running series may be very significant. In other cases, it may be more beneficial, commercially and creatively, for the producer to allow the composer to retain the music publishing rights in return for receiving a low fee for the composition, than to fight difficult battles for control of the music publishing rights when the potential revenues from a single production may not be of great consequence.

(It is usual, when music publishing rights are being acquired, for the agreement with the music publishing company to be attached as a schedule to the composers' agreement).

4.2   Performing rights

The agreement must expressly provide for the grant of performing rights in the music, with revenues being administered and collected through the PRS (see *Paragraph 1.3* above).

4.3   Synchronisation rights

The agreement must expressly provide for the producer to be granted a worldwide synchronisation licence in the composition for the purpose of including the music in the programme. As a general rule, this will be an exclusive worldwide licence, i.e. the music cannot be used in synchronisation with any other production.

The agreement should also specify whether the exclusive synchronisation licence is for the use of music in the programme or series for which it is initially being commissioned only, or whether it extends to the use of the composition in sequel or spin-off series.

Recording the music   4.4

It is usual to do a package deal with the composer whereby, in return for a single overall fee, he or she composes the music and produces the sound recordings of it for the production. The composer's fee covers the rights in the composition, as outlined above, and the rights in the sound recording, which may be the assignment of copyright in the recording or the grant of a synchronisation and dubbing licence. The fee also covers all the fees payable by the composer in respect of the use of the studio, engagement of musicians and so forth. The contract makes the composer liable for all these contracts, and payments to musicians under the Musicians' Union agreements.

If the composer's agreement is not structured as a package deal, the contract must specify whether the producer or the composer is responsible for booking studios, musicians and so forth for the purpose of recording, and which party is responsible for contracting and making payments.

THE INTERNET/ON-LINE MATERIAL: Chapter 11
COPYRIGHT AND SERVICE AGREEMENTS

The Internet and digital technology have probably been the most significant audio-visual developments since the invention of television itself. As the technology develops and, in particular, as the long-awaited roll-out of broadband comes about, facilitating the swift downloading of films and programmes, the current structures, practices and economics of the audio-visual industry are likely to undergo a sea change. Many production companies now have their own website and are planning programme-related websites. E-commerce possibilities are also being explored. Deal structures are having to be devised to address these new forms of programme and usage.

To write definitively about the type of deal structures a producer may encounter is impossible because they will be evolving for years to come. However, just because the technology is new does not mean that existing legal and commercial structures aren't appropriate for it. In very many cases, with a bit of tinkering with the wording, they are.

This chapter gives a brief description of copyright issues relating to material shown on the Internet and intended for on-line uses and to the structure of agreements for websites and e-commerce. Agreements with UK broadcasters for Internet showings and for commissions for digital channels are addressed in *Chapter 17*.

KEY TOPICS & ISSUES

C11

1 COPYRIGHT AND THE INTERNET

There is a tendency for people to assume that because material is on the Internet it is, so to speak, in the ether, and usual terrestrial copyright laws do not apply. They do. The laws which apply to reproducing copyright material on the Internet are no different to those which apply in any film or television programme. The same procedures for the acquisition of rights and clearances have to be observed. The same laws apply to the ownership of copyright in material specially created for use on websites.

Obviously copyright law is being developed to keep pace with Internet and digital developments and this is being done through the World Intellectual Property Organisation (WIPO) which is an agency of the United Nations responsible for developing global policies and treaties in relation to intellectual property (copyright material). These treaties are being adopted by many countries with the aim of providing consistent protection for copyright works and performances disseminated in digital form since, to be effective, legislation related to the Internet will need to be observed internationally. To date, some court judgements in different countries on the same Internet issues have been at significant variance, which could lead to a practice of disseminating material on the Internet from a different country in order to take advantage of a more lenient jurisdiction.

Piracy is one of the major problems with digital technology, but it appears likely that in the near future a means will be found of encrypting data which will prevent the unauthorised use of copyright material recorded in digital form.

2 DOMAIN NAMES

Domain names are part of website addresses (which are technically known as URLs – Uniform Resource Locators). Computers connected to the Internet have unique numerical addresses so that the electronic information is delivered to the right place. The domain name system translates the numerical addresses of computers into more user-friendly and memorable names such as www.pact.co.uk

2.1 Registration

It is inexpensive and easy to register a domain name. There are various ways it can be done but it is usually through an Internet Service Provider (ISP) or through an organisation called Nominet.UK which is described as the UK Internet Names Organisation.

What are described as 'top-level' domain names such as .com, .org, .net, .name, .info, .biz can only be registered by registrars accredited by ICANN (Internet Corporation for Assigned Names and Numbers), a non-profit making organisation based in the USA working in collaboration with WIPO.

Under UK copyright law, as with titles and names, there is no protection for domain names. Protection against the unauthorised use of a domain name comes under the laws relating to trade marks and passing off (see *Chapter 1, Paragraphs 6.4 and 7.6*).

2.2 Cybersquatting

In the early days of the expansion of the Internet a practice emerged known as cybersquatting. An individual registered the names of a whole range of organisations and individuals which did not, at that stage, have websites or e-mail addresses, including such household names as BT, Marks & Spencer, Virgin, Sainsbury as well as the names of some well-known individuals as domain names. When these organisations/individuals discovered that their name had already been registered as a domain name and, thus, it was not possible for them to use the name in a website address without first purchasing it from the cybersquatter, litigation swiftly followed and the test case found against the cybersquatter. Cybersquatting is now much less common but it does still happen because, in order to have the registration ruled illegal, the organisation/individual has to take the cybersquatter to court. Cybersquatters have discovered that companies would rather pay them (£500, say) for the name than incur legal costs of several thousand pounds in taking them to court. An alternative is to refer the dispute to the arbitration panel of WIPO which adopts the policy that, if it is found that the person making the registration has no legitimate interest and is using a name in bad faith, the registration can be cancelled. This costs approximately £1,000.

As domain names are registered on a first come, first served basis, it is sensible practice, when producing a television series or a film, to register the title as a domain name before there is any public knowledge of the title. There is no requirement for the domain name to be registered as a trade mark in order to protect against cybersquatting. Successful actions can also be brought in 'passing off', when it can be demonstrated that members of the public mistakenly believe that the registered domain name is linked to a very similar trading name.

CONTRACTS WITH INTERNET SERVICE PROVIDERS 3

Many domestic Internet Services Providers (ISPs) offer all sorts of services free of charge: domain name registration, e-mail addresses, web space etc. However, particularly for a commercial website, it is advisable to enter into a formal contract with the ISP covering such issues as guaranteed availability for the website, back-up on a reserve server if the server fails, stipulations as to level of traffic, responsibility for the security of the website, fault reporting procedures and performance levels.

A European Union copyright directive has recently ruled (rather surprisingly) that an ISP does not have the same legal liability in relation to material included on a website which may be in breach of copyright or libellous, defamatory, obscene and blasphemous as publishers and broadcasters in the UK who are responsible for the content of material which they 'publish'. The responsibility lies with the producer of the website. The ISP should, however, be placed under an obligation to act promptly to remove or disable access to any such material if requested to do so by the producer.

CONTRACTING FOR WEBSITES 4

Arrangements with broadcasters for websites linked to programmes are outlined in *Chapter 17*. When setting up a website, care needs to be taken to ensure that the necessary rights in the design and all material shown on the site have been acquired and cleared. If the site is offering goods for sale, such as books and videos, the e-commerce procedures need to be observed. Key issues are as follows:

Contracts for design of the site 4.1

The work involved in designing and setting up a website is as long as the proverbial piece of string. A website for promoting a programme can be designed very simply using a desktop PC and stills and clips from the programme. There is copyright in the design of the site so the producer should ensure that he or she obtains the necessary written assignment of copyright from whoever is doing the design. Necessary clearances will have to be obtained for the use of still photographs, although so far as agreements with the talent unions are concerned, promotion on a website is no different to other forms of promotion and as such does not attract additional payment.

For more sophisticated websites a designer or developer may be engaged to create it. The first owner of the copyright in the original design, source code and other materials is the creator. It is, therefore, necessary to enter into a written agreement with the designer providing for an assignment of copyright in all materials created for the website. The contract will also need to set out a design specification including availability and bandwith, performance levels, security, testing and delivery procedures and a timetable for completion and delivery, with the staging allowing aspects of the design to be changed before the website is launched.

4.2   Engagement of 'talent'/clearances

At present there are no union agreements covering writers, actors and musicians who are being engaged to render services on material being commissioned specially for a website. The usual arrangement is to agree a fixed fee providing for the assignment of copyright/granting of consents, and provide, as a minimum, that the fee is a buyout in respect of the use of the material in all formats, by all means and in all media now known or hereinafter invented. It is usual for there to be a time limitation on the use of the material, possibly three years, but the producer should ensure that the contract provides for the entitlement to extend the usage for a further term on payment of a fixed fee.

The contracting of music tends to be particularly difficult. Blanket agreements do not cover Internet usage and terms for Internet usage have not, at the time of writing, been negotiated with the Musicians' Union. Because of the current ease of pirating music on the Internet it is likely to take some time for arrangements to be agreed, by which time it may well be possible to encrypt music to prevent any unauthorised recording.

Archive and library footage needs to be cleared for use on all on-line formats. A licence covering all forms of television dissemination now known or hereinafter invented would give this clearance.

4.3   Live web cams

If the website has live web cams, be careful to ensure a slight time delay to remove/edit material which participants may introduce, such as photographs and music, which may infringe copyright.

4.4   Linking and framing

It has not yet been determined whether linking, that is linking one website to another, and framing, that is displaying another website in a smaller window, infringes copyright. It would, however, be advisable to obtain permission from each website to which there is a link or frame.

4.5   Copyright notice

The website should display a copyright notice and a warning that no reproduction of material on the site is permitted without prior consent.

5   E-COMMERCE WEBSITES

If the website (or interactive TV service) is offering goods or services for sale the producer is advised to seek specialist legal advice to ensure that the arrangements conform to the rules relating to e-commerce which are being formulated through EU directives. Key matters to be addressed are:

The user must be informed in easily accessible, direct and permanent form of:

i   business name and address;

ii   full particulars including e-mail and postal address;

iii   VAT details;

iv   terms and conditions and obligations of the consumer;

v   prices clearly and accurately displayed; and

vi   all additional costs.

The producer's liability should be protected by setting out in a prominent place, on the home page and selling page of the site and on any documentation the following:

i   terms and conditions for selling, use of website/interactive service and marketing devices;

ii   disclaimers for liability; and

iii   policy relating to confidentiality, privacy and data protection.

Other matters to be addressed include password protection to check customers' identities, security procedures for electronic payment, cyber-tax issues and jurisdiction.

Advertising on the Internet is governed by the Advertising Standards Authority.

THE DATA PROTECTION ACT 1998   6

The Data Protection Act 1998 provides that every individual and business in the UK involved in processing personal data either on a computer or on paper (described as a data controller) must comply with the principles of data protection set out in the act. The rules apply to all processing of personal data which relates to or may identify a living individual. The act provides, amongst other things, that those processing data do so fairly and lawfully, taking appropriate technical and organisational measures to protect the security of personal data and only transferring data outside the European Economic Area where the country of destination ensures an adequate level of data protection.

Under the act individuals have the right to be informed as to whether a data controller holds data about them and what this comprises. They also have the right to object to the processing of personal data for direct marketing purposes and if it is likely to cause substantial damage or distress.

It will be seen that all this may have particular relevance to processing information for a website, such as visitors' e-mail addresses, forums for exchanges of information and information stored about individuals' tastes and preferences. It would be advisable for a producer setting up a website to seek detailed advice about obligations and liabilities under the act. In the first instance each data controller must, on payment of an annual fee, register with the Data Protection Commissioner, providing a description of the personal data to be processed and the purpose for which it is being done. (More information can be obtained from the Information Commission, www.dataprotection.gov.uk)

UMBRELLA AGREEMENTS Chapter 12

An 'umbrella deal' is a term which is used very loosely in the television industry to describe all sorts of collaborative deals between producers. Strictly speaking, however, an umbrella deal is one where a small and often relatively inexperienced production company is working under the protective umbrella of a larger and more experienced outfit. These types of arrangements are becoming increasingly common for a number of reasons. Broadcasters are much less likely to take risks than hitherto with inexperienced production companies and will frequently stipulate, when indicating that they may commission a project, that the production company must work under the auspices of a company with more experience of producing programmes in the particular genre. As the industry becomes evermore competitive many less experienced production companies feel that they stand a better chance of getting a project considered if it is submitted by an established production company.

Each umbrella deal is going to be unique, since terms will vary in each case, depending on a large number of different factors. Before writing this chapter, however, a certain amount of informal research was carried out with a range of umbrella companies to try to identify customary parameters for these deals amongst UK producers.

KEY TOPICS & ISSUES

PRELIMINARY ISSUES 1

Written agreements 1.1

It is crucial for both sides embarking on an umbrella deal to enter into a written agreement in respect of the arrangements. In cases where the broadcaster has committed to the project and it is going straight into production, the agreement may be short and simple, confirming the key issues such as roles on the production and entitlements to shares of production fee, profit shares and, if applicable, ownership and control of format rights. Whatever arrangements are agreed must, of course, dovetail with the broadcaster's contract for the production.

In cases where the parties are intending to work together on the development of the project, prior to approaching the broadcasters, the agreement will be more complex since the relationship is likely to be much more open-ended. The agreement will need to address questions such as ownership of rights in the development work, responsibility for the development costs, procedures for raising production finance, anticipated roles on the production and, most importantly, turnaround provisions in the event that the parties are not jointly successful in raising finance for production and one party wishes to proceed without the other.

The following preliminary factors need to be taken into account when negotiating each deal. (In the interests of simplicity the production company which is to be the umbrella company is referred to as Company A; the company seeking the umbrella deal Company B.)

Level of broadcaster interest 1.2

Clearly this is the most crucial matter. If a broadcaster has confirmed an intention to commission, Company B will be in a strong bargaining position, since nothing is more valuable to any production company, whatever its size, than a broadcaster commitment. If, however, broadcaster commitment has not been obtained and Company B is looking to Company A to bring in the broadcaster, Company A can name its terms for doing so.

Development work required 1.3

The amount of pre-existing development work is highly relevant. If the development work already carried out by Company B constitutes a 'work of copyright', that is to say it has been written up in considerable detail in a form ready to be presented to a broadcaster and/or it includes third-party material (for example, a script or research material) with Company B having contracted for the necessary rights, this should be recognised in the deal and have a significant bearing on the rights and entitlements of Company B. If, however, the development work constitutes little more than an idea for a programme and Company A is being expected to undertake the development work prior to submission to a broadcaster, then Company B will obviously have less entitlements.

Production experience 1.4

This can be a sensitive issue. The only non-subjective criteria for assessing experience and reputation is actual production company credits for the particular type of programme. If Company B can demonstrate that it has already successfully produced a programme(s) of the type proposed, then it would be reasonable for it to expect to have a producer role on the proposed production. If it is not able to demonstrate credits in the field, it is fair to argue that the production will be relying heavily on the experience of Company A and the deal will need to reflect this.

C12

1.5   Nature and type of production

This is obviously significant, both in terms of the level of experience required to obtain a commission for the type of programme on offer, and because, in any commercial consideration of the deal, Company A is going to need to work out the likely financial return from its involvement. If it is a single, low-budget documentary it may simply not be financially viable for Company A to take a lower than usual production fee and possibly relinquish charges for individual services on the production, particularly when, if Company B is inexperienced, it may involve Company A in a very considerable amount of additional work. If, however, the project is a high-budget drama series there is obviously a much larger 'cake' to be shared out.

2   KEY TERMS FOR AN UMBRELLA DEVELOPMENT AGREEMENT

The following are the principal commercial issues to be addressed in the agreement(s) between Company A and Company B.

2.1   Preamble

As previously explained, it is important for an agreement to be drawn up at the outset if the parties intend to work together on the development of the project prior to its submission to potential financiers. Whereas production is finite, development can take forever and it is very easy for recollections of where the project began, and who was expecting what from it, to become distorted over time. For this reason it is useful for the development agreement to contain a preamble recording which party originated the project and which party approached the other.

2.2   Rights in the development work

The agreement should record:

i   which party owns rights in the existing development work;

ii   the arrangements for the further development work: is it to be jointly undertaken, or by one party only?

iii   who is going to be responsible for the costs;

iv   whether the rights are to be jointly owned or owned by one party only;

v   what the entitlement of each party will be to recover development costs. (In the normal course the only development costs which are allowed in production budgets are direct costs paid to third parties and, where development has necessitated travel and research costs, some provision for these as well. Rightly or wrongly, it is not industry practice on any type of production deal to allow the recovery of indirect development costs, such as salaries, office rental, phones etc.)

2.3   Roles on the production

This matter should be addressed at the outset of the intended relationship and it must be remembered that ultimately the financier (broadcaster) will require final say in the choice of individual producer: the choice will not be at Company A's discretion. In most circumstances Company B will probably be expecting to be the individual producer of the project. If Company A does not intend this and/or does not think that it would be able to persuade the financier to agree, it should make this completely clear before things go any further, so that Company B can decide whether or not to remain with Company A or take the project to another company which may not have the same reservations. A compromise can sometimes be arrived at whereby Company B's individual producer may be guaranteed an alternative role on the production (such as associate producer or consultant) in the event that the financier will not accept them as individual producer.

Approaches to potential production financiers 2.4

It is important to have a clear strategy for approaching production financiers, since it can be damaging to the project if the same financiers are approached about the same project by different individuals. The agreement should address the following matters:

i   which party is to be responsible for making approaches to whom and whether these are to be made jointly or singly;

ii   the company identification and copyright notice to be shown on any written treatment submitted to production financiers.

The party responsible for approaches should be under an obligation to keep the other party informed of responses and consult about the terms of any financing deal prior to its conclusion.

Turnaround on development work 2.5

There are potentially few more difficult situations for production companies than those which can arise when two parties have made copyright contributions to the development of a project and, thus, jointly own the copyright in it, and then decide that they no longer want to work together. As the principal purpose and value of any contract is to address what happens when things go wrong, it is absolutely essential that there should be agreement at the outset as to each party's entitlement to take the project into turnaround.

To this end the agreement should provide for a fixed term during which the parties agree to work jointly on the project. Obviously the length will depend on the nature and complexity of the project, its topicality and the amount of development work required to render it suitable for submission to financiers. As a very general rule, anything less than 12 months would probably be too short.

The agreement can then provide that either the parties can mutually agree to extend the term or if they don't so agree, one company is in first position to proceed without the other company, the usual proviso being that the non-proceeding company is entitled to recovery of its contribution to direct costs of development. These are repayable on first day of principal photography. The non-proceeding company is also entitled to a share of the producer's net profits from sales. If within a certain period – say 18 months – the company in first position has not succeeded in setting up production, then the other company should be entitled to do so, accepting the same obligations to the other party for the repayment of direct development costs and net profit share. (In either case it should be remembered that the broadcaster will require final approval of the cost of development which can be recovered from the production budget.)

The question of which party should be in first position to take the project into turnaround may be contentious. In circumstances where Company B originated the project and carried out the bulk of the development work it would seem fair that it should be in first position. If, however, Company A has funded and carried out a large amount of development work then it would seem fair that Company A should be in first position.

The development agreement should go on to make provision for the arrangements for production, as outlined below, clearly stating that the agreed arrangements will be subject to financiers' approval and with the parties agreeing to negotiate in good faith in the event that the arrangements require variation in the light of the eventual financing arrangements and the requirements of the financiers.

3 KEY TERMS FOR AN UMBRELLA PRODUCTION AGREEMENT

3.1 Contracting with the production financier

This obviously determines the structure of the whole deal since the company contracting with the principal financier will be contractually liable for delivering the production in accordance with the budget, schedule and editorial specification and it must, therefore, have ultimate control over all aspects of the production. There are some examples of Company B contracting with the financier but this usually happens only in cases where the broadcaster has stipulated that the production must be supervised by an individual executive producer supplied by Company A, as distinct from the production being managed by Company A.

Financiers, or certainly the mainstream UK broadcasters, will rarely agree that Company A and Company B can contract jointly with them for the production. From their point of view, it is administratively much more straightforward to contract with one company and, if things do go seriously wrong, it is preferable to have one party, rather than two, to sue!

Sometimes Company A may be reluctant to let Company B see the production contract. Whilst Company A may have particular reasons for keeping the contract confidential, this can cause mistrust and resentment. If Company B is supplying the services of the main producer it would seem proper that they see the contract (and the budget). Some of the biggest problems on umbrella productions result from paranoia caused by lack of transparency on the production arrangements.

Financiers are extremely reluctant to get involved in the negotiations between Company A and Company B in respect of their entitlements on the production, even when they have decreed that the marriage should take place. If real problems arise between the two companies, commissioning editors will very occasionally be prepared to conciliate, but the business affairs negotiators almost never get involved.

It is important to ensure that the contract between Company A and Company B meshes with the contract with the broadcaster, particularly in the areas of ownership of rights and warranties and undertakings. Broadcasters recommend that, if arrangements are agreed between Company A and Company B which directly relate to the terms of production agreement, the broadcaster be advised of the position.

3.2 Production fee

Share of production fee is generally the deal term of most concern to producers. Where Company B has secured broadcaster commitment (or significant production finance) before entering into the deal with Company A, it is in a strong bargaining position since the broadcasters generally will not specify that the production must be produced under the auspices of one named production company, but allow Company B to choose so it has the opportunity to explore which potential umbrella company may offer the best deal. A broadcaster will, however, require approval of the umbrella production company and in some fields the number of suitable, and willing, umbrella companies may be small and Company B's opportunity for shopping around for the best deal may be limited.

The informal survey of big name UK companies most frequently involved in umbrella arrangements showed considerable consistency in relation to production fees. All these companies make the point that they carry significant ongoing overhead charges which are met from production fees and only a small percentage proportion of any production fee can be said to represent profit to the company. If Company A is expected to give away a significant amount of the production fee to Company B the deal may not be financially viable since it is preferable for them to devote company time and resources to productions on which they will receive the full production fee.

Many companies are unlikely to offer any share of production fees if Company B does not have a track record as an independent production company, does not have offices and overhead charges and is to all intents and purposes a 'loan out' company for the supply of services of the individual freelance producer.

Where Company B is a bona fide production company, but the particular project needs to be more fully developed and pitched to broadcasters by Company A, the proportion of production fee offered to Company B is unlikely to be more than about 10%.

If considerable development work has already been done by Company B and it has experience of production of the same type of programming, the share offered might rise to around 20-25%.

Where Company B has obtained broadcaster commitment prior to the approach to Company A, anything is negotiable. A number of the major companies do, however, set a ceiling of 30% on share of production fee and some are only prepared to 'umbrella' for much less, around 15%. Companies with a less full production slate may, of course, be prepared to offer much more, although it is probably fairly rare in any circumstances for Company B to be offered more than 50-60% of the production fee.

In all cases the production fee needs to be defined as the amount of the fee actually received by the production company since, if there is an overspend on the production, the broadcaster will have the right to withhold the overspend from the production fee otherwise payable to the production company.

Some production companies will expect to recover development and other costs not provided for in the production budget from the production fee, prior to shares being paid. This can be contentious and it is advisable for it to be made clear at the outset of the umbrella collaboration that this is what Company A will be expecting and agreement reached as to the allowable deductions. As a general rule, these should be limited to direct costs paid to third parties in respect of development work for the production which have not been recovered from the production budget.

Sharing of underspend and overspend   3.3

All the Company A companies surveyed said that they did not offer Company B a share of any underspend on the grounds that problems can arise if Company B is incentivised to achieve savings on the production budget. If the broadcaster believes that these savings have been achieved at the expense of programme quality, it is Company A, as the contracting party, which takes the risk.

Generally Company A will be solely responsible for any overspend and so will need to be able to claim overspends from the production fee. If both parties are responsible for the overspend, the total overspend should be deductible from the production fee, with the balance of the fee being split in accordance with the agreed division of shares.

3.4 Ownership of copyright in the completed production

For programmes which are fully funded by the broadcaster (or other financier) almost invariably the copyright in the completed production will be owned by them and the question of ownership between Company A and Company B will not arise. When this is not the case, usually when the production companies themselves have brought finance to the production, the copyright is generally jointly owned in proportions equal to the financial contribution which each party has brought to the cost of production.

3.5 Control of distribution rights

Where the agreement with the broadcaster allows the production company to retain the distribution rights in the programme, the parties need to agree who is responsible for control of them. In many cases it is likely that this will be Company A, but it is reasonable to make provision that Company B will be consulted about the choice of distributor and the terms of the deal with the distribution company. A good compromise can be to provide for joint control of the rights. Alternatively, if one company is granted control of the rights but within a specified period – say two years – has not licensed sales to specific territories, the other party may be entitled to request a grant of rights in those territories to see if it can achieve sales.

3.6 Control of format rights

Regarding ownership of the format and other underlying rights in the programme, these are likely to be governed by the terms of the agreement with the broadcaster. But as a general rule agreements with broadcasters provide for ownership of the format to be retained by the production company, albeit the broadcaster may have a continuing entitlement to commission further programmes based on the format and to a profit share from exploitation overseas.

In cases where Company B originated the format and obtained commitment from the broadcaster prior to the collaboration, it would be reasonable for the agreement between Company B and Company A to be limited to a first series only and for Company B to retain ownership and control of the format rights. If this is the case, it needs to be addressed when contracting with the broadcaster since in the usual course, if the broadcaster is contracting with Company A, the broadcaster would be entitled to commission Company A to produce further series.

Company A may, of course, make a strong case that if the format works it is largely due to its production expertise and it should, therefore, have first opportunity to be the production company on any future series and be entitled to control the format rights.

Where the format was developed by Company B prior to the collaboration with the umbrella company and the two companies subsequently worked together on further development prior to its submission to the broadcaster, Company B should be consulted about the terms being negotiated with the broadcaster. The agreement between Company A and Company B should provide for an entitlement for Company B to have a role on any future commissions of programmes based on the format. Further, if the contract with the broadcaster provides for format rights being controlled by the production company, Company A and Company B need to agree which party is entitled to ownership or control of the format rights. They need also to agree each party's entitlement to participate in revenue from exploitation of the format rights. In some cases this will be dealt with straightforwardly by providing that the parties jointly control the rights and share revenues 50:50 after deduction of commission and costs by the party (or the agent) responsible for the exploitation of the rights.

These format negotiations are obviously complex and before embarking on them producers should be satisfied that the programme has an identifiable and unique format which may be capable of further exploitation. For more information on format deals see *Chapter 7*.

Shares of net profits   3.7

It is usual for both companies to share the producer's share of net profits from sales of the production. This should apply even in cases where Company B is not being offered a share of the production fee since, unlike production fees which are required to meet ongoing overheads, most companies regard net profits from sales as being a bonus if and when they come in. Whilst in many cases the division of net profits will be agreed in the same proportions as the share of the production fee, there is a certain amount of custom and practice for the share offered to Company B to be higher than its share of production fee.

It will be seen from the foregoing that there can be no standard terms for umbrella deals. There are too many variables in each situation. Companies cannot, however, be too strongly advised always to negotiate an agreement in respect of terms for an umbrella deal at the outset of the collaboration with the written agreement being signed by both parties. When drawing up the agreement the parties should not duck resolving potentially sensitive issues, such as roles and entitlements on the production, and the agreement must always provide for clear termination provisions in the event that the parties no longer work together. If these steps are followed the chances are that the umbrella arrangements will work well since through attempting to sort out these matters at an early stage the parties will form a very good idea as to whether or not they will be able to work together happily.

C13

PREPARING AND SUBMITTING PROGRAMME PROPOSALS

Chapter 13

There is much angst among producers as to the procedures for submitting programme proposals. Understandably so, when livelihoods are dependent on winning the highly chancy and competitive game of targeting the right commissioning editor with the right proposal at the right time. Luck obviously plays a large part but good management goes a long way towards generating good luck.

Good management in this context involves, firstly, researching not just what the producer wants to make, but what production financiers actually require and, thus, are prepared to fund. A considerable amount of information on this is available. PACT regularly organises briefing days when commissioning editors from the various UK broadcasters, as well as the burgeoning number of digital channels, will outline their requirements. Most of the channels now issue occasional commissioning briefs which are distributed to the PACT membership. In addition to these sources, even very basic, inexpensive research such as careful evaluation of all programme listings can reveal a great deal of information about how the different channels make up their schedules and hence what their likely requirements are.

If it is planned to raise pre-sale or co-production finance from outside the UK, it is of great value to talk through with distributors what the tastes and requirements of particular overseas markets may be. All too often producers think that if they introduce, say, a Scandinavian element into the production, money from Scandinavia will flow in, only to find that what they have painstakingly devised is just the kind of thing which is complete anathema to a Scandinavian buyer! Tapping into the kind of detailed knowledge which distributors have of overseas markets can avoid such all too common pitfalls.

This chapter explains basic procedures for submitting programme proposals.

KEY TOPICS & ISSUES

C13

1 TELEVISION PROPOSALS

1.1 Preparing a programme proposal

It is very important in all circumstances, but particularly when dealing with the UK broadcasters, to have developed a programme idea to the extent that it can attract copyright before approaching a broadcaster. The terms of contracts offered to producers are significantly different for programmes which have been originated by the producer and those which are considered to have been originated by the broadcaster and suggested to the producer. The BBC definition of programmes originated by the producer are those where "the fundamental idea has been developed in sufficient detail in the form of a format, outline treatment, screenplay or is otherwise of such nature as to qualify for copyright or other legal protection". In other words, the programme idea must be written up to attract copyright protection.

1.2 Protection of the proposal

Given the necessity to develop a programme proposal to a certain extent before submitting it to broadcasters, there is always a concern that the proposal may then be turned down by them, only to subsequently emerge on-screen as an in-house production or, even worse, by another independent producer. Whilst no one could claim that proposals are never plagiarised, it probably happens far less frequently than producers tend to suppose. There are very few truly original ideas – it is for this reason that ideas as such do not have any protection under copyright law. It is not uncommon for commissioning editors to receive a number of almost identical proposals based on the same basic idea within the space of a few weeks. The producer's idea may have been triggered, perhaps subconsciously, by a news event or a newspaper article or a television programme which has sparked off exactly the same train of thought in others. After all, ideas for documentaries are, by definition, drawn from subject matter which is in the public domain and it is often said that there are only seven basic dramatic plots. As has been explained in *Chapter 7*, it is very difficult to claim that a drama format is truly original until it has been fully scripted.

This does not mean that a producer should not take certain steps to safeguard the programme proposal and this can be done by the following means.

Early in development the programme proposal should be written up to contain as many specific details as possible. The more there is in written form about the producer's own original plans and thoughts for the style and content of the programme, the greater the likelihood of protection under copyright law.

Although there is no requirement in UK law for a copyright notice, in order that no one can be in any doubt that the producer claims copyright in the programme proposal a © copyright notice identifying the producer as the owner, together with the date, should be clearly shown on each page of the proposal. As further precaution, each copy of the proposal can be numbered and the cover sheet should stipulate a ban on any reproduction of the proposal.

If the producer is a member of PACT the proposal can be lodged with PACT's script registration service. Alternatively, it can be dated and sent to the producer's solicitor or bank with the request for a written, dated acknowledgement of receipt.

Programme proposals developed for the US market can be registered with the US Copyright Registration Office at the US Library of Congress in Washington. As explained in

Chapter 1, Paragraph 6, these devices do not afford any protection against infringement of copyright: they simply make it easier to prove (if ever it should be necessary to do so) that the producer had devised the proposal by a certain date.

Proposals should always clearly state that they are being submitted in confidence. The single major successful case which has been brought in the UK concerning the theft of a programme idea was the case the three originators of the format for the *Rock Follies* drama series brought against Thames Television, which produced the series during the 1970s. The format had been devised by three actresses as a vehicle for themselves and was submitted to Thames in confidence. Thames did not enter into any agreement with the actresses in respect of the format and commissioned a writer to write the scripts and engaged three different actresses to play the lead parts. Two series were produced and were very successful. The actresses who had devised the format brought the case on grounds of breach of confidence. They claimed that they had developed the format to further their careers and for financial gain and, by producing the series, Thames had breached the confidence in which the format had been submitted. The court awarded very substantial damages to the actresses for the losses of potential earnings and opportunity to enhance their reputations.

The broadcasters' terms of trade generally contain an acknowledgement that any original programming ideas submitted in writing are confidential and the sole property of the producer.

In the last analysis, although it is recognised that it may not be feasible for the producer to do this in all circumstances, the most effective means both of protecting the programme proposal and establishing that it originated with the producer is for the producer to have secured, prior to submission, a hold on rights in any underlying rights material, or on the services of a key contributor or artist integral to the programme proposal. If the producer's contractual position on key, pivotal elements is secure, it will be extremely difficult for the proposal to be plagiarised. Procedures for optioning literary works are set out in *Chapter 4* and for securing a contractual measure of protection for ideas in the public domain in *Chapter 8.*

The majority of US stations, and some UK broadcasters, frequently include, in a letter acknowledging receipt of a programme proposal, wording to the effect that they will be under no liability to the producer in the event that they subsequently produce a programme similar to the proposal which has been submitted. A number of US stations (including the Discovery Channel which frequently contracts with UK producers) go further and require producers to sign a document confirming their acceptance of this before the station will agree to consider the proposal.

These practices cause considerable anxiety amongst producers. It is understandable that broadcasters and TV stations want to protect themselves against tiresome claims of infringement of copyright from producers who have submitted proposals based on material in the public domain which may be virtually indistinguishable from several other unsolicited proposals, but it is profoundly disturbing for a producer. In the end the producer has to make a judgement as to whether or not he or she is prepared to allow the proposal to go forward to a commissioner who makes these stipulations, since no amount of resistance on the part of the producer is likely to persuade the commissioner to agree a change in procedures.

The only consolation is that, in the last analysis, infringement of copyright is illegal and no amount of disclaimer letters carry any weight in a court of law if it can be proved that by producing the programme the broadcaster has infringed the producer's rights of copyright.

1.3 **Submitting programme proposals**

Timescale

Some broadcasters' terms of trade give a timescale to the commissioning process, but in practice these rarely seem to be adhered to. However, when broadcasters are giving details of their commissioning briefs, they will frequently indicate a timescale which is usually linked to the timing of their programme budget rounds, so producers should watch out for these and try to work towards them. Occasionally a commissioning editor will indicate that they want to commission a programme but that it will have to wait to come out of the next year's budget. In these circumstances, the producer should try to negotiate a development deal so that some formal commitment is made to the project and it is kept 'live' until production funding is available.

Who to approach and how

Proposals should, in the first instance, be submitted to commissioning editors. Lists of the various commissioning editors are regularly published and updated by PACT and weekly reading of the trade press is also essential to keep abreast of who is where.

If a programme proposal is to be submitted by post, it is a matter for individual judgement as to whether to dispatch a multiple submission to all the UK broadcasters or send it to commissioning editors one by one: there is no 'correct' procedure.

Although the proposal should be written up in some detail, ensure that the first pages contain a succinct outline so that by reading a couple of pages the commissioning editor can learn its subject and nature; suggested length; estimated cost; possible scheduling slot; and, if the producer is not known to the commissioning editor, something about the producer and the production company. Commissioning editors are disinclined to wade through pages of documentation to find essential facts: if the basic idea appeals and appears to fit their programme requirements, they will call for a meeting to discuss the producer's plans in detail.

If the producer has a meeting set up with a commissioning editor, for the reasons explained in *Paragraph 1.1* above, the programme proposal should, nonetheless, have been prepared in writing prior to the meeting. If the proposal needs further development work the producer should go into the meeting with a clear idea of what is required and what the cost might be.

In the USA the 'pitch' to the commissioning editor has always been critical. US stations do not really consider written proposals: decisions are taken on the basis of the producer's face-to-face sales pitch. US producers spend a great deal of time perfecting their pitch in order to sell the concept in the couple of minutes a busy commissioning editor might be prepared to give them.

Whilst a US-style pitch might seem rather bizarre in this country, in an era when the marketing of a product is of huge importance, it is very important for producers to have rehearsed a selling line for the project in advance of their meeting with commissioning editors. The importance of being able to go into the meeting and make a fluent, persuasive presentation of the proposal cannot be overemphasised.

Finally, always follow up a meeting with a written note to the commissioning editor confirming what was discussed and, if the concept for the programme changed during the course of the discussion, the producer should refer to the alterations in such a way that it is clear that the new plan originated with the producer.

Commitment to production   1.4

If the programme proposal appeals to the commissioning editor and he or she wants to make some commitment to it, the broadcasters' standard procedures for commissioning independents should be brought into play. There are some variations in these between the broadcasters but, as explained in detail in *Chapter 15*, in the first instance, the producer will be expected to submit the budget for the further development work which may be required or, if no development is called for, for the production itself. These budgets will be scrutinised by the broadcaster's cost accountants and it is only following formal approval of budgets that a draft contract for development or production will be issued. Unless and until this procedure has been followed, the producer should not make any assumption that even the most enthusiastic expression of interest by a commissioning editor is going to lead to a commission: a good meeting is not a commitment to production. To quote a former director of programmes at Channel 4: "'I love it' is not a commission!".

The commissioning editor may request the producer to undertake further work on the project before making any formal commitment (or payment) in respect of the project. This is a difficult situation for a producer. On the one hand, he or she does not want to jeopardise the chances of the project being commissioned if the further work is not carried out; on the other, there are any number of commissioning editors requesting more and more work only to then reject the project without having paid a penny for the work undertaken at their behest. These are difficult commercial judgements for a producer to make. The bottom line is that account should be kept of the costs of the additional work and, if and when the project does proceed to production, the costs which have been speculatively incurred should be included within the production budget or otherwise be taken into account in terms negotiated for the production deal.

FILM PROPOSALS   2
Submitting film proposals   2.1

The questions of which financiers to approach and how to to go about it with a feature film proposal are far less clear cut than for television. Public funding is largely distributed through the Film Council and its subsidiary bodies. They have funding available for various levels of development, from writers' loans to funding for full development. The two UK broadcasters with feature film arms are BBC (BBC Films) and Channel 4 (FilmFour). They too fund development. It is worth approaching the major independent feature film production companies, who are always on the look out for new projects. Sales agents and distributors may very occasionally fund development.

The producer should always ensure that they have a formal contractual hold on a feature film project before approaching financiers. 'Chain of title', i.e. the necessary ownership of copyright in the underlying rights in a feature film, is a very major consideration at every stage of a film's development and the producer should ensure that agreements for the treatment or script are in place before approaching third parties. Details of procedures are set out in *Chapters 4 to 7*.

C13

3 NON-DISCLOSURE/CONFIDENTIALITY AGREEMENTS

Some producers are now issuing a 'non-disclosure' or confidentiality agreement which the person or organisation to whom the proposal is being submitted is asked to sign. These agreements give a definition of the confidential information. They also place an obligation on the recipient that the proposal will be treated in confidence; that they will not reveal its contents to any third party without the consent of the producer; and that, in the event that they wish to commission a production based on it, this will be subject to good faith negotiation of terms under which the producer/production company will be commissioned to produce the programme. Agreements go on to place the recipient under an obligation to return the confidential information and to indemnify the producer as a result of any losses by the producer as a consequence of any breach of the confidentiality.

Given how commercially competitive the industry now is, it is understandable that producers may feel they require this level of protection, particularly if it is a highly commercial idea, and no one should be criticised for seeking to protect their commercial interests. However, this procedure has to be weighed against the fact that a non-disclosure agreement implies that the person or organisation to whom the proposal is being presented may not be trustworthy, and this may not be the most felicitous way to embark on a new relationship.

C14

DEVELOPMENT AND OUTPUT AGREEMENTS

Chapter 14

The great value of any development deal offered by a third-party financier is that it gives a programme proposal credibility. It is not just the producer who thinks it is a good project, but a potential financier thinks so too. Even if the development money is small, it is always high-risk and the potential financier will, therefore, be more motivated to try to progress it to production than they may be for a project developed at no financial risk to them. As a general rule, if development money is on offer, take it – provided the terms for the deal are such that the producer's position on the production is safeguarded.

Across the industry the key terms for development deals offered by broadcasters and other financiers, including feature film financiers, are broadly similar. They are outlined here.

KEY TOPICS & ISSUES

C14

1 TELEVISION DEALS

Drama or situation comedy development deals are likely to be staged so that the first stage development is confined to the commission of a treatment and/or first script. If this is accepted, the development moves to a second stage, which may include the commission of further scripts together with the preparation of a production budget and schedule, suggestions for key casting and choice of director.

With documentaries there will probably be only one stage of development, entailing research and recces, the preparation of a full treatment and of a detailed production budget and schedule.

For game shows and factual entertainment programmes such as cookery, gardening and chat shows, development will frequently involve the commission of a pilot programme or pilot material demonstrating the style of the programme and the proposed presenter.

In the case of programmes which are intended to be 100% or majority funded by the UK broadcasters, this further development work is likely to be paid for by the broadcaster. For direct access deals with the ITV Network Centre, as it does not have development funding, such funding will have to be found by the producer, either from his or her own resources or through third-party investment funding. Likewise, the producer is likely to have to fund, or at least partially fund, the development of programmes destined for licence fee deals with the other broadcasters.

Some EU Media funding is available for the development of certain types of television production. Information can be obtained from the UK Media Desk (see useful addresses). Some major television distributors are prepared to fund development in return for being granted distribution rights if the project proceeds to production. This latter route works particularly well on ITV direct access projects and other licence fee deals, where the producer retains control of distribution rights in the production outside the UK and is in a position to license the rights to the distributor.

1.1 Development budgets

Common to any agreement for third-party development funding will be the requirement to draw up a budget for development costs. The extent to which a third party will agree to fund the development will obviously vary, but the following elements are generally allowable items in development budgets.

Rights payments

Generally producers will be refunded from the development budget for any direct costs for the acquisition of rights, i.e. option payments, script fee and other rights fees, incurred by the producer prior to entering into the development agreement. If such costs are not reimbursed, under the terms of the development agreement the producer should retain part ownership of rights in the development work and/or the producer's contribution to the cost of the rights should be regarded as investment in the production (and be repaid from the production budget).

Legal costs

It is usual for a development financier to be prepared to refund reasonable legal costs which the producer may have incurred on contracting for the acquisition of underlying rights in the project, prior to entering into the development agreement. A provision of about £750 up to about £2,000, if the arrangements have been particularly complicated, is generally accepted. Fees in excess of about £2,000 would probably only be allowable if the development work called for specific legal advice over and above that required for the drawing up of routine contracts.

Producer fees

Unless the development work is particularly labour intensive and/or clearly requires the full-time services of the producer, for example if the producer were required to travel overseas to research and recce the project, it is very unlikely that a charge for the full-time services of the producer will be accepted. On drama developments, during the scriptwriting period, it would be usual to allow approximately one day per week for producer services. The calculation of producer fees should be based on the rates customarily paid for freelance producers on the type of production being developed.

Researcher, script editor and other services required on development should similarly be costed at the usual UK freelance rates.

Office overheads

Office overhead charges are, by their nature, problematic. They obviously vary from production company to production company, although from the financier's point of view there is rarely any justification for paying one company more than another. Further, even when the production company keeps complete costings for its overheads, it is almost impossible to apportion these charges accurately between its various projects. As a very approximate guide, financiers may accept an overhead charge of approximately £300 per week for each week of the development period, i.e. from commission of the development work to date of delivery. These charges would represent a contribution to office rent, lighting, heat, stationery, secretarial and accounting (other than production budgets), script typing, photocopying, postage, telephones, faxes, couriers.

Expenses

It is usual to allow some provision for direct out-of-pocket expenditure on couriers, travel, hospitality etc. If the writer works a considerable distance from the producer a special provision may be agreed for travel costs. As a rough guide, on a drama development budget of approximately £15,000 a provision of about £750 for miscellaneous expenditure would probably be allowable.

Production budget and schedule

If production budgets and schedules are required, they will generally be commissioned at a second stage of development, after the script has been delivered. A charge of £1,500 to £2,000 for a drama production budget and schedule would usually be allowable: a documentary budget would probably be expected to cost about half that.

Casting and location recces

Casting and/or recces would similarly be likely to be called for only at a second stage of development. It is usual to allow approximately £1,500 a week for a casting director and a similar amount, plus travel and out-of-pocket expenses, for location recces.

Production fees

Production fees are not paid on development budgets. If the project proceeds to production, the costs of the development work are included within the overall production budget and so are taken into account in the calculation of the production fee.

Indirect costs

Generally producers are unable to recover indirect costs incurred prior to obtaining third-party commitment to fund development. It is, however, important for producers to endeavour to agree a valuation on these costs with production financiers to ensure that, even though they may not be paid at development stage, when negotiating recoupment and profit shares, account is taken of the financial contribution the producer has made to the production through funding of indirect development costs.

Development cash flow

There is no standard staging for cash flow payments beyond the usual requirement that a portion of the development funding not be released until delivery of all the items of development work. As a general rule, the funds are paid in about three instalments: on commencement; at about the half-way stage (or on drama projects, on delivery of the first draft script); and on delivery of all development materials. The instalments are rarely equal: the first payment is usually the largest, since the producer will need to have funds to commission the script and/or services, pay the legal fees on negotiating contracts and so forth. Whilst a financier will expect the cash flow to bear some resemblance to the stages at which payments fall due, the producer should bear in mind that, once the financier has made a commitment to fund development, the timing of the release of those funds is generally of less importance to the financier than it is to the producer.

Development bank account

It is usual for the producer to be required to open a separate trust account for the development funding. The producer will be expected to account for the development monies. A number of financiers require repayment of any unused funds.

1.2 Development agreements

Once the development budget has been agreed the development agreement will be issued. The following key matters must be addressed in development agreements.

Rights

It is standard form in broadcasters' agreements for development for the broadcaster to take what, on the face of it, appears to be a rather alarming charge over the copyright in all the development materials, including a charge on the copyright, or whatever rights may have been obtained, in the underlying rights in the project. This charge is a security for the broadcaster's financial investment and protects the broadcaster against any double-dealing by the producer during development.

The development agreement will usually go on to stipulate that if and when a commitment is made to production, the ownership and control of rights in the production will be negotiated in good faith and the agreed arrangements will apply retroactively to rights in the development work.

That is to say, in the event that the copyright in the eventual production is jointly owned with the producer and/or the producer retains certain secondary or reserved rights in the production, that arrangement applies retroactively to the rights in the development work. In circumstances where the producer is not being refunded direct costs of development, such as payments made for the acquisition of underlying rights, the producer should negotiate for joint ownership and control of the copyright in the development materials.

On development agreements with distributors, which are more in the nature of a joint venture, the rights in development work may either remain vested with the producer conditional on him or her meeting certain obligations to the distributor, or they may be held jointly by the producer and the distributor. As the producer may be required to assign rights to a production financier in order to raise production finance, in such circumstances the distributor must be under an obligation to release its interest in the rights in return either for being granted distribution rights in the production or being reimbursed development funding plus interest on first day of principal photography.

Option for production

Producers should always be very careful to check that the development agreement specifies that if the development work proceeds to production, the broadcaster (or other financier) will commission the producer to produce the production and if the producer is not so commissioned the development work goes into turnaround. Some broadcasters' agreements are slightly ambiguous on this point, simply referring to the broadcaster 'commissioning production' and not specifically stating that it is the producer who will be commissioned to produce the production. Although broadcasters will insist that it is always the intention that the producer will be commissioned, there have been unfortunate cases when, without the specific wording, this has not been honoured. Given the usual requirement that copyright in the development work is assigned to the development financier, it is very important for a producer to check the wording of the development contract very carefully.

Some broadcasters (most notably Carlton) require the producer to confirm its acceptance of all the principal terms of the production agreement at the time the development work is being contracted.

Turnaround

It is important to ensure that the development agreement contains a turnaround provision. These provisions specify the procedure whereby if, following delivery of the development work, the financier does not want to proceed further with the project, the producer has the right to continue the development and offer the development work to third parties. The financier undertakes to assign its rights in the development work to the producer subject to the producer repaying the financier for the sums received for the development work whenever third-party funding for production becomes unconditional or on first day of principal photography whichever is the earlier date.

The monies to be repaid usually attract interest at 2% above bank base rate between date of release of funds and date of repayment. Some financiers also seek repayment of an overhead charge.

In practice, these turnaround payments rarely present a problem for the producer, provided they only fall due when a third-party financier has fully committed to the project. All financiers have similar turnaround repayment provisions within their own development agreements and are, therefore, prepared to accept the obligation to make turnaround payments when they are imposed by another financier. Provision for such repayment is routinely provided for within production budgets.

The contract should specify the date by which the producer will be notified of the financier's intentions and when, in the absence of such notification, the project can go into turnaround. Depending on the nature of the project, the financier should use best endeavours to notify the producer as to whether or not it wishes to proceed further within about six months of delivery of the development materials and, if such notification is not received, the development work can go into turnaround within about 12 months of delivery.

C14

The BBC standard form agreement provides that the turnaround period is triggered from acceptance of the development work but it does not provide for a mechanism or time period for notifying the producer of acceptance. Consequently, some developments have gone into limbo because there has been no trigger date for the start of the turnaround period. Always insist that the turnaround period starts either from the date of acceptance or, if no notification of acceptance is received, within, say, six weeks of delivery of the development materials.

For development work carried out for one of the ITV franchise holders, producers should try to ensure that the contract provides that, if the ITV Network Centre turns the proposal down, the rights go into immediate turnaround, unless the producer is prepared to allow the ITV company to approach other broadcasters with the project.

Some of the ITV companies, and other development financiers, seek to include provisions whereby, after the project has been released into turnaround, the producer is nonetheless placed under an obligation to give them the opportunity to match any offer the producer may subsequently receive for funding of a production based on the development material. The producer should beware of such provisions. Matching offers are very onerous, since the producer can go to enormous lengths to elicit a commitment from a third party, only to have to say, "Hang on before we do a deal – I have to give X company the opportunity to match the terms we've agreed". If X company matches the offer, the deal, and probably the relationship with the third party, collapses altogether. Even if company X chooses not to match the offer, the procedure nonetheless hinders the commissioning process in an unacceptable manner.

2 FEATURE FILM DEVELOPMENT DEALS

The development process for feature films is far more protracted than for television programmes, because so much work is generally required on the screenplay, firstly with the writers and then with the writers working with the director. Thereafter, the process of scheduling, casting and budgeting, not to mention raising finance, can take ages. Development, therefore, tends to take place in different stages and frequently with different, or additional, financiers at each stage.

The Film Council and other public bodies funding development will supply detailed information of their development processes. Essentially, however, development budgets and contracts are broadly similar to those for television programmes, as set out in *Paragraph 1* above. In some cases the financiers may not take an assignment of rights in the way broadcasters do, but the contract will nonetheless grant them a lien on the rights which will prevent the producer disposing of them without meeting repayment obligations.

The turnaround arrangements do not generally apply, but the producer may be entitled to buy the financier out of the development on repayment of the development monies and with the financier having a continuing entitlement to a share of producer's net profits from the film, generally 5%. Buy-back terms are likely to include a premium for the financier of as much of 100% of the monies advanced for development, plus interest, as well as a net profit share and probably an end credit in respect of the contribution to development.

Sometimes the repayment provisions can seem quite onerous in relation to the relatively small amount of money being advanced for development and a negotiating ploy is to provide that the net profit share and other entitlements are directly linked to the relative amount the financier may contribute to the development.

OUTPUT DEALS   3

Output deals are a form of development deal which may, in some cases, guarantee that a certain amount of programming will be commissioned over a fixed period. For all but the most spectacularly successful production companies, output deals are probably the most hoped for and elusive form of production deal. They do, however, occasionally happen. Whilst they are by their nature bespoke arrangements, there are a few key points to address when negotiating an output deal.

Level of commitment   3.1

There are various degrees of output deal. The most sought-after output deal is one where the broadcaster guarantees to commission a certain number of programmes/ series of programmes over a fixed term. These are likely to be linked to the producer not only having a glittering reputation as a producer of successful series but to the company also having a contractual hold on a stable of established writing and/or format devising and/or star talent. By definition these deals are very scarce.

The most usual type of output deal is a development deal where the broadcaster makes a commitment to develop a certain number of projects during each year of the deal with the intention, as distinct from a contractual obligation, that one or more will proceed to production.

The deal is structured so that the producer receives an annual payment for 'seed development' which is used to fund the commission of treatments, acquisition of options and so forth for possible projects, say six per year. The broadcaster is then given the first opportunity to commission further development/production of the seed development projects and the deal sometimes provides that the broadcaster will guarantee the commission of not less than a certain number of such full developments each year of the deal. If the broadcaster does not elect to commission further work on a seed development project the producer is free to take it to third parties subject, perhaps, to an obligation to repay development costs on production.

Broadcasters disconcertingly frequently approach independents for output deals which do not carry any guarantees for the producer by way of development funding and/ or commitment to production, but which the broadcaster clearly thinks the independent should gratefully accept for the honour of being able to say they have a deal with them. These type of output deals effectively give the broadcaster a free first opportunity to acquire the producer's projects. A commercial judgement has to be made as to whether it is worth agreeing this in order to have a 'foot in the door' or whether, as a matter of principle, no-one running a business should give someone something for nothing! (In these circumstances, 'nothing' also means that the broadcaster has no financial motivation to proceed with projects since no development money has been put at risk.)

Exclusivity/first look   3.2

Unless the production company was being offered an amazingly generous deal, it would be extremely unusual for any output deal to be completely exclusive, that is to say, the production company was accepting an obligation to make programmes only for that one broadcaster/financier. The deal might, however, be exclusive for certain specified genres of programmes only. As a general rule, output deals are limited to 'first look' with the producer being free to deal with other financiers if the broadcaster does not elect to proceed with any 'first look' project. It is important for the contract to provide for clear time periods during which the broadcaster can take up a first look proposal: say four weeks from submission of the proposal to elect to commission further development/production.

3.3 Payment

Obviously the payment and other benefits from an output deal will vary hugely from case to case. If it is a development deal, as outlined above, it is usual to agree an annual payment which is made up of a negotiated contribution to the producer's overheads and the direct costs of initiating projects. When these proceed to full development, a full development budget, as set out in *Paragraph 1.1*, is then agreed.

It is also usual for output deals to specify the terms which will apply if projects proceed to production, and this too is subject to negotiation in each case.

3.4 Term

Given the time that development, commitment to production, production and scheduling all take, it is usual for output deals to be structured to run over a minimum period of about three years: anything shorter and it is hard to see how a judgement can reasonably be made as to whether the arrangements are working effectively.

AGREEMENTS FOR FULLY-FUNDED INDEPENDENT PRODUCTIONS

Chapter 15

Although fully-funded independent commissions by the UK broadcasters may be becoming rarer all the time, the terrestrial broadcasters are likely to remain the principal source of commissions for the independent sector for some time to come. It is reasonable to assume that, whatever upheavals the industry may be experiencing, broadcasters' respective procedures for independent commissions are not going to change overnight or even during the working lifetime of many producers. The key terms of trade are likely to remain, at least as benchmarks, for the negotiation of most types of production deal which a broadcaster may be wholly or majority funding. This chapter deals with procedures set out in the terrestrial broadcasters' terms of trade and the key terms of contracts. For more detailed information copies of the terms of trade for the BBC, Channel 4 and Channel 5 are available direct from the broadcaster. The ITV Network Centre issues information about its licence fee deals (see *Chapter 16*). The ITV companies do not have standard terms of trade although individual companies may issue statements about their contracting procedures. (Terms for fully-funded deals for the digital channels are set out in *Chapter 17*.)

KEY TOPICS & ISSUES

C15

1 PRELIMINARY PROCEDURES

There is often an unsettling period of uncertainty between the commissioning editor giving the producer the glad news that they intend to commission the production and the producer actually receiving formal notification that the commission is confirmed.

1.1 Letter of intent

When a commissioning editor says he or she intends to commit to a project, in some cases a letter of intent will be issued which confirms that, subject to approval of budget and underlying rights contracts, the broadcaster intends to commit to production. It is not, however, completely standard practice for letters of intent to be sent out and frequently producers may have to press for one to be issued.

1.2 Approvals procedure/programme finance committee

Whether or not a letter of intent has been sent out, the next stage in the commissioning process is for the producer to be asked to draw up a budget for the production. This budget will then require approval through the broadcaster's system for confirming commitment to the commission and the budget. As a general rule, the system involves approval of the project by the broadcaster's programme finance committee which is made up of commissioning editors and legal and business affairs executives. Until confirmation has been received that the project has been approved by the committee, the producer should not enter into any commitments in respect of the production: projects can and do fall at this final hurdle.

In addition to approval of the budget, the broadcaster's lawyers require prior approval of the terms of any agreements for the underlying rights in the project, for example, if it is based on an existing book, the agreements for the book rights and for the scriptwriter. Such approvals are not a formality: if the terms of the contracts are not acceptable to the broadcaster's lawyers they can and do insist that the contract be renegotiated before the commission can be confirmed.

1.3 Trust letters

As the approval procedures inevitably take several weeks, and only thereafter will a draft contract will be issued, it may be necessary in some cases to commence production before production contracts can be finalised. In such cases (although increasingly rarely) the broadcaster may be prepared to issue production funding on a trust letter in order that the start of production is not delayed. These trust letters invariably start with the wording, "In view of your urgent need for funds", which tends to make the producer feel he is standing in rags on a street corner. The trust letter goes on to provide that the funds must be placed in a trust account; that the parties agree to negotiate in good faith the terms of the production agreement; and that, in the meantime, rights in all materials acquired or created by the producer will be the property of the broadcaster. It is by no means unknown for entire productions to be funded on the basis of trust letters, with contracts only being concluded after the programme has been transmitted.

1.4 Producers Rights Agency (formerly PIRS)

As soon as the commitment to production has been received, the producer should set up a meeting with the Producers Rights Agency (formerly Producers Industrial Relations Service) to establish the appropriate arrangements for contracting technical crews and talent. Whilst it is no longer necessary for crews to be members of the appropriate union as a pre-condition of employment, as a general rule, it is more straightforward to contract crews, artistes, contributors, limited rights material etc. on the terms and conditions of the standard form agreements provided by Producers Rights Agency. These standard form contracts have been approved by broadcasters and if, for any reason, those being contracted require variations to the standard contractual provisions, the producer should obtain the broadcaster's prior approval to such variations.

PRODUCTION AGREEMENTS   2
Negotiating the contract   2.1

The customary format of broadcasters' production agreements is for the agreement to be divided into two principal sections: one section is variously described as the 'special terms', 'special conditions', 'programme specification' or similar, and the other is generally described as the broadcaster's general terms and conditions, which are standard to all productions. Attached to these two sections will be various appendices covering such matters as detailed delivery requirements, facilities house letters, inducement letters, details of distribution commissions and so forth.

If the producer is hoping to secure contractual terms which are different in certain respects to those specified in the broadcaster's terms of trade, it is advisable to raise these with the business affairs executives dealing with the contract at a very early stage, in advance of the draft production contract being issued. It can be argued that the further down the road the production is, the stronger the producer's negotiating position. In practice the negotiations then tend to end in an impasse, over which the ultimate power of the broadcaster, and their ability to withhold production payments until the matter is settled, loom large. As a general rule, the broadcasters are more likely to be accommodating if they are aware from the outset that the producer has certain specific contractual requirements than if these requirements are brought up at a stage when the broadcaster believes that everything has been settled.

Further, on a fully-funded commission, the producer must demonstrate valid reasons for seeking variations to the general terms and conditions. These are generally non-negotiable, unless circumstances are exceptional. Obviously, if the producer is unfamiliar with production agreements, it would be sensible to study the broadcaster's terms of trade and to take legal advice on the production agreement. Unless, however, there are particular reasons for doing so, it is rarely worthwhile attempting to negotiate variations to standard contractual provisions for fully-funded productions which, for better or for worse, have generally come to be accepted as the norm.

That being said, there are certain points which are open to negotiation even on a fully-funded deal, in particular the production fee, the net profit share, the control of distribution and secondary rights and the treatment of format rights. Some strategies for negotiation are outlined below.

Special terms and programme specification   2.2

The special terms set out the details of the programme being commissioned: type, length, number of programmes, delivery date, budget, production fee, clearances required, broadcaster's representative, distribution arrangements and profit shares, and the extent to which it is agreed to vary any of the clauses contained in the general terms and conditions. The special terms also generally include a programme specification setting out all key elements: the names of the producers; director; scriptwriter; key cast; production manager;

production accountant; locations; studios; production dates; delivery date; technical medium; names of labs; and facilities houses.

It is a pre-condition of production agreements that the broadcaster approves all the key elements in the programme specification. After such approval, any subsequent changes are subject to the express prior approval of the broadcaster.

2.3   Rights in the production

Copyright in the production

All the broadcasters require assignment of copyright in the programme throughout the world in perpetuity and a similar assignment of rights in all the materials included in the programme (to the extent that such rights are acquired by the producer) and all physical materials created in connection with the programme. They also acquire all rights in rushes, offcuts and so forth.

Primary broadcast rights/clearances

Notwithstanding the assignment of copyright to the broadcaster, the terms of trade generally provide that the broadcaster is granted unlimited showings of the programme in the UK without any further entitlements for the producer in respect of this exploitation of UK rights, but with revenue from any sales of the programme outside the UK forming net profits, as described in *Paragraph 2.8* below. In the case of the BBC, the agreement provides that it is entitled to unlimited showings on its licence fee funded channels.

Given that the UK secondary market has expanded out of all recognition since the terms of trade containing these provisions were drawn up, the producer's entitlement to participation from further showings on the broadcaster's own digital channels, as well as shares of revenue from sales to UK channels operated by other broadcasters/service providers, is a matter which is under active review by PACT in its ongoing discussions with the broadcasters on terms of trade issues. Producers are, therefore, advised to try to negotiate a provision whereby it is accepted that, following the initial transmission, subsequent showings in the UK will be treated as sales, from which the producer is entitled to receive net profits.

Clearances – under current talent union agreements, and the usual provisions of licences for existing archive/library material, it is not usual to acquire more than a limited number of UK transmissions and the production agreement will specify the number of clearances which have to be obtained, and paid for from the budget. Any further showings in the UK will be subject to payment by the broadcaster of any residual, royalty or copyright fees which fall due in respect of the further showings.

Internet rights

At the time of writing, procedures for the treatment of Internet rights are being worked out and have not been definitively established. It is, however, likely that, on fully-funded commissions, the broadcasters will insist on retaining Internet rights and the rights to related websites. The producer should seek a contractual entitlement to be commissioned to produce website material and also to have the entitlement to use programme material on the production company's own website. For more details on negotiations with broadcasters and Internet issues refer to *Chapter 17*.

Distribution and secondary rights

All broadcasters' agreements provide for the distribution rights in fully-funded productions to be vested with the broadcaster, although in some cases the broadcaster undertakes to consult with the producer as to the arrangements for the exploitation of the rights and may, in exceptional cases, agree that the producer may have control of the rights. In such cases, the producer would need to demonstrate that it had the necessary mechanisms in place to exploit the rights effectively and collect and distribute revenues from sales.

In increasingly few cases Channel 4 categorises productions as Category C commissions where all rights, except the UK rights, are assigned to the producer following satisfactory delivery of the programme to Channel 4. These programmes are generally low-budget and are regarded as having extremely limited potential for overseas sales.

Format rights

The important exception to the assignment of rights should be the treatment of format rights. Under the BBC terms of trade, where a format has been exclusively created by the producer all rights remain vested with the producer; where the format for the programme has been jointly created by the independent producer and the BBC the format rights are jointly owned. Under these arrangements the BBC has a limited exclusive opportunity to commission further series based on the format. Almost identical arrangements are set out in Channel 5's terms of trade.

So far as Channel 4 and the ITV companies are concerned, in the first instance, the assignment of copyright to the broadcaster generally includes format rights. In many cases, however, it is possible to negotiate a position whereby, if the broadcaster does not commission further production based on the format within a period of approximately two years from the date of transmission of the last production, the format rights will revert to the producer who will be free to exploit them elsewhere.

In all cases where the format might have possibilities for wider exploitation the producer should aim to retain ownership and control of the changed format rights. For more information on negotiating format deals with broadcasters see *Chapter 7*.

Editorial control   **2.4**

Broadcasters always retain final editorial control. In order to be able to fulfil the terms of the statute, charter or licence under which they operate, it is necessary that they do so, as it is in relation to their position in law as 'publishers' of material which may be libellous, defamatory or obscene, or might otherwise give rise to legal action.

In the case of potentially contentious material, the producer is required to warrant that no such actionable material is included within the programme. There are, however, instances where the subject matter of the programme may, by its very nature, lay the broadcaster and the producer open to such claims. In such circumstances, it is sensible for the producer to try to negotiate a 'reverse indemnity' with the broadcaster whereby, provided the producer follows the advice of the broadcaster's own lawyers as to the inclusion of potentially contentious material, the broadcaster will indemnify the producer against such actions.

The production agreement sets out the procedures under which the broadcaster exercises editorial control in consultation with the producer. In some cases, particularly those where the producer may have had to make certain undertakings to those contributing to the programme as to its portrayal of them and their activities, the producer may seek the right to closer collaboration in the editorial process than may be provided for within the standard form production agreement.

Codes of practice

The ITC issues a 'programme code' and the individual broadcasters also issue their own codes of practice, or compliance manuals, which set out procedures to be followed to ensure that the completed programme will not breach the provisions of the Broadcasting Act and other regulatory requirements for UK television transmissions. This is done with particular reference to due impartiality, the portrayal of violence, taste and decency and so forth. Producers are advised to familiarise themselves with the provisions of these codes and, when producing material which may be of a sensitive nature, to work closely with the broadcaster's compliance lawyers to avoid any possible breach.

2.5 Budgetary control

Programme budgets and cash flows are usually drawn up on standard forms supplied by the broadcasters and appended to the contract. The producer will be required to open a separate trust account at a bank approved by the broadcaster into which funds for the production are paid. A bank mandate must be prepared, under which the broadcaster will have the entitlement to require all cheques drawn on the account to be countersigned by a representative of the broadcaster. (In practice this rarely happens, unless it appears to the broadcaster that the accounting may be going seriously adrift.) The producer will be under an obligation to place funds not immediately required for production into an interest-bearing deposit account and the interest will be credited to the production account and can be used to defray any overcost and thereafter form part of the underspend.

The procedures for budgetary monitoring and control will be laid out in detail in the production agreements and it is obviously essential that these are closely observed.

Overcosts

The contract will specify procedures to be followed if an overcost on the production is projected. As a general rule, these state that, in the first instance, the producer's production fee will be applied to reduce any overall overcost (that is, after applying savings in other budget areas and contingency). Provided, however, the contractual procedures are observed and the overcosts are not the result of negligence on the part of the producer, the broadcaster may agree to meet the overcost, but the contract will not place them under any unequivocal obligation to do so.

In extreme cases of overspend or if there is some major mishap or upheaval on the production, the broadcasters will have the right to take over and complete production.

If a producer is aware that an overcost is inevitable, it is important to draw this to the attention of the broadcaster's cost controller immediately and work with them on ways of reducing it. There is an increasing tendency on the part of all the broadcasters to recover any overcost out of the production fee and their contracts allow them to do this, even when the producer has not been negligent.

Underspends

Underspends on the budget (excluding savings on contingencies) have customarily been shared 50:50 between the broadcaster and the producer, unless the broadcaster can demonstrate that the underspends have been achieved at the expense of the quality of the completed programme. Some of the ITV companies do 'cap' the producer's entitlement to underspend to an amount equivalent to a percentage of the production fee or to a fixed maximum sum.

Goods and materials bought for the production which have some second-hand value will be sold off after completion and the sums received set against the cost of production to defray any overcost and thereafter form part of the underspend.

Production fees   2.6

Production fees have customarily been calculated as a percentage of the approved total budget for the programme, including fees for the services of the producer on the production and office overheads, but excluding contingency. They are, in effect, an additional payment for the producer which Channel 4 originally introduced so that producers have some funds to draw on in order to be able to remain in business when not actually in production.

The Channel 4 scale of production fees is as follows:

Direct and Overhead Costs £000	Production Fee %
0–50	Up to 25
51–100	20
101–500	15
501–1,000	12.5
Over 1,000	10

In most cases, Channel 4 pays production fees according to the above scale.

The BBC terms of trade provide "that the production fee will be negotiated with regard to prevailing market conditions and any published industry scales". For small-scale commissions the BBC pays a proportionately larger production fee than for large-scale commissions, which are negotiated case by case. For some years the BBC has, as a general rule, only been prepared to agree production fees which are significantly lower than the Channel 4 scale fees.

The practice of the ITV companies varies from adherence to the scale to no observance of it at all: Carlton, for example, negotiates a fixed amount for the production fee, which is not calculated as a percentage of the production budget (although in practice works out at rarely less than 5% and never more than 7.5%). In negotiating (arguing) such a fee it would be reasonable to use the Channel 4 scales as the benchmark for normal industry practice.

If the producer has more than one project in production with the same broadcaster, the broadcaster may lump the total cost of the productions together in arriving at the production fees. This is known as 'aggregation'. This too can be a matter for hard negotiation (although most producers would welcome the luxury of being in a position to have to do this).

The production fee is paid in instalments at key stages during production with a final payment, usually between 10% and 20% of the fee, being made on delivery and acceptance of the programme.

Note: Producers do occasionally grant a share of the production fee to associates who may, for example, have suggested the idea for the programme or who have some role on the production. When agreeing any such arrangement a producer must always bear in mind that if there is an overcost it may have to be met out of the production fee and should, therefore, make it clear that the share can only be of the production fee actually received by the producer.

2.7   Budgets for ITV network programmes

When the producer is being commissioned to produce a programme for an ITV company which is in turn delivering it to the ITV Network Centre, the ITV company negotiates a licence fee for the production from the ITV Network Centre. This fee may not cover the production budget and even if it does, the ITV company may take the view that it does not cover all its direct costs relating to the production. Such direct costs may include the PACT levy, the company's contributions towards the costs of blanket licence agreements, production audit fees and so forth. In addition to these the company may also wish to charge an indirect overhead cost, calculated as a sum equivalent to up to 5% of the budget. If these costs are not recouped from the ITV Network Centre licence fee the ITV company may seek to recoup these costs (plus interest) in first position from revenue from sales of the programme. This can be a matter for tough negotiation.

2.8   Net profit shares

The entitlement of a producer to receive shares of net profits from overseas sales and any spin-offs from the programme is generally recognised. The terms of trade for Channel 4 and BBC provide for an entitlement to the producer of 30%. The shares offered by ITV companies vary and Channel 5 negotiates shares case by case.

The usual definition of net profits is gross distribution revenues from all sales of the programme (excluding, for the avoidance of doubt, the commissioning broadcasters' UK transmissions), less distribution commission and expenses (which will be detailed in the production agreements), residual and royalty payments in respect of overseas sales and the recovery of any excess cost, plus interest, on the budgeted cost of production.

Where a producer has undertaken a significant amount of development work at their own risk or where the producer has been instrumental in bringing funding to production, the producer should try to negotiate a higher share of the profits. Production budgets may be partially funded by the broadcaster's distributor, with the distribution advance being recouped in first position from first sales revenue, thus, putting back yet further the likelihood of the producer ever receiving any monies in respect of the net profit entitlement. If it appears that the broadcaster's UK television service is, thus, getting the programme at a bargain price, the producer should try to negotiate for a higher than usual share of net profits to compensate for the fact that the possibility of receiving any revenues from the net profit share has been put back while the broadcaster's own distributor recoups.

2.9   Insurance

Insurance requirements will be laid out in the contract, but (depending on the nature of the production) are likely to include principal personnel including cast; negative all risks; employer's and public liability; producer's errors and omissions. The broadcaster will require approval of the arrangements made by the producer who should generally be able (although should not be obliged) to use the broadcaster's own insurers.

Completion guarantees

Although standard form contracts refer to completion guarantees, these are only called for on the most expensive television productions and even then generally only when these are co-financed or co-produced. For an explanation of completion guarantees see *Chapter 18, Paragraph 7*.

Production monitoring 2.10

All production agreements specify arrangements for production monitoring. Needless to say, it is very important for the producer to follow closely all the procedures laid out within the agreement. The producer should set out in writing reasons for a variation from the programme specification, schedule or budget and ask for written confirmation of the broadcaster's agreement. If the programme, or the budget, goes awry and the broadcaster can claim that the producer is in breach of contract because the programme does not conform to the agreed proposal, schedule or budget or the producer has not followed correct procedures, the producer's liabilities can be potentially very onerous (not to mention the damage which may be done to the producer's standing with the broadcaster).

Use of broadcasters' facilities 2.11

Broadcasters recognise that they cannot stipulate that producers use their facilities on independent production deals (although there may be occasions when the producer may judge that in the interests of getting a commission it could make tactical sense to offer to do so).

If broadcasters' facilities are to be used, the method of arriving at an agreed budget for the purpose of settling the production fee is for the producer to draw up a notional production budget and schedule, based on a costing of the use of outside facilities. The broadcaster will expect to approve this in the usual way. The producer will be responsible for contracting and supplying the above-the-line elements in accordance with the budget provisions and the production fee will be calculated as a percentage of the notional budget. The broadcaster will then provide the 'below-the-line' crews and facilities, in accordance with the requirements of the agreed production schedule, at whatever the internal cost may be to the broadcaster.

Care must be taken to ensure that account is taken of any variation between the broadcaster's union agreements for rostering, working away from base, meal breaks, overtime and so forth, and those which apply under independent sector agreements. Delays and changes in availability can sometimes be a problem and terms must be settled in advance with the broadcaster for the cost, or responsibility for costs, if production requirements turn out to exceed those provided for within the schedule.

Mixed crewing, i.e. employing technical staff under different union agreements, is not generally permitted, but it may sometimes be possible to use crews on different agreements on recording and post-production.

ITV NETWORK COMMISSIONING PROCEDURES 3

After the award of the ITV franchises in 1991, the Independent Television Commission (ITC) introduced major changes in the network scheduling procedures which, up to that point, had been something of a free-for-all between the 15 ITV companies, with the five largest players invariably coming out on top. The ITC decreed the establishment of an independent Network Centre with its own programme budget and headed by a network director responsible for the commission and scheduling of ITV network programming.

The ultimate governing body of the Network Centre is its council. Composed of the chief executives of all the ITV companies, the council determines the overall programme strategy, the number of hours of programmes to be provided for the network and the annual network programme budget (which is funded by all the ITV companies in proportions equal to their respective shares of overall advertising revenues). Thereafter, the network director has the day-to-day responsibility for commissioning and scheduling network programmes and determining the price to be paid for them.

At the time of its inception a statement of principles and code of practice were drawn up for the operation of the Network Centre. These provide that both independent production companies and the ITV companies have equal direct access to the commissioning staff at the Network Centre. The code of practice in relation to direct access and to the selection, commissioning and contracting of programmes applies to all programme proposals submitted to the Network Centre, whether by an independent producer directly, by an ITV company or by an ITV company in conjunction with an independent producer.

Thus, the Network Centre provides a level playing field on which producers have the same rights of access as ITV companies to the commissioning procedure for programmes for the ITV network. If the Network Centre elects to commission the programme, it is a direct access commission, i.e. in the commissioning process the producer is in no way beholden to one of the ITV companies (although, and as explained in *Chapter 16*, an ITV company subsequently has to become involved in programme compliance, so that the ITC is not in breach of certain statutory obligations under the 1990 Broadcasting Act).

Further, and largely in response to the representations made by PACT to the Office of Fair Trading about the practice of the ITV companies of insisting on ownership of copyright in independent productions, the trading arrangements with the Network Centre are such that, in return for the licence fee, the Network Centre acquires no rights other than UK terrestrial rights for a limited period. On a direct access commission the producer, thus, retains ownership of copyright in the programme and all exploitation rights other than the UK transmission rights licensed to the Network Centre.

However, in order to be able to take advantage of the direct access route, the producer has to fund the development of the project since the Network Centre has no funds available for development. Particularly in the case of drama, the cost of development can be very substantial and it is risk money, since the Network Centre rarely makes binding commitments to production until all the development work has been completed: it is under no obligation to do so and from its point of view there is no good reason why it should.

If programmes are commissioned on the direct access route, the licence fee is only payable by the Network Centre on delivery of the completed production. The producer, therefore, has to find means of cash flowing the production budget. If there is a deficit the producer has to find ways of funding it. Any overspend must be met by the producer since the licence fee is a fixed price deal (see *Chapters 16* and *18*).

For these reasons, and also because, notwithstanding the stated policy of equal access, some producers believe that they will have a better chance of obtaining a commission if it is submitted to the Network Centre through an ITV company, many producers continue to follow that route. However, it should be borne in mind that, even if the ITV company expresses tremendous enthusiasm and support for the project, it is not itself in a position to guarantee a commission, since that decision is made by the commissioning editors at the

Network Centre and at that stage the ITV company is in no better or worse position than a producer following the direct access route. (How long the ITV barons will allow this state of affairs to continue, particularly when the number of franchise holders has been reduced to two, is a matter of continual industry speculation.)

If the producer decides to submit the proposal to the ITV company and it wishes to proceed further, the ITV company will generally fund the development work which it considers may be required. (It may seek to get some indication from the Network Centre of its likely eventual interest in the project before doing this.) Thereafter, the ITV company will have to obtain commitment from the Network Centre to the commission, before it can contract the independent producer to produce the programme.

If the ITV company obtains the commitment from the Network Centre it will then negotiate the price which the Network Centre will pay and the ITV company will cash flow the production budget and, if necessary, provide deficit financing. In return for this the ITV company will treat the production in exactly the same way as a fully-funded commission for which the terms explained in this chapter apply.

LICENCE FEE AGREEMENTS Chapter 16

There are various forms of licence fee deals which are negotiated with UK broadcasters. The ITV Network has a formal system for licence fee deals on direct access commissions which is followed for every such commission; the BBC Terms of Trade give details of a similar structure for licence fee deals but in practice it is virtually never adhered to; Channel 5 also has terms of trade for licence fee deals but most of their deals are negotiated case by case. Channel 4 does not have any terms of trade for licence fee deals but will enter into them when the producer is bringing significant funding to the cost of production. Licence fee agreements are sometimes negotiated on deals for the new digital channels where budgets may be so low that, from the producer's point of view, the deal is only viable if a limited licence is being granted.

This chapter outlines the arrangements for the ITV Network Centre licence fee deals and sets out key terms to be negotiated on other types of licence fee deals.

KEY TOPICS & ISSUES

C16

1 ITV DIRECT ACCESS LICENCE DEALS

An explanation of the ITV commissioning structure and the difference between a direct access commission from the ITV Network Centre and doing a deal through an ITV company is explained in *Chapter 15, Paragraph 3*. This chapter deals with the arrangements for direct access licence fee deals which are negotiated for many independent productions produced for the ITV network.

1.1 Development

The ITV Network Centre does not fund development of projects. Its commissioning editors may be prepared, at an early stage in a project's development, to give an indication of likely interest in the fully developed project, but the Network Centre only commits to production on the basis of fully developed proposals. The producer is solely responsible for carrying out and funding the necessary development work. As explained in *Chapter 14, Paragraph 1*, television distributors are a possible source for development funding for Network Centre projects.

1.2 Budget

If the commissioning editor at the Network Centre wishes to proceed with a commission, the producer will initially be asked to submit a budget for the production in order that negotiation of the licence fee agreement can commence. A key aspect of direct access licence fee deals is that the fee is only payable on completion and delivery of the programme and the producer, therefore, has to arrange for bank or other finance in order to cash flow the cost of production.

The budget should include all customary charges and the costs the producer has incurred on development, a production fee calculated in accordance with industry practice and the 'cost of money', i.e. costs incurred in securing financing for the cash flow of production funds, plus interest and, if applicable, completion guarantee costs. The producer should also allow a reasonably generous provision for legal costs, since the producer will have to meet the legal costs of contracting for financing for the production. To meet the requirements of the financiers who will cash flow the production the budget will also need to contain contingencies amounting to approximately 10% of budget. (The Network Centre will not generally agree that the licence fee, even if it covers the budget, should also extend to the contingency element).

1.3 Licence fee

On receipt of the budget the Network Centre will negotiate the licence fee it is prepared to offer for the production and the number of UK transmissions which it expects to be cleared and paid for from the fee directly with the producer. From time to time the ITV Network issues guide prices for licence fees for different genres of production, but each fee is negotiated individually. In some cases the licence fee will cover the cost of production; in others there may be a shortfall which the producer will have to make up through funding from distribution advances, pre-sales and/or co-production funding (or from its own resources).

The licence fee is payable on the fifth working day of the month following delivery of the programme. The producer has, therefore, to put in place arrangements for cash flowing the cost of production from pre-production until completion and delivery of the programme. The arrangements which banks and other financiers offer for such cash flowing are explained in *Chapter 18*.

Rights/term   1.4

It is a fundamental condition of the Network Centre's Code of Practice that "the Network Centre will not acquire any rights other than UK broadcasting rights and non-UK simultaneous re-transmission rights needed for the programme to be shown on the ITV network".

In practice the Network Centre normally acquires the sole and exclusive right to three UK showings over five years. These are currently defined as "the simultaneous or non-simultaneous broadcast of the programme in the UK from some or all of the transmitters broadcasting the ITV service". The Network Centre will have the option to extend the term for a further consecutive period of two years on payment to the producer of a sum equivalent to 6% of the original licence fee, which excludes the residual costs of the repeat showing. (At the time of writing it is proposed that the wording of the agreement is amended to provide that the licence also covers on-line showings which are simultaneous screenings of the terrestrial transmission, but this arrangement has not yet been finalised.)

All other rights in the UK, i.e. terrestrial rights (after expiry of the licence term), pay cable, subscription and satellite television, video, theatric and non-theatric rights, as well as all overseas rights, are reserved to the producer on condition that there is no exploitation of any of the other UK rights prior to the first transmission of the programme on ITV.

Since the introduction of ITV2 the ITV Network Centre has frequently acquired an extension to the licence for a showing on ITV2 for a payment equivalent to 1% of the original licence fee.

In the event that the licence fee does not cover the repeats and residual costs which may be due to writers and performers on the second and subsequent showings licensed to the Network Centre, the Network Centre undertakes to reimburse the producer for these costs on transmission (or to be precise, on the fifth working day of the month following transmission) of the repeat.

The Network Centre has the sole and exclusive option to commission sequel programmes to the production. This option must be exercised either 12 months from date of transmission of the programme or, if a series, the last episode of the series, or 13 months from delivery of that programme, whichever is the earlier date.

Tripartite agreement   1.5

Once the budget and licence fee have been agreed and a compliance company selected (see procedures below), the Network Centre will issue a 'deal letter' to the producer confirming all the key elements of the production: title; length; description; principal personnel; director; writer; principal cast; delivery date; licence fee; licence period; and number of transmissions. When certain pre-conditions have been met, generally the confirmation that specified production personnel/talent are available; that all necessary underlying rights have been acquired; and that sufficient finance is available and committed to complete the programme, the parties will proceed to enter into the 'tripartite agreement' between the Network Centre, the producer and the compliance company for the production.

The terms of the tripartite agreement will need to be approved by the financiers with whom the producer will be contracting for cash flow for the production.

C16

When these arrangements were first introduced, considerable difficulties were encountered in reconciling the contractual requirements of banks and other third-party financiers with the contractual requirements of the tripartite agreement, particularly in relation to the Network Centre's entitlement not to release the licence fee in the event that the programme was not produced or delivered in accordance with the terms and conditions of the contract. These early difficulties have largely been resolved, and the process is now much smoother, certainly when working with those banks who are accustomed to direct access deals. It is, nonetheless, an intrinsically more complicated procedure than commissioning procedures for fully-funded productions. Even with all concerned working at full tilt, it takes time to complete all the paperwork and conclude all the agreements to the satisfaction of all parties. Further, third-party financiers responsible for cash flowing the production will not release monies on trust letters, as broadcasters may do when production needs to commence before contracts are finalised: all agreements need to be fully executed before production funding is forthcoming.

1.6 Compliance company/editorial procedures

When the Network Centre opens negotiations for the licence fee terms, the producer must, at the same time, make arrangements for one of the ITV franchise holders to act as the compliance company for the production. This arrangement is necessary if the Independent Television Commission (ITC) is to fulfil its statutory obligations under the 1990 Broadcasting Act to ensure that ITV is structured on a regional basis and that its programmes do not, for example, offend against good taste or decency; incite to crime; lead to disorder; offend public feeling; lack impartiality; contain subliminal messages; and that they generally conform to the ITC's published codes relating to programmes, programme sponsorship, advertising standards, technical performance and the Broadcasting Standards Council's Code of Practice. The ITC can only achieve this observance of the act through its contractual relationship with its franchise holders, the ITV companies, not through the Network Centre with which it does not have a contract.

Therefore, whilst the Network Centre contracts direct for the network commissions, the commissioning contract is a 'tripartite' agreement between the Network Centre, the producer and the ITV company appointed as the compliance company.

The ITV Network Centre will indicate to the producer the ITV companies which may act as compliance licensee and will approve the arrangements for compliance. The producer's views on the compliance company will be taken into account but the ITV Network Centre has the final say.

The compliance company receives a fee direct from the Network Centre for its compliance role. The fee is calculated as a small percentage of the budget and this varies in relation to the genre of programming and the consequent volume of compliance work for the franchise holder. The fee is agreed between the Network Centre and the compliance company and does not form part of the budget for the programme.

In practical terms, the role of the compliance company is to monitor the editorial content of the programme to ensure that it does not breach the provisions of the Broadcasting Act in relation to programme content or otherwise infringe the various ITC codes; to check that the producer's contracts for rights in the production are secure; to approve the contracts with financiers for the cash flow of production funding and for deficit finance and to monitor the cash flow to ensure that funds are being expended in accordance with the provisions of the budget; to ensure that the programme is produced in accordance with the programme specification; and that all the delivery requirements are met and that the programme conforms to the required technical standards.

These various functions are carried out by the compliance company's own compliance officer, its in-house lawyers, cost controllers and technical and presentation staff, as appropriate. The producer, therefore, needs to maintain a continuous dialogue with the compliance company but, unless compliance problems arise on production, the relationship is far more tenuous than that between producer and commissioning company on a fully-funded production. In particular, the editorial role relates to ensuring compliance with the Broadcasting Act: it does not involve advice and consultation on purely creative aspects of the production, as it would on a fully-funded commission. Consultation on creative matters is between the producer and the commissioning editor at the Network Centre.

Producers should be aware that under the tripartite agreement publicity for the production in the UK is under the control of the Network Centre, and this function is generally dealt with by the publicity department of the compliance company. In some cases this arrangement has proved problematic for the producer. The compliance company obviously does not have the same interest in promoting a programme which is not one of its own as it does for its own in-house or commissioned programming. In cases where the Network Centre is satisfied that the producer has the in-house capability to handle productions, it is prepared to allow the producer to handle publicity.

From the producer's perspective, producing on the direct access route is contractually, administratively, financially, creatively and psychologically very different to producing a fully-funded production. The producer is in complete control. Although there are checks within the procedures for the commissions, fundamentally the producer carries all the responsibility and all the financial risk, and ultimately reaps the rewards.

LICENCE FEE DEALS WITH OTHER BROADCASTERS   2

As explained in the introduction, the BBC and Channel 5 have published terms of trade for licence fee deals. These are, however, almost never used and are, in any event, due for review. As things are at present, it is preferable not to try to relate terms to those provided for in the terms of trade, but to negotiate case by case, as outlined below.

Licence fee and acquisition deals   2.1

Licence fee deals and acquisition deals are essentially the same: the broadcaster is granted a licence for a certain number of showings of a programme in a certain territory over a fixed term. In practice, in dealings with the UK terrestrial broadcasters, there is a distinction between them. Licence fee deals are negotiated prior to commencement of production when the producer is bringing significant funding to the production budget, usually by way of co-production or pre-sale monies. The broadcaster's licence fee is used to partially fund the production budget and the broadcaster has creative and other involvement in the production. These are sometimes referred to as 'hybrid' deals (particularly by the BBC), that is to say, part commission, part licence. An acquisition deal is entered into after the programme has been completed (and financed) and thus, there is no opportunity for creative input from the broadcaster.

It must be said that broadcasters frequently have a very grasping approach to licence fee negotiations. The producer will have had to go to very considerable lengths to develop the project and to raise finance and the broadcaster's business affairs executives are rarely prepared to fairly recognise this work, the risk involved and the fact that they are getting a programme which, to all intents and purposes, has been commissioned by them at a far lower price than they would otherwise have had to pay. On the contrary, they frequently appear to exploit a situation where, having made enormous efforts to raise third-party funding, the producer is even more desperate than he or she might otherwise be to secure a deal. Further, the great stumbling block with negotiating licence fee deals is that there are no agreed scales for the relative value of UK transmission rights which can be applied to carving out a fair deal.

The only advice to offer is that the producer should do considerable research into the amount the broadcaster would normally pay for fully-funded commissions for the same slot and work out, in advance, a clear strategy for the key terms for the deal in relation to the amount the broadcaster is prepared to contribute (see *Chapter 24*).

Key terms are as follows:

2.2 Territory

Normally the territory would be the UK, and possibly the Republic of Ireland, only. On some deals the broadcaster's distributors are granted control of distribution rights in other territories and this should be subject to a separate distribution agreement between the producer and the distributor.

2.3 Rights

It is critical to identify the transmission rights. These can generally be divided as follows (using non-technical/contractual parlance):

i   transmissions on one of the broadcaster's own channels only;

ii   transmissions on all of the broadcaster's own channels;
     (For the BBC this can also be split between transmission on licence fee funded channels and/or commercial channels such as UK TV.)

iii pay TV channels, which can be split between satellite, cable, digital channels, video-on-demand (and possibly on-line);

iv   on-line transmissions, which can be split between simultaneous showings of the broadcaster's own transmission and non-simultaneous web casting;

v   video-on-demand, or similar;

vi   video sale and rental;

vii secondary rights; and

viii ownership of the UK copyright in the production.

All these different possibilities allow much scope for negotiation. The minimum position is obviously (**i**), the maximum (**viii**). In between there is the possibility for a number of certain types of showing and/or for the broadcaster to have the entitlement to showings on other channels subject to the producer receiving a share of the revenues from any such sales; for there to be a holdback of negotiable length on the producer selling to the other UK channels so the broadcaster has a window of exclusivity in the UK. The broadcaster may acquire control of the UK video rights and even control of the secondary rights or these could be controlled by the producer with, possibly, the broadcaster being entitled to a share of revenues.

Particular care has to be taken over on-line rights. Broadcasters generally ask for these, but it is risky to grant them since on-line transmissions cannot be limited territorially. Any grant of the on-line rights to a broadcaster might conflict with the exclusive rights in another territory granted to the co-financier. For more details on the treatment of on-line rights see *Chapter 17*.

Term/exclusivity   2.4

The length or term of the licence is negotiable: usual parameters would be a minimum of a year to a maximum of five years. Exclusivity during the term is also negotiable. When the producer is retaining other UK rights it could, for example, be an exclusive licence for two years and non-exclusive for the remaining three years, so during the non-exclusive period the producer would be entitled to make other UK sales of the programme.

Number of runs   2.5

This too is negotiable: anything from one showing to unlimited transmissions. Two or three runs are quite common. The question of clearances also has to be addressed. If the broadcaster is requiring multiple transmissions the agreement must provide that, whereas a certain specified number of clearances will be paid for from the budget, the broadcaster must be responsible for the clearance costs of further showings.

Licence fee   2.6

The level of licence fee will obviously be a matter for hard negotiation. The broadcaster is likely to want approval of the budget and to see the terms of the deals with other financiers to ensure that the financing arrangements are in order.

A key factor in negotiating the licence fee will be the staging of payments. Sometimes broadcasters are prepared to cash flow the licence fee into the production or pay it in stages, for example: 25% on signature; 25% on commencement of filming; 25% on completion of filming: 25% on delivery. On some deals they may only agree to pay the licence fee on delivery; on other deals they may be prepared to cash flow the budget for the whole production in advance of the third-party's contribution being paid. The terms negotiated for other key terms of the deal, as outlined above, will obviously relate, not only to the level of the fee, but also to the extent to which the staging of the payment of the fee is, or is not, to the producer's benefit.

AGREEMENTS FOR INTERNET   Chapter 17

SCREENINGS AND DIGITAL CHANNELS

At the time of the dot.com boom during 1999 and 2000, the television industry went into a frenzy about on-line services as it dawned on the industry that, with the advent of broadband, the terrestrial broadcasters' primary means of transmission could in future be by way of on-line services; that it was feasible for anyone to set up an on-line television service to compete with the existing services; and that there was potential to earn huge revenues from sponsorship and advertising on programme-related websites. From a business affairs point of view the most valuable potential asset became the on-line rights. Channel 4 was the first to respond to this frenzy by inserting draconian wording into its standard form contract under which it acquired all rights and revenues from any form of on-line exploitation whatsoever of its programmes for ever and ever. This provoked a storm of protest from independent producers and more reasonable terms were eventually agreed between Channel 4 and PACT (Producers Alliance for Cinema and Television).

It has now become clear that, however much people enjoy surfing the net for information or for playing computer games, when watching television programmes they generally prefer to relax, with friends and family, in an armchair in front of a conventional television. The two different means of using a screen are accurately described as 'lean forward' and 'lean back' activities. Interactive TV is a 'lean forward' activity. There are currently some very interesting developments in interactive programming but it is fair to say that the general public is being fairly slow to respond to them.

Similarly, the audience for digital channels has been far more elusive than expected and this has raised major doubts about the feasibility of mounting commercially successful on-line television services. Few websites have yet demonstrated that it is possible to earn serious revenues. None of this is to say that on-line services are not going to have a major impact, particularly in areas such as education, news and other specialist fields, but it is going to take longer than anyone was predicting for existing viewing habits to change significantly. There is, therefore, no immediate necessity to re-write the existing terms of trade but on-line rights do need to be treated with care in negotiation.

So far as the digital channels are concerned, under their operating licences there is an obligation on them to commission not less than 10% of production from independent producers. There are, however, as yet no agreed terms of trade for such commissions: the terms of trade for the primary channels do not apply. Negotiations are tough, particularly in relation to the limited funding which is made available. This chapter addresses key issues in programme contracts.

agreements for internet screenings and digital channels

KEY TOPICS & ISSUES

AGREEMENTS WITH BROADCASTERS FOR INTERNET/ON-LINE RIGHTS   1
Simultaneous web casting   1.1

This is the on-line transmission of broadcasters' services and it is generally accepted that to fall within the primary rights customarily granted to broadcasters in their standard production contracts whereby they have the right to transmit the programme in their broadcasting services however such services are delivered. 'On-line' is simply another 'platform' for transmission of the service. Under talent union agreements and production contracts no additional payment is made for simultaneous on-line transmissions.

There can, however, be problems in granting simultaneous on-line transmissions when the programmes are being co-funded from other territories in return for exclusive rights in those territories. Means of addressing this are dealt with in *Paragraph 3* below.

Non-simultaneous web casting   1.2

This is the transmission of the programme at times other than the broadcast transmission and does not necessarily fall within the definition of broadcaster's primary rights. 'Non-simultaneous' can mean many things and the definition needs to be worded with care. Non-simultaneous may be non-commercial, such as a 'catch-up' service, where viewers can have the opportunity to see programmes on the broadcaster's own channels at a different time, but very close to, their first transmission: or commercial, where the programme is transmitted as part of an on-line pay TV service, or offered as 'video-on-demand' where viewers pay a charge to view and possibly download the specific programme. It could even be sold on to a third party's on-line television service, when such services exist.

The broadcasters are trying to establish that catch-up services do not attract any additional payments. There is no standard practice at this stage, but it is reasonable to argue that a genuine catch-up service is one where the programme is re-transmitted within, at most, two weeks of its original transmission and there is a strict limit on the number of showings, probably not more than two. Any later and/or further showings should attract an additional fee.

In the case of commercial non-simultaneous services, the contract should provide for the producer to receive a share of the broadcaster's revenues from exploitation on any such services, in the same way as producers are customarily entitled to receive shares of net profits from conventional overseas sales. The talent unions also require additional payment for this type of usage.

Promotional websites   1.3

The use of clips of the programme (of up to four minutes duration) and other programme material on the broadcaster's own promotional website has been accepted by the talent unions as being another form of publicity for the programme and, as such, does not attract additional payments. Although there was some initial resistance, broadcasters now generally agree that the producer is similarly entitled to use material from the production on the production company's own website.

Programme-related interactive websites   1.4

When a series is proving highly popular, programme-related websites might well have considerable potential to earn additional revenues. The *Big Brother* website was the first to attract an immense number of 'hits'. Websites are now being launched where television game shows can be played interactively from home, for a fee, at the same time as the programme is going out, the most recent one being the *Fifteen To One* interactive website. More and more programme ideas are now being devised which allow the programme to be viewed conventionally with an interactive website being launched alongside the terrestrial transmissions. Arrangements for these types of websites need to be carefully negotiated and should address the following points:

Right to launch the website

Does the independent producer or the broadcaster have the right to launch the website? If, as is likely, the broadcaster requires the right in the first instance, the producer needs to ensure that he or she is commissioned to produce the material for the site (although this may be conditional on the producer demonstrating the necessary know-how or engaging those with the necessary experience to work on it).

Budget/costs/shares of revenues

What is the budget for material being produced for the website? It is important to ensure that it provides for a production fee for the producer. How is the cost of mounting the website to be met? Will it be wholly funded by the broadcaster or will the costs be shared between the broadcaster and the production company? If the website is, or becomes, a commercial website, how are the revenues to be shared between broadcaster and producer and what costs in respect of the creation of the website are to be recouped from revenues before any share? Who is responsible for collecting the revenues and accounting for them?

Term

How long should a website be allowed to continue after transmission of the programme or series has ended? What are each party's entitlements if the website becomes an ongoing commercial enterprise in its own right? What happens if the broadcaster has ceased to commission the programmes but the website continues?

1.5 **Websites and programme formats**

Where the producer retains the format rights in the series, it is important to ensure that the contract provides that the producer has the sole and exclusive right to use the programme format on a website, albeit the broadcaster's agreement to this may be subject to an entitlement to a share of revenues from the website. Any such entitlement should be limited to a share of those revenues received during the term of the broadcaster's television licence in the format (see *Chapter 7*).

1.6 **Domain names**

Broadcasters' standard contracts generally provide that the programme title is registered by them as a domain name. This should be resisted when the broadcaster is being granted only a limited licence in the programme and/or in the format for the programme. For more information on domain names see *Chapter 11, Paragraph 2*.

2 **COMMISSIONS FOR INTERACTIVE AND ENHANCED MATERIAL**

It is anticipated that terms of trade will shortly be negotiated with broadcasters for the commission of interactive and enhanced material. In many respects the arrangements for the production of interactive material, rights of copyright, budgeting, editorial controls and approval can be similar to existing arrangements for conventional commissions. The exploitation rights are, however, another matter. It is important to specify the intended uses of interactive material; whether the broadcaster is acquiring the right only to use it in connection with transmissions of the programme; in what other formats the broadcaster may be permitted to use the material; if the broadcaster wants to use it in more formats/ markets, what additional payments will this attract for the producer?

The most critical issue relates to the 'source code' for the interactivity. In some cases the producer may be acquiring a licence to use an existing source code. In cases where the source code is being specially devised, the agreement will need to address the question of ownership of the code and what each party's entitlements are in the event that it is subsequently used, or licensed for use, on other interactive programmes.

It is too early in the commissioning of interactive material to be able to give examples of how these matters are customarily being dealt with. The key thing which producers should always bear in mind when negotiating deals for any form of programme material is to ensure that, in the event that the material proves to have possibilities for forms of exploitation other than those envisaged and paid for at the time it was commissioned, the producer will have an ongoing entitlement to receive benefits.

INTERNET/ON-LINE RIGHTS VIS À VIS CONVENTIONAL DISTRIBUTION RIGHTS   3

The problem with Internet rights is that, as things stand, it is not possible to limit showings on a territorial basis, whereas much funding for television production is now raised by granting production financiers exclusive rights in the programme in specific territory(ies). The grant of Internet rights to one party obviously infringes this exclusivity. Business affairs executives have been very reluctant to recognise this practical problem, issuing contracts which routinely provide that Internet rights are granted to the broadcaster even where co-finance is being raised from other territories. It is essential for producers to ensure that there is no conflict between the terms of agreements with the commissioning broadcaster and co-financiers. Possible strategies are as follows:

Holdback
Negotiate a holdback on any exploitation of the on-line rights at least until after first conventional transmission in each co-financier's territory; or

Limitations on Internet showings
Provide that the only permitted Internet showing is by way of simultaneous web casting on each co-financier's television service; or

First opportunity
Provide that the majority financier has a right to the first transmission on-line; or

Approvals
Provide that any exploitation of the Internet rights is subject to the agreement of all the co-financiers, with each financier being entitled to a share of revenues from sale of the Internet rights proportionate to their respective contribution to the cost of production.

Formats
Game show and other format rights are licensed on a territory by territory basis. When the deal with the broadcaster provides that the producer is retaining the format rights in the programme, the agreement should not permit the broadcaster to exploit its programmes on the Internet because this could cut across the exclusive territorial rights which a producer would be granting to a changed format licensee.

C17

4 DIGITAL CHANNELS

There are currently no terms of trade for commissions for the digital channels. The deal structures are more akin to those customarily offered for corporate video commissions, being a fixed price deal which is a complete buyout in respect of the assignment of the copyright in the programme to the commissioner. It must be said that these are some of the toughest deals around and many producers have walked away from them since they do not represent a viable way of making a living, let alone a profit. As a general rule, budgets are astonishingly low. Many are achievable only on a 'volume discount' basis, when a large block of programmes is commissioned. Even then, a producer's ingenuity will be stretched to the limits to find ways of doing everything more cheaply. Instead of being properly rewarded for the level of skill required to produce quality material on a tight budget, the operators' approach to negotiations is aggressively grasping and the producer needs to adopt a similarly aggressive stance as to what would make the deal acceptable.

4.1 Rights

The commissioning body generally requires the producer to grant a complete assignment of copyright in the completed programme throughout the world for the full period of copyright. This entitles the commissioner to exploit the programmes by any means they see fit without any further remuneration accruing to the producer. Even the customary entitlement to 30% of net profits does not generally apply.

Although a producer may feel they have no alternative but to agree an assignment of copyright, there are ways in which he or she can negotiate an improved position. Various alternative strategies are as follows:

Payment

Make sure that the payment is in respect of the initial transmissions on the commissioning body's service only. Any exploitation of the programme on another channel or service is subject to additional remuneration, either by way of a further fee or profit shares for the producer.

Term

Limit the time period for exploitation of the rights to two to three years. Negotiate the possibility of an extension to the period for a fixed fee.

Number of showings

Limit the number of showings which can be made without further payment.

Reversioning rights

Ensure that the contract provides that only the producer can be commissioned to carry out any reversioning of the programme for other forms of exploitation, at fees to be agreed.

Format rights

If it is not possible for the producer to retain control of the format rights, try to negotiate for joint ownership and control and a 50:50 share of revenues.

4.2 Budget

Production fees are rarely on offer and are increasingly subject to a cost controller's blue pencil. As is the practice in other countries, producers should be looking at ways of weighting the budget to provide for a built-in profit element which is not as easy to identify as a production fee and, thus, delete from the budget.

Budget deficits

If the producer's budget cannot be met, insist that the shortfall is treated as the producer's contribution to production funding with the producer being entitled to recover the sum of the shortfall, with interest, in first position from revenue from subsequent exploitation of the programme.

Cost reporting

Resist any obligation to have to spend time and money providing detailed cost reports on a budget when it is, in effect, a fixed price deal with no possibility of any additional funding being made available to the producer if it goes into overspend. Similarly, there should be no obligations to share any underspend, in the highly unlikely event that one can be achieved.

Co-funding

In many cases it will be necessary for the producer to find co-finance in order to fund production. Even in these cases, however, the commissioning bodies are looking to acquire all rights that the producer does not have to grant to third parties in order to raise finance. This practice is completely inequitable and should be strongly resisted. On any commission where the producer is bringing a financial contribution to the cost of production the terms of the deal should be on the lines of a licence fee deal (see *Chapter 16*).

SOURCES OF PRODUCTION   Chapter 18

FUNDING IN THE UK

Feature films have traditionally been financed in a multiplicity of ways, from advances from sales agents and distributors through studio funding, tax break schemes, subsidy funding, equity investment and product placement, not to mention producers deferring fees, mortgaging homes and selling the family silver. In contrast television production has, until recently, financed itself from the sums broadcasters are prepared to pay for the programme, the money which can be raised from pre-sale and co-production deals and revenues from distribution advances. It is a worrying reflection on the economic health of the television industry that producers are increasingly having to cast around for alternative sources of 'non-trade' finance in order to be able to meet deficits on available production finance.

There are a limited number of alternative sources of funding. The bulk of National Lottery funding available for film is dispersed through the Film Council, Scottish Screen, Sgrîn, Wales and the Northern Ireland Film and Television Commission. A welcome source of alternative funding for production was brought about in 1997, when the 1992 Finance Act was amended to allow sale and leaseback deals on films with a lower cost than the previous threshold of £15 million, thus, making sale and leaseback deals available for lower-budget feature films and for television programmes. Regrettably, at the time of going to press, April 2002, the Chancellor announced that sale and leaseback schemes can no longer apply to television productions, but will remain for films planned for theatrical release. Over recent years there have been other tax break schemes which can be applied when deficit finance is needed for production. Another alternative, although a difficult one, is sponsorship for which the rules have been somewhat relaxed.

This chapter sets out current parameters for these types of deals. It also explains loan facility agreements and completion bonds, which are increasingly required when alternative forms of finance are being contracted for production.

KEY TOPICS & ISSUES

NATIONAL LOTTERY FUNDING   1

The Film Council   1.1

The Film Council was appointed by the Government to take over the previous functions of the British Film Commission, the British Film Institute's Film Department, British Screen and the Arts Council's Lottery Film Department with effect from April 2000.

The Film Council now receives the bulk of revenues from the National Lottery allocated to film and contributes funds towards the development and production of a wide range of films. As a general rule, the producer is expected to bring other funding to the development and production; in the case of production funding it is a condition of the funding that a distributor is attached to the film. In all cases the funding is repayable, with a premium and a profit share, when the film goes into production. Detailed information can be obtained from the Film Council website www.filmcouncil.org.uk/funding.lasso.

Scottish Screen, Sgrîn, Wales and   1.2
the Northern Ireland Film and Television Commission

Scottish Screen, Sgrîn, Wales and the Northern Ireland Film and Television Commission have lottery funding available to contribute to the development and production of films originating in their respective national regions or destined for production there. There are also area funds such as the Yorkshire Media Production Agency, the South West Media Development Area and the East Midlands Arts Board.

Media Plus funding   1.3

Media Plus is the European Union's funding scheme for the film and television industry and makes funds available for development as well as promotional, training and distribution activities. Information can be obtained from the UK Media Desk, based at the Film Council offices, england@mediadesk.co.uk. Media Antenna are also located in the offices of Scottish Screen, Sgrîn, Wales and the Northern Ireland Film and Television Commission.

SALE AND LEASEBACK TRANSACTIONS   2

Sale and leaseback deals are usual in a number of different industries. In the film industry they are deals in which the owner of the copyright and master negative of a production sells all the exploitation rights in the production to a purchaser (the lessor) who immediately leases the rights back to the original owner (the lessee) in return for an annual rental fee, payable over a leasing period of 10 to 15 years. The lessee can then license the production for distribution in the usual way.

The benefit to the lessor is the entitlement to set the cost of the purchase against profits and thus, claim 100% tax relief on the value of the transaction; to the lessee it is the financial return from the sale (after deduction of the rental payments and the costs of the transaction).

At the end of the rental period the lessee will have the right to extend the lease for a second, unlimited term, on payment of a single, nominal, rental fee.

Parties to a sale and leaseback transaction   2.1

To enter into a sale and leaseback deal the lessee needs to be the owner of the copyright and master negative in the production. In the case of most feature films this is likely to be the production company, although the film's financiers may require that revenues from the transaction be set against the film's recoupment.

The lessor is likely to be an equity partnership of individuals who have been brought together by entrepreneurial firms of accountants or financial managers in order to purchase the rights in the production. Each individual in the partnership will be able to set his or her contribution to the cost of the transaction against their individual tax liabilities.

2.2 Qualification requirements

To qualify, each individual scheme needs to be approved by the Inland Revenue, in accordance with its Statement of Practice. This is not a case of rubber stamping; there are examples of approval not being given. The equity partnership arrangements and the deals themselves are scrutinised by the Inland Revenue to make sure all the requirements for claiming tax relief are met fully.

To meet the regulations the partnership has to demonstrate that it carries out business in the exploitation of films and in order to do so will require some entitlement to net profit participation from the subsequent exploitation of the production.

The key element required to qualify is that the production must be classified by the Department of Culture, Media and Sport (DCMS) as a British film. The rules for classification are varied from time to time. Currently, key requirements relate to the nationality of the production company which must be incorporated in the UK or in a member state of the EEA; 75% of the labour costs must be expended on UK, EU and Commonwealth nationals and 70% of the production cost must be incurred in the UK.

It is possible for films produced as co-productions with other countries to receive classification as a British film if they receive DCMS classification under the terms of the UK Government's official co-production treaties with Australia, Canada and New Zealand. European co-productions can also obtain DCMS classification as British if they meet the similar requirements of the European Convention on Cinematographic Co-Production (see *Chapter 19, Paragraphs 5.1*). Information on all these procedures can be obtained from the DCMS website: www.culture.gov.uk.

The final certificate of British nationality can only be obtained after completion of production and presentation of the audited cost of production. It is not, therefore, possible to conclude a sale and leaseback deal before the production has been completed and, thus, revenues are not available to finance actual production. It is, however, now possible in certain cases to raise bank finance against the expectation of sale and leaseback revenues (see *Paragraph 2.5*).

2.3 Sale and leaseback payments

At the time of going to press, the rules for the calculation of the sale price (which has to be approved by the Inland Revenue) have just been changed to restrict it "to production expenditure which has been paid at the time the film is completed, or is unconditionally payable within four months of the date the film is completed". This seems to rule out inclusion of any deferred fees. It is likely that costs directly attributable to financing production will not be allowable, nor business overheads not directly attributable to production.

If the production has been exploited prior to the transaction, the calculation of the sale price is based on an assessment of its remaining commercial value at the time of purchase. For this reason, unless the production enjoyed a spectacular success, it is preferable to do the deal before any post-production sales are entered into, since such sales will obviously reduce its residual value. (Paradoxically, if certain territories have been pre-sold in order to finance production, or if the rights have already been licensed to a distributor, these might not necessarily be deducted from the cost of production when calculating the sale price, as long as significant markets remain to be exploited.)

The rental payments payable in each year of the lease are negotiable. The total payments have been as low as approximately 88% of the sale price, but about 92% is probably now more usual. They are payable in annual instalments at the end of each financial year during the term of the lease.

Agreement needs to be entered into with a bank for a guarantee for the rental payments which, unless the production company has significant assets, will involve the company placing the total sum of the rental payments in an escrow account with the bank providing the guarantee, from which only the rental payments can be made. The rental payments attract interest which is met from the interest earned on the funds in escrow.

Cash benefit from the transaction   2.4

In the calculation of the sale price and rental payments, provision will need to be made for the sale price to cover the legal and accounting fees incurred by the production company in completing the deal. Account also needs to be taken of the costs of the bank guarantee. The production company needs to remain in existence through the term of the lease and if, as is frequently the case, the transaction is through a special purpose company set up solely for the production, account should also be taken of the costs of keeping the company in existence and providing annual audits to Companies House.

After deduction of the above costs and the rental payments, the remaining balance – generally between about 8-10% of the sale price – is the actual cash value to the production company of the transaction.

It will be seen from this that it is rarely worthwhile doing a sale and leaseback deal if the cost of the production is less than £1 million and it would be difficult to find investors for anything with a lower budget.

Sale and leaseback revenues as deficit finance   2.5

A production company is fortunate indeed to be in a position where it is the owner of the copyright in the production, the production is fully funded and the sale and leaseback revenues can, therefore, be retained by the company.

Notwithstanding the fact that a sale and leaseback transaction can only be effected after completion and delivery of the production, it is increasingly the case that the likely revenues from the eventual sale and leaseback deal will be relied upon to fund a deficit on the production budget.

Where the sale and leaseback revenues are required to fund a deficit, it may be possible to raise bank financing against the completion bond company having given assurances that the production will meet the qualification requirements administered by the DCMS and, thus, sale and leaseback revenues can be relied upon. Only a few banks are prepared to enter into this kind of arrangement and other criteria will need to be met before it is agreed, but it is achievable.

Sale and leaseback arrangements have now been extended until 2005 but the rules and regulations remain subject to variation. Before embarking on a transaction the production company should establish the current qualification requirements of the DCMS and consult a lawyer and an accountant experienced in sale and leaseback transactions for production.

3   TAX BREAK SCHEMES

There are other forms of tax break funding, which generally relate to relief on an individual's capital gains liabilities. The rules for such tax break schemes are varied too frequently by the Inland Revenue for them to be written about here with any certainty that they will still apply in a few months', let alone years', time. Currently, the structure of the deals is that a bank or financial partnership (the investor) will cash flow the entire cost of production with sums committed by the broadcaster and other production financiers being immediately returned to the investor. Any deficit on the production finance is cash flowed by the investor against a first position recoupment from revenues from distribution of the production.

To enter into this type of arrangement the investor will need to approve not only the amount of funding committed to production, but sales estimates and the choice of distributor. The production will also require a completion bond. The investor will require the distributor to distribute the production for a rate of commission significantly below the norm until the sum of the deficit (sometimes with interest) has been recouped. Distributors may be prepared to do this in return for not having been asked to put up an advance to acquire the distribution rights. Following recoupment, distribution commission will increase to its usual percentage (or, in some cases, higher) and the investors will be entitled to a profit share from subsequent sales.

These arrangements can work well, although from the producer's point of view he or she can almost certainly wave goodbye to the prospect of ever seeing any profits from sales of the production.

3.1   Enterprise investment schemes

These are tax break schemes designed to help small businesses raise investment. Small businesses sell shares in their 'enterprises' to investors who become shareholders in a similar way to which individuals are shareholders in plc companies. The investors can claim tax relief on the subscription cost of the shares. Current regulations do not allow an enterprise to raise more than £1 million per year but a number of production companies have used this mechanism to fund production of low-budget features.

4   EQUITY FINANCE

Very few producers can demonstrate any success in raising equity finance for production. Equity investors' conventional requirements for a percentage return on the investment and an 'end date' by which the investment will be recouped, can rarely be satisfied. Neither the high street banks nor merchant banks can be persuaded to invest: at best they will cash flow productions against contracts guaranteeing payment of production funding.

Whilst conventional sources of equity finance are generally closed to the producer, wealthy private individuals are often attracted by the idea of taking a gamble on projects which may be of particular appeal or interest to them, in much the same way that 'angels' invest in theatre productions. They are drawn by the glamour of film and find it more exciting to risk funds surplus to their immediate requirements in films than in stocks and shares. Finding this type of funding obviously requires a high degree of initiative, cheek, contacts and luck on the part of the producer, but it does happen more frequently than most sensible people might think possible!

If the producer does secure this form of investment, it is important to have a carefully drawn up agreement which provides not only for the manner in which the investor is to recoup his or her net profit entitlement, but wording under which the investor acknowledges that the investment is a risk investment; that the producer is under no liability to the investor either in relation to the quality and profitability of the completed film or in respect of reimbursement of the contribution in the event that the film itself does not generate sufficient revenues to repay the investment. However friendly and generous the investor may be at the outset, it is disconcerting how swiftly generosity can turn to animosity when things don't work out and in these circumstances a simple written agreement can prevent an awful lot of problems.

SPONSORSHIP   5

On the face of it, sponsorship from manufacturers is an obvious form of alternative finance. For feature films it generally takes the form of product placement, whereby manufacturers supply props, sometimes of enormous value, to the production free of charge in return for the on-screen exposure. Product placement is not, however, permitted on television programmes.

Sponsorship of programmes on all commercial channels regulated by the ITC is governed by the ITC's Code of Programme Sponsorship. All sponsorship on these channels has to be approved by the ITC and it will only consider applications for approval when these are submitted by one of its licensees. The BBC Charter has similar principles to those of the ITC relating to programme sponsorship. BBC procedures require prior clearance of sponsorship which entails rigorous checking to ensure that the programme's editorial content is not influenced by the sponsorship.

Any producer proposing to seek sponsorship for a production planned for a mainstream UK broadcaster is advised, in the first instance, to obtain the ITC Code of Programme Sponsorship (www.itc.org.uk). The individual broadcasters also have their own codes of practice relating to programme sponsorship.

This is not to say that broadcasters are not interested in securing production finance through sponsorship. They are. The possibility of a programme having good prospects for sponsorship revenue is likely to carry considerable weight with commissioning editors constantly on the look out for ways of achieving savings on their budgets. If, therefore, a producer believes that a project might attract sponsorship it would be well to emphasise this when presenting the project to a commissioning editor. However, the regulations laid down by the ITC Code of Programme Sponsorship and the BBC Charter make it extremely difficult, not to say impossible, for a producer to be able to contract for sponsorship finance without the full co-operation of the broadcaster. Further, commercial channels regard sponsorship revenue as their own as it comes out of the same pot as advertising revenues, and they are extremely reluctant to allow independent producers to access these revenues direct. Leaving aside the regulations, on a purely practical level it is ultimately only the broadcaster who can contractually commit to deliver to the sponsor what they may require in terms of credits, exposure, slot time and so forth.

As things stand at present, the advice to producers is by all means explore the possibility of sponsorship, since this could clinch the commission. Do not, however, attempt to negotiate any deals for sponsorship without involving the commissioning broadcaster. In this connection, be very cautious when, as quite frequently happens, independent producers are approached by sponsorship brokers offering to set up sponsorship deals with manufacturers in return for a handsome commission. These arrangements may work for programmes which are to be funded and produced speculatively, but are extremely difficult to negotiate when it is planned that the production will be commissioned by a mainstream broadcaster.

6   LOAN FACILITY AGREEMENTS

For direct access deals with the ITV Network Centre (see *Chapter 16*) and for other deals where it is necessary to obtain bank financing to cash flow production, pending payment of committed production finance, it may be necessary for the producer to enter into a loan facility agreement with a bank. In fact, not many banks are prepared to negotiate facility agreements for production finance but the principal banks currently offering to do so are Barclays Bank Media Branch, Soho Square; The Royal Bank of Scotland, Cavendish Square Branch; The Leumi Bank; and Coutts Bank.

6.1   Pre-conditions

The following pre-conditions are likely to be attached to a facility agreement: Acceptance/approval by the bank/bank's lawyers of:

i   a certified copy of the producer's company's Memorandum and Articles of Association, and of appropriate board resolutions authorising the facility agreement;

ii   the contracts for underlying rights in the production (e.g. contracts for scripts and/or literary works on which the production is based);

iii   agreements for key individuals: usually the individual producer, the director, key cast and composer;

iv   budget and cash flow;

v   policies for production insurance, including errors and omissions insurance;

vi   pledgeholder agreements, in favour of the bank, with laboratories and/or facilities houses holding visual and sound materials relating to the production;

vii   the licence fee agreement (in the case of ITV licence fee deals, the tripartite agreement) and agreements with other third parties for production finance;

viii   written approval by production financiers of the terms of the producer's loan facility agreement; and

ix   a deed of assignment whereby, as further security, the benefit of the producer's agreements with production financiers is assigned to the bank.

(With some contracts, particularly those for key cast and the composer and the pledgeholder agreements, it may not be possible for the producer to supply these in advance of finalisation of the loan agreement since the services/facilities may only be contracted after commencement of production. In such cases the facility letter may stipulate by which date such contracts need to be approved by the bank and the producer will not, thereafter, be able to drawdown further funds unless the bank's approval has been given.)

Structure 6.2

Loan facility agreements are for negotiation in each case but the basic structure is as follows:

Arrangement fee

The bank charges an arrangement fee calculated as a percentage of the loan: the percentage is a matter for negotiation but is generally between 1.5-2.5%. The arrangement fee is included in the budget and is generally paid to the bank on signature of the facility agreement, with the sum of the arrangement fee being included within the loan.

Bank interest

Loans attract interest for the bank at a percentage above either the nominated bank base rate, or LIBOR (the London Interbank Offer Rate, which is the rate at which a bank is able to borrow money on the London interbank market from lending banks). There is much custom and practice for interest being calculated at 2% above base/ LIBOR, but this too is negotiable. The interest is calculated from date of drawdown of loan funds to date of repayment.

Legal costs

The producer pays the bank's legal costs (as well as his or her own) in arranging the facility. (It is important to try to negotiate a 'cap' on these legal costs, since lawyers can have a field day with the volume of legal work required to conclude a loan facility agreement.)

The charge

The bank will require a charge over the production, whereby the copyright in the production and the underlying rights (and revenues) are assigned to the bank as security for repayment of the loan. The charge is registered at Companies House (and will be discharged on repayment of the loan). The wording of the charge needs to be checked carefully to ensure that it only relates to the actual production and not to any other assets the producer may have.

Takeover

The agreement will have very specific procedures relating to the bank's entitlement to take over and complete production, in the event that there is a breach by the producer of the terms of the agreement. It can sometimes be quite difficult to reconcile these requirements with those of other third-party financiers, who may require similar forms of protection in relation to their investment or interest in the production. It is for this reason that it is important to arrange loan facilities with banks and other financiers who are accustomed to dealing with film and television productions, since the deal can become a legal quagmire if those involved are not experienced in hacking out these forms of agreement.

COMPLETION GUARANTEES/BONDS 7

Completion guarantees (sometimes called completion bonds) are a form of insurance whereby the completion guarantor guarantees to take over and complete production if, for any reason at all, it becomes apparent during the course of production that the production cannot be completed within the approved total budget. By this means the financiers' investment in the production, or loan, is safeguarded. The producer is also protected, since the completion guarantor is responsible for financing the cost of

C18

completing the production if it goes into overcost (whether, thereafter, the producer would ever again be acceptable to completion guarantors is another matter).

The completion guarantors guarantee that the production will be completed and delivered by a certain date (although give no guarantees as to the artistic quality of the completed production). If the production is not delivered by the due date, the completion guarantor will reimburse production financiers for their investment.

Before undertaking to guarantee a production, the completion guarantor will require approval of all key production elements: producer, director, script, principal cast. This approval is not confined to the terms of the contracts with the key production personnel, but extends to approval of the choice of individual, since certain directors and actors (and even producers) may have well-earned reputations for behaviour on set which might raise the completion guarantor's level of risk to unacceptable heights.

The production budget will be subject to particularly careful scrutiny by the completion guarantor to ensure that it is adequate for the production and in any event must include a general contingency of 10%. The terms of the production financing agreements will also require prior approval.

The completion guarantor's charge is negotiable, but is usually in the region of 3-6% of budget. A rebate on a portion of the charge will be payable if the completion guarantor is not brought in and this rebate will usually be set against recoupment by production financiers of the cost of their investment.

As with sale and leaseback financing, it would be extremely unusual to be able to obtain a completion guarantee for a production with a budget lower than £1 million. The amount of work and expense involved in effecting the guarantee cannot be justified if it is for less than this amount.

Throughout the world there are a limited number of companies offering completion guarantees. The principal guarantor for UK productions is Film Finances.

Completion guarantee agreements are very lengthy and somewhat technical. It is, therefore, important for the producer to engage a media lawyer with extensive experience of this particular form of work to deal with the agreement.

C19

RAISING PRE-SALE AND CO-PRODUCTION FINANCE OUTSIDE THE UK

Chapter 19

With increasing pressure on production budgets there is an ever-growing need for producers to be able to raise co-finance from other territories to be able to fund production, particularly for major drama and documentary projects. This chapter gives suggestions on: methods of approach; the basic structure of pre-sale and co-production deals; how to work with a 'finder' in raising funding; and how to start making contacts.

A comprehensive guide to likely sources of co-production and pre-sale finance would undoubtedly be a book in itself (and would almost certainly be out of date by the time it was published). This chapter aims to give some pointers to possible sources of pre-sale and co-production finance.

KEY TOPICS & ISSUES

1   PRELIMINARIES

Unless the producer is very well established and/or has excellent overseas connections and even if the project appears to have obvious appeal for a particular overseas territory, as a general rule, it is extremely difficult for a UK-based producer to obtain pre-sale or co-production funding from outside the UK without having first obtained a firm expression of interest from a UK financier. All producers know how difficult it is to get a response, let alone a commitment, to a project from broadcasters in the UK and will, therefore, appreciate that it is virtually impossible to raise funding in another territory without the credibility that a positive expression of interest from a third-party financier in the producer's home territory gives to the producer and the project.

2   COMMITMENT FROM UK BROADCASTER/FINANCIER

If the producer is able to overcome the first hurdle of obtaining interest, in principle, from a UK financier to partially fund production, he or she must first ascertain the level of funding on offer and the rights that will be required in the production. The producer is then in a position to know the amount of co-funding needed and what rights and entitlements he or she will have to offer potential third-party co-financiers.

Unfortunately, none of the UK broadcasters appears to have any recognisable procedures which come into play when it is interested, in principle, in a production, but where co-finance must be raised. Cost controllers and business affairs executives are understandably reluctant to do any work on a production until they know that it is actually happening. It is sometimes the deal-making equivalent of pushing a boulder through a maze to obtain satisfactory documentation relating to the broadcaster's potential contribution and required rights, which will enable the producer to enter into sensible negotiations for co-finance. (It is even more difficult to get the broadcaster to accept that the producer's role in successfully raising finance for production should be properly recognised in the terms of the eventual production deal.)

In the first instance, the commissioning editor and/or the producer may approach the broadcaster's own distributors to see whether they would contribute the balance of the funding as an advance against overseas distribution rights and/or whether, through their co-production contacts, they would be able to secure the additional funding through pre-sale or co-production investment. If the broadcaster's distributor is able to do so the deal effectively becomes a fully-funded commission by the broadcaster from the producer's point of view. The main point for negotiation is placing a fair value on the broadcaster's UK transmissions, thereby establishing the amount the broadcaster's distributor is actually contributing in respect of the overseas rights and what they will recoup in first position, from revenues from distribution, before the producer receives a net profit share.

If the broadcaster's own distributors are not prepared to contribute the balance, the producer is then left to do it. It would be unwise of a producer to start doing so unless a letter of intent is received from the broadcaster confirming that, subject to the producer being able to raise the balance of finance, it will commit to production. Having obtained a formal, in principle, commitment it is sensible for the producer to maintain a dialogue with the commissioning editor on the progress of the fundraising efforts, to ensure that the project remains on the commissioning editor's list of anticipated future commissions.

BASIC STRUCTURES OF PRE-SALE AND CO-PRODUCTION DEALS AND DISTRIBUTION ADVANCES 3

Pre-sale agreements 3.1

Pre-sale funding is funding which an overseas broadcaster or other television station is prepared to put into the production at an early stage to acquire exclusive transmission rights in the completed programme in its home territory. The pre-sale financier will not have any involvement on the actual production, although the funding is likely be conditional on the production meeting certain creative and editorial requirements.

Pre-sale funding is only likely to be forthcoming for programmes which will fit neatly into one of the financier's existing programme strands or for prestigious or very commercial programming, for which there might be considerable competition for transmission rights, and/or where the financier may score some prestige public relations points from association with the production.

Pre-sale funding for documentaries may be found at the stage where there is a detailed treatment available, but for dramas it would be unusual for it to be forthcoming before the programme is fully scripted and principal cast and director lined up.

The terms of the licence granted to the pre-sale financier are negotiated in relation to the level of their contribution to the overall production budget and the customary values attached to the sales of programmes in the same genre to the pre-sale financier's territory.

Rights

The usual arrangement would be to negotiate that the pre-sale financier holds an exclusive licence in the production in its home territory for, say, two transmissions over a two- or three-year period, with there being a holdback on the exploitation by the producer of other rights in the territory until after first transmission by the pre-sale financier.

The agreement will need to specify which television rights are being granted: some or all of terrestrial; satellite and cable subscription; video; non-theatric. Sometimes all rights will be granted: other times they will be limited to certain rights only. If not all forms of television are being granted, it would be usual to provide a limited holdback on the exploitation of other rights in the territory, at least for the first year of the licence period.

It is important, if satellite rights are being granted, to ensure that there will be no conflict between the overspill on these into other territories from which pre-sale revenues may be raised. It is also important to exclude on-line rights since the grant of these rights could conflict with rights granted in other territories. If this is a problem see *Chapter 17, Paragraph 3* for possible solutions.

If the pre-sale contribution is considerably in excess of prices usually paid in that territory, the financier may seek to acquire wider rights, e.g. all rights in its home territory and/or control of distribution rights in certain additional territories and/or an entitlement to a share of net profits from sales of the production outside its territory.

Payment structure

The timing of the release of the pre-sale funds is a crucial factor in these negotiations. As pre-sale funding is required to finance production it is desirable that it should be paid in stages during the course of production: e.g. 25% on commencement of pre-production; 25% on commencement of filming; 25% on completion of filming; 25% on delivery of the programme. In some instances, however, the pre-sale funder may only be prepared to pay on delivery of the completed programme.

It is important to establish in which currency pre-sale funding will be paid and, if it is in a foreign currency, to make allowances within the production budget for fluctuations in the exchange rate.

Credits

A pre-sale funder may require a credit on the production, which is generally in the form "Produced in association with…". The commissioning editor may require an individual executive producer credit.

If there are a number of pre-sale agreements the credits may be tricky to negotiate and it is frequently a good idea to make provision for different credit sequences in each pre-sale territory, with one agreed credit sequence for the 'international' version being sold outside the territories of the financiers.

3.2 Co-production funding terms

Co-production funding is funding which comes in when an overseas producer or broadcaster actually shares responsibility for aspects of the production, has editorial input and contributes to the production costs, either through cash or facilities or both. The production is likely to have to be structured to allow major creative input from nationals from each (or all) of the co-producers' home territories; for example, if the script has been written by a UK writer, the co-producer may require that the director is a national of its home territory and the nationality of the cast may be divided between territories.

Rights

A co-producer is likely to expect complete ownership of rights in the programme in its home territory, where the programme will probably be screened as locally originated material, credited as being a co-production between the financier and the UK producer. Depending on what proportion of funding the co-producer brings to the production, the co-producer may also control certain distribution rights outside its home territory and be entitled to profit shares from the production, which are generally calculated in accordance with the proportion of the contribution to the production budget brought by the co-producer.

For detailed terms for co-production development and production agreements see *Chapters 20* and *21*.

3.3 Distribution advances

Distributors are sometimes prepared to offer an advance against control of distribution rights before production has commenced to secure exclusive distribution rights in the eventual production. A distribution advance is, however, unlikely to be forthcoming until the programme plans have been fully developed to the extent that the distributor can make an informed commercial judgement as to the programme's likely sales potential and until sufficient production funding has been committed to ensure that, with the additional funding from the distribution advance, production will proceed.

The distributor recoups the sum of the advance from first income from sales, after deduction of the distributor's usual commissions and distribution costs. It is sometimes possible to negotiate payment of the advance in stages during pre-production (as described for pre-sales), but advances will frequently not be payable until delivery of the completed programme to the distributor. More information about distribution advances is given in *Chapter 22*.

HOW TO FIND FUNDING 4

There are two alternatives open to a producer:

i   to use a distributor or an agent to act as a 'finder' in raising finance for the production; or

ii   to make the contacts and 'go it alone'.

Using a 'finder' 4.1

Distributors are in contact with overseas broadcasters on a day to day basis and at the many international programme markets. It is their business to know who is looking for what, what types of programming will have appeal in particular markets and territories and who are the key programme decision makers in each organisation. They are, therefore, well placed to find pre-sale and (to a lesser extent) co-production funding. There are also a growing number of agents and packagers, commonly known as 'finders', who are prepared to raise funding in return for a fee.

Care has to be taken when appointing a finder. There are many unscrupulous bounders around juggling with projects, and it is easy for a programme proposal to become 'shop-soiled' and, therefore, unappealing to potential production financiers through being offered around indiscriminately by individuals who have no real commitment to it and who are just out to get the best deal for themselves.

If the finder is also a distributor, their main interest usually lies in acquiring material for their sales catalogue and they may, in addition to receiving a finder's fee, want to retain distribution rights in the programme in territories which are not sold off for production funding. This needs to be treated with care, since there can be some conflict of interest between the need to sell off territories to secure funding and the distributor's wish to retain the widest distribution rights possible.

For co-production deals the producer must stay particularly close to the finder and, once an initial expression of interest has been secured, be present at all meetings where the production is to be discussed. Creative considerations obviously play an enormously important role in any co-production deal. Even the best-briefed and most artistically sensitive finder will not be equipped to discuss production arrangements and volunteer or accept suggestions for ways in which the production can be structured so that it is creatively satisfactory to both parties. The producer must avoid being in the position of being presented with a co-production or pre-sale deal which is conditional on all sorts of undesirable criteria, both in terms of creative requirements and the physical arrangements for production.

Never let anyone, be they an established distributor or a freelance individual, represent a project without entering into a written agreement as to the terms under which they are to operate, as follows:

Agreements with a finder 4.2

Finder's fee

The most frequently used method of arriving at a finder's fee is to calculate it as a percentage of the sums the finder is being asked to raise (not as a percentage of the production budget). The percentage is negotiable, but it is usually worked out on a sliding scale (like production fees): the larger the sums to be raised, the lower the percentage. Very approximately it should be about 5% if the finder has to raise sums in excess of £1 million and up to about 15% for sums less than approximately £100,000.

The finder should be expected to raise the cost of the finder's fee in addition to the sums needed for production funding, i.e. if the production requires £1 million, the finder should raise £1,050,000 to cover a 5% fee.

The finder's fee must cover any direct costs and expenses incurred by the finder in raising the money. The finder, not the producer, should be at risk for these costs if the finder is unable to raise the required sums. (It is quite common for finders to ask producers to meet their costs. If pressed into this, the agreement must expressly state that the producer will only meet costs which are agreed, in advance, in writing.)

Exclusivity/territories

During the term, the finder usually has the exclusive right to raise the finance, or the right to raise finance in certain specified territories. This right needs to be exclusive, since it is damaging to a project for more than one person to be chasing the same sources of production finance.

Term

The agreement must specify a finite term (usually about 12 months) during which the finder can look for funding. If they are not successful in raising the required sums within that term, then the producer must be entitled to terminate the agreement.

Consultation/approvals

The producer must be kept informed of all approaches being made by the finder and responses received, and have the right to approve the terms of the deals before finalisation and to be a signatory to the contracts.

No liability

The contract must contain a 'no liability' provision for the producer in the event that the finder raises the required sums but the producer is not, for whatever reason, able to proceed with production.

Termination

If the producer terminates the agreement, provision is generally made for the finder to continue to be entitled to receive finders' fees in the event that the producer contracts for production finance with a financier introduced to the producer by the finder during the term of the agreement.

4.3   'Going it alone' to find funding

Unless, through previous production or other experience, the producer has had the opportunity to build up contacts overseas, raising funding can be a daunting task. It requires a high order of determination and tenacity. There is little more soul-destroying than going to overseas sales markets and buttonholing potential financiers, who then gaze abstractedly into the middle distance or greet every second person passing by, while the producer attempts to outline cherished production plans. There are no easy routes or short cuts and, as with most things, luck plays an important part.

Firstly, unless the producer has a particular entrée, it is rarely worth approaching potential overseas end-users direct. All producers know how difficult it is to get responses from the UK so it's not hard to imagine how much more difficult it is to get one from an overseas broadcaster who knows nothing about the producer or the company.

A valuable initial step is to seek advice from distributors. The relationship between distributors and producers is naturally symbiotic: producers want to make programmes and distributors want programmes to sell. The roles are complementary. There can be benefits for both sides in building up a working relationship. In circumstances where a producer needs advice on likely sources of co-production or pre-sale funding, a distributor is well placed to be able to suggest approaches and contacts.

Another important step is to make contact with producers in territories which are likely to be interested in the type of programming the producer intends to produce, to establish whether collaboration might be possible.

For European co-productions, the EU Media Programme runs various courses which enable producers to make contacts with producers in other European territories. Further, all member states have a Media Desk in their own countries, which is able to supply information on producers and production companies in their territories.

The European Broadcasting Union runs biannual conferences on co-production in Europe and the Council of Europe also organises gatherings.

The Sharing Stories Conferences, which take place annually in Scotland, are funded by the Scottish Development Agency with the aim of bringing together participants with co-production experience from all over the world.

During some of the major markets, such as MIP, the organisers occasionally run seminars where producers can exchange information on the programming requirements of their territories and the opportunities for co-production.

Regular seminars and conferences designed to disseminate information and provide a forum for producers to meet are held by PACT and other interested organisations.

No one pretends that any of this is easy: it takes a great deal of drive and energy to network effectively, but the results can be very worthwhile. One of the most valuable assets a producer can have is a good working relationship with a producer in another territory who has the same programme-making interests and an ability to raise finance from his or her territory for development and production.

SOURCES OF PRE-SALE AND CO-PRODUCTION FINANCE   5
Europe   5.1

It is clearly not possible within the framework of this book to give definitive information on likely sources of pre-sale and co-production finance. The various television services are now in a constant state of change because of the plethora of new digital channels; feature film financing has always been a constantly moving feast (or famine) and, for both television and feature films, rules for subsidy funding and tax break schemes are kept under continuous review. The following aims to give a few pointers for possible routes for funding in different territories.

There tends to be, often well-founded, sensitivity and defensiveness among European producers about British 'imperial' attitudes towards co-production since, all too often, the British approach European co-production on the basis that "we make better programmes better than you do and, therefore, we are going to produce it our way". (The Americans tend to take a similar attitude towards the British.) When approaching potential European partners it would be wise to do everything possible to dispel concerns about this.

Nearly all the European countries have some form of state subsidy for the production of audio-visual works. Under EU rules these funds are technically accessible by nationals of other member states although, in practice, it is probably only feasible for a UK producer to access them by working with a producer in the country granting the subsidy.

Eurimages

This is the principal pan-European fund. It is an initiative of the Council of Europe in Strasbourg and is funded by contributions of some of the member states of the Council of Europe. Subsidy funding of up to approximately €1 million or 20% of the budget is available for feature films which, to qualify, need to be trilateral European co-productions; and funding of approximately €150,000 or 15% of budget for bilateral European co-productions of documentary films. A pre-condition for qualification is that the co-producers are independent producers who are European nationals, with, in the case of feature films, the majority co-producer contributing no more than 70% of the funding and the minority co-producer no less than 10%; for documentary films the ratio is 80:20.

European Convention on Cinematographic Co-Production

This too is an initiative of the Council of Europe and sets out rules for European productions to qualify as co-productions under the European Cultural Convention. This qualification is required to access certain European subsidy funds (and to qualify as a British production for the purpose of sale and leaseback funding).

EU Media Programme

At the time of writing the European Union has launched Media Plus, which is the third phase of the European Union Media Programme. Although Media Plus does not make funds available for production, it does make them available for development, which includes funding to identify industry partners, co-producers and financiers. Further information can be obtained from the UK Media Desk.

National subsidies and tax break schemes

The most lucrative subsidy schemes, and those most likely to be accessible to UK-based producers, are the various federal and regional subsidies offered by the German authorities. The federal schemes generally carry a requirement for a German producer and involvement of German creative talent; the regional schemes (the principal ones are for Berlin, Hamburg and Nordrhein-Westfalen) require a proportion of filming or post-production work relative to the value of the subsidy to be carried out in the region granting the subsidy. Many of these funds are designed primarily to fund the production of theatrical features, but an increasing number of drama productions are being funded from both theatrical and television sources.

In Germany there are currently tax break schemes for feature film financing whereby partnerships of individual investors fund the entire cost of the film, subject to the feature film company guaranteeing a return of 50% of the investment on completion of the film and to it obtaining satisfactory estimates from the sales agent and meeting certain other criteria, and set the cost against their individual income tax liabilities. This tax break funding has been accessed for UK and US productions without any requirement for German involvement in the actual production arrangements. A point of contact for these tax break schemes is the Film and Television Division of the Deutsche Bank AG.

In France a number of schemes operate around the Centre National de la Cinematographie – commonly known as CNC funding. These require a high proportion of the talent and crew to be French and a significant amount of the production funding to be spent in France. Subsidy funding is also available through SOCIFICAS (Sociétés pour le Financement des Industries Cinematographiques et Audiovisuelles) which are tax break schemes where individuals can obtain tax relief on investment in film production.

It must be said that the regulations governing the French subsidy schemes are extremely complicated, as are the ways in which French producers work around their regulations. A UK-based producer requires a trusting relationship with a French producer in order to successfully access these schemes to the benefit of both parties.

The Irish Film Board provides subsidy funding for development of screenplays and will contribute to finance for productions which are being shot in Ireland, involving Irish talent. Ireland also has a Section 481 tax break scheme for funding for feature films, under which contributions amounting to approximately 12% of the budget can be obtained for a feature film being shot in Ireland.

Virtually all the other European countries have subsidy funding available for various forms of audio-visual production (and co-production). Many carry criteria relating to language and the specific cultural requirements of the territory. As a general rule, the sums available, although sufficient to facilitate the production of programmes primarily designed to meet the tastes and interests of the particular domestic market, are rarely substantial enough for programmes which are intended for wider distribution. The return would not generally justify the necessary work.

Commercial funding

For sources of commercial funding it would be sensible for a producer to access these through establishing a working relationship with an independent producer working in that country. France and Germany have the most significant sums available. The French terrestrial channels and Canal Plus contribute substantial amounts for high-quality drama and documentaries and there are a number of well-established independent production companies in France which are accustomed to working with UK partners.

In Germany it is probably easier to access co-finance for feature film production rather than television. German broadcasters rarely co-produce television programmes since their prime requirement is for programming which reflects German domestic life, rather than wider horizons.

The cultural subscription channel ARTE co-funds 'artistic' productions for its cross-border transmissions in France and Germany.

With other European territories pre-sales are likely to be a more profitable route than co-production, since (as with subsidy funding) the amounts of money available are frequently too limited to justify the hassle of co-production.

Co-production treaties

The British Government has entered into co-production treaties with France, Germany, Italy, Norway as well as with Australia, Canada and New Zealand. These provide that, so long as the co-production arrangements have sufficient 'points' from each co-producer's territory, the production comes within the provisions of the treaty between the two governments. The production is then entitled to benefit from the subsidy funding and other financing schemes which may be available to assist production in the respective co-producers' countries. In some cases the co-production treaties provide for co-production between nationals of three countries.

Treaty points are calculated on the nationality of key talent and crew: director; scriptwriter; composer; director of photography; sound engineer; editor; art director; and leading artists. Other key points relate to the proportion of the production budget being contributed by each country and where recording/filming and post-production will happen.

Co-production treaties are administered by officials in the Films Division of the Department of Culture Media and Sport (DCMS), who in turn liaise with their opposite numbers in the co-producer's territory. If it is planned to bring a co-production within the ambit of a co-production treaty, it would be wise to contact the DCMS at a very early stage in the planning to ensure that the production arrangements can be structured to fulfil the treaty requirements.

For many years qualification under the treaty only brought benefits to a UK producer in that it enabled a co-production partner to access subsidy schemes in their own country; none were available in the UK. Qualification is now hugely significant in relation to qualification for sale and leaseback funding (see *Chapter 18*).

5.2   USA

Firstly, most co-production deals with the USA are really pre-sale deals: there must be very few, if any, examples of true co-productions with the USA, with production companies sharing the responsibility for physical production of the programme. Before committing any funding to production, US funders will require script approval, which may entail major re-writes, and are likely to lay down other specific creative requirements. There is little point in looking for production funding in the USA when production plans have reached a stage where they cannot easily be altered, since significant funding is unlikely to be forthcoming unless the US end-user has had the opportunity to ensure that the production can be tailored to meet their requirements.

Network television – ABC, NBC, CBS (and the Fox Network)

Network television is virtually a closed door for British productions. Whilst there have been some successful British changed format series on the US networks, only two British-originated drama series have actually been co-produced in association with major US companies for transmission on the US network. The difficulties for an individual producer of approaching, let alone cracking, this market cannot be over-estimated. In most cases the only possible route is by working through one of the large US studios which regularly produces for the network, and the usual procedure is for a US agent to approach the studios with the project and probably a talent package. Apart from any other considerations, the networks generally only consider projects written by 'network A list' writers and it will be almost impossible to contract such a writer as, once they are on the A list, they will almost certainly be tied to an exclusive deal with one of the major studios.

Public Broadcasting System (PBS)

The PBS system is a non-profit making organisation funded by money from foundations. There is a network of regional PBS stations across the USA. The major stations producing 'strands' of programmes for the PBS network are interested in co-financing possibilities. The two principal PBS stations which have a long tradition of 'co-producing' with the UK are the Boston-based station WGBH, which through its Masterpiece, and also Mystery, Theatre strands has participated in the production of many major British-originated drama series, as well as (particularly science-orientated) documentary programmes and series; and WNET in New York, which has been involved in many documentary productions, particularly one-off documentaries which fit its travel strands, and also music and arts programming.

The PBS stations can rarely be persuaded to contribute more than approximately $150,000 per hour for documentary material and $250,000 per hour for major drama. For this they are likely to require exclusive US standard rights on the PBS system for four runs over three years, home video rights and holdbacks on exploitation of US non-standard rights and on sales to Canada and Mexico, at least until after first transmission on PBS, and sometimes for a year or so longer. The PBS stations require a considerable level of editorial input into a production (more than some may consider is warranted by the level of contribution to funding) and the procedures for this input, the delivery requirements and so forth need to be carefully reconciled with the requirements of the other financiers.

Subscription (pay cable) services

The emergence and growth of the US subscription services continues apace and offers possibilities for pre-sale/co-production of expensive programming of a type and quality which is generally equally acceptable to the British and US markets. Home Box Office, The Showtime Networks, the A&E Television Networks, The Disney Channel and Turner International (CNC) (with operations in Europe as well as the USA) are all interested in high-quality television drama, comedy, music and documentary and, in some cases, children's programmes. Discovery Communications, which has operations in both the USA and Europe, is increasingly co-funding documentary programming originated in the UK, as does The History Channel. Nickelodeon co-finances children's programming.

As a general rule, if the subject matter fits their programming requirements, the subscription services will make a very significant contribution to production costs in return for exclusive non-standard US television rights with multiple runs over the licence period. They are likely to require considerable creative input and editorial control over the version of the production to be shown in the US.

Canada   5.3

A number of UK independents have formed compatible working relationships with the mainly Toronto-based Canadian independent producers who supply programmes to the Canadian Broadcasting Corporation and the commercial stations in Canada. The two major Canadian distributors/producers, Alliance/Atlantis Communications and Nelvana International, are interested in co-producing with UK partners. Largely because of Canadian sensitivities to US dominance of the television services, public subsidies are available for Canadian production, principally through Telefilm Canada. These are available for co-production with UK-based producers, provided that the requirements laid out in the co-production treaty between Canada and the UK are met (see *Paragraph 5.1*).

Australia and New Zealand   5.4

The Australian Broadcasting Corporation and the major commercial networks in Australia, The Seven Network, the Nine Network and Network Ten, have all mounted Australian/UK co-productions, generally in popular drama. A number of major Australian independent companies have too. The cultural ties of the UK and Australasia, and the common language, form a good basis for co-production partnership.

The Australian Film Finance Corporation has significant funding from the Australian government for investment in production in Australia and this funding can be accessed for both feature film and major television drama co-productions which have sufficient Australian content, are primarily filmed in Australia and which meet the criteria of the UK/Australian official co-production treaty.

The New Zealand Broadcasting Corporation, and its film subsidiaries, are interested in co-productions in the fields of drama, documentary and children's programming. The amount of funding available from New Zealand is limited, but it is, nonetheless, useful and there is considerable cultural compatibility as to programming requirements. There is a limited amount of government subsidy funding available for co-productions which have the requisite amount of New Zealand content.

5.5   Japan

There have been a number of major co-productions, particularly in the field of documentaries, with NHK, the Japanese equivalent of the BBC. It must, however, be said that whilst co-production and pre-sale finance can be secured from Japan, the intricacies of the Japanese hierarchical systems and the preoccupations with the status of the individual or organisation with whom they are dealing, render it extremely difficult for an independent producer (unless he or she has particular knowledge of, or contacts in, Japan) to make successful approaches for production funding. There can also be considerable resistance to programming which is regarded as having too Western an approach and the producer must be prepared to work towards reconciling the sometimes very different cultural requirements. As a general rule, it may be sensible for an independent producer to collaborate on contractual dealings with Japan with the UK broadcaster with whom the programme may be being co-produced.

C20

CO-PRODUCTION Chapter 20

DEVELOPMENT AGREEMENTS

Attitudes towards co-productions have swung like a pendulum over the last 20 years or so. In the early 1980s, when there was the first downturn in revenues, co-productions were suddenly the name of the game. However, in many cases the results were Euro or mid-Atlantic puddings which, by trying to satisfy all tastes and needs, met none. For years thereafter it was the kiss of death for a project to pitch it to a UK broadcaster on the basis that it was suitable for international co-production.

Economic necessity has now swung the pendulum back the other way. Without co-production revenues it is almost impossible to fund high-quality drama and documentary programmes. For the independent sector, competition is so stiff that producers have to look to every means of achieving an edge on their rivals, and this edge can be the ability to bring in co-production finance.

In the rest of Europe, as well as Australia, New Zealand and Canada, there is even greater interest in co-production than there is in the UK because the size of potential audiences in the individual territories and, consequently, available production revenues, is generally smaller. Therefore, not only are UK-based producers looking to work with co-production partners, but overseas producers are similarly seeking out UK partners. There is no question that it can be enormously advantageous for producers to establish and carefully foster co-production relationships with producers in other countries.

These co-production relationships are by their nature complex. Further, the process of setting up co-productions is generally much slower than for fully-funded production. The importance of producers doing preliminary groundwork before entering into a co-production agreement and thereafter entering into a proper agreement for development, cannot be overemphasised.

This chapter deals with key matters to be addressed at the outset of a co-production relationship.

KEY TOPICS & ISSUES

C20

PRELIMINARY ISSUES   1

When either seeking, or being approached by, co-production partners it is important, before opening negotiations, to check out the potential co-producer and the project. Film and television are creative businesses and contain more than their fair share of individuals whose creative talents lie more in making exaggerated claims for themselves and their productions than in actually making them. It is hard to exaggerate the problems that arise when a co-production partner turns out to be unreliable. Unless the partner is well-known to the producer, it is advisable to explore the following points before proceeding further:

Company search   1.1

In most countries systems exist for registering companies to which companies are required by law to make annual returns. On application (and payment of a fee) it may be possible to obtain background information such as the date it was founded, names of directors, shareholding structure, whether accounts have been filed on time and whether there are any charges on the company's assets.

It may be possible to check details of the company on the databases of the producers' association in the co-producer's home territory. In EU it may be possible to get information from the Media Desks for the EU Media Programme. In certain countries, banks will carry out a check and divulge limited information on the viability of a company.

Production credits   1.2

Previous credits are obviously relevant in gauging whether or not the potential co-producer has the necessary production experience for the proposed project. It is generally possible to check these by contacting one of the other parties or individuals credited on the same production. A number of film and television trade journals, such as *Screen International*, carry regular listings of films and television programmes in production, giving details of key production personnel as well as cast and crew.

With any of the above matters, if there are inconsistencies between information gleaned from these checks and from the individual, query them and if a satisfactory explanation is not forthcoming, be extremely wary of proceeding further. "When in doubt, don't" is a good maxim when approaching something with such potentially wide-ranging and long-term consequences as a co-production partnership.

History of the proposed co-production   1.3

If being approached to co-produce, always enquire about any approaches which may already have been made to potential financiers/other co-producers. It is not necessarily a cause for concern if a project has been around for some time but, before agreeing to become involved, it is important to be aware of the extent to which likely sources of production finance/collaboration have already been explored and exhausted.

Underlying rights in the project   1.4

Often the proposed co-production will be based on an existing script, book or other source material in which copyright exists. As a precondition to any agreement, establish that the co-producer owns the rights or holds an exclusive option to acquire them. Check also how long the option has to run, the price and whether any conditions are attached to the grant of rights which may be unacceptable to financiers (see *Chapter 4*).

Provisional financing plan   1.5

The potential viability of the co-producer's finance plan is a good pointer as to their likely reliability as a co-production partner. For example, proceed with great caution if the co-producer is planning to raise a significant part of the finance from outside the co-producer's territories, since this is generally an unrealistic expectation.

Caution is also required if the proposed financing scheme is very elaborate. It is rare for co-producers to have the time, skill, resources and level of dedication and tenacity required to draw a complex web of financing contracts to a successful conclusion.

1.6 Estimated cost of development/production budget

A judgement needs to be made as to the reasonableness of the projected costs of further development work and the anticipated level of the production budget. These may be unrealistically high or unworkably low.

If funding has already been committed, ask to see the contracts or letters of intent. The vast distinction between an 'expression of interest' and a 'commitment to fund' is all too frequently glossed over. It is understandable if commitments to funding have been made conditional on a number of factors being met, but little value should be attached to documents which, in essence, offer no more than 'interest in principle'. This is often used as a slow way of saying "no".

1.7 Timescale

There is a universal tendency to be over-optimistic about the time it takes to secure co-production finance and mount a production. Therefore, it is important to recognise that, for the majority of co-productions, particularly those with high budgets involving a number of partners, it can easily take two to three years, frequently longer, to bring a project to production. If a production has to take place within a certain time frame, for example, to coincide with an anniversary or because the rights are only available for a finite period, an assessment needs to the made as to whether this is likely to be achievable.

1.8 Benefits to the co-production partners

A very careful assessment needs to be made of the likely creative and financial return to the individual co-producer on the proposed deal. Co-productions can frequently impose financial and legal responsibilities on the co-producers out of all proportion to the potential benefits accruing from the co-production. In some cases these may amount to nothing more tangible than an on-screen credit.

2 CO-PRODUCTION DEVELOPMENT AGREEMENTS

A development agreement is required when co-producers have agreed to collaborate on further development work and/or to raise development or production finance. All too frequently co-producers disregard the need to draw up an agreement at this stage, considering that it is only necessary to go to the trouble and expense of doing so as and when production plans are being finalised. This is folly. Development can be very protracted, and over time recollections of oral agreements can become extremely hazy or distorted.

Failure to ensure that the development stage is underpinned by a signed agreement can cause endless confusion and difficulties over respective responsibilities for development work and for approaches to third parties for production finance; later on over critical questions of ownership, roles and financial participation on the eventual production.

Further, producers should bear in mind that in a number of European countries oral agreements are deemed to be as binding as signed contracts. If it is not clearly on record that certain matters require resolution before the parties can be said to have reached agreement, failure to proceed may constitute breach of contract and as such carry legal consequences. When negotiating co-production arrangements a careful written record must, therefore, be kept of decisions and this documentation should make clear that a contract will not be entered into unless and until agreement is reached on all matters.

The development agreement must make clear that the co-producers will only proceed to production when all the financing for production has been secured. The agreement should also provide that, when production finance is committed, a further agreement will be entered into between the parties for the co-production. This agreement will contain the same terms for production as those contained within the development agreement, unless there is mutual agreement to vary the terms.

The following are the key matters to be addressed when negotiating a co-production development agreement.

Development work   2.1

Preamble

Development can last a very long time. When a development agreement is drawn up it should contain a preamble which clearly records the origins of the co-production: who initiated it; who approached whom; and what the co-producers' intentions are. If there are subsequent disagreements, the underlying basis for the arrangements can be very relevant in arriving at a fair resolution.

Planning

The co-producers should itemise the further development work and set the dates by which it should be completed. For example:

i the commission of a script/re-write of the script/commission of other programme material/the choice of writer or contributor;

ii planned delivery/completion date;

iii research/recces/location finding – which countries, when to be carried out;

iv raising production finance/application for subsidies; and

v timescale.

Roles and responsibilities for development

The co-producers must determine who is responsible for the different elements of the development work, including the responsibility for entering into agreements and for renewing options on underlying rights material.

The development agreement should provide that, in the event that an individual is unable to carry out the development, the co-producers are to be informed and consulted about or, if appropriate, have the right to approve the choice of replacement.

Term

The co-producers must agree a reasonable period during which they will work together to set up production. This time period will account for the following factors:

i the timescale for approaches to other sources of production finance. In some cases national broadcasters publish a schedule for their decision making process. The dates of international television festivals and markets should also be taken into account as well;

ii if subsidy funds are being sought, the timescale required for completion and processing of applications. The funds' documentation for applications will usually give details of the timetable for considering and announcing decisions on submissions;

C20

iii   the time required to carry out necessary further development work such as the preparation of a script or other programme material; and

iv   the need, if any, to mount the production at a certain time.

As a general rule less than about 12 months would hardly allow sufficient time and anything more than three years might be unduly lengthy. The best method is to agree a fixed period, after which the arrangement may be extended by mutual agreement or otherwise the agreement terminates.

2.2   Production

Production arrangements

As a pre-condition for entering into a development agreement, co-producers must in principle agree their respective roles, responsibilities and entitlements on the eventual co-production, recognising that, notwithstanding this agreement, they may be placed in a position of having to vary the arrangements to meet the requirements of production financiers. It is no solution simply to leave it that the arrangements will be agreed when finance is secured: this can (and distressingly frequently does) result in co-producers discovering, when the time comes to sort things out, that they have quite irreconcilable expectations of their involvement in the co-production. Lawyers, the courts or even a mutually agreed arbitrator cannot resolve such a situation to the satisfaction of everyone.

The development agreement should state that, subject to each co-producer being able to bring its required share of funding to the production and subject to the approval of production financiers, it is the intention that co-producer X will perform role X and co-producer Y, role Y. If co-producer X and/or co-producer Y is not able to contribute the required share of production funding, the role of that co-producer may be reviewed, with the co-producer undertaking either to withdraw or to accept a different or lesser role to allow for an alternative and/or additional co-producer to be engaged on the production, as may be required for the purposes of finalising production finance.

Similarly, if any of the co-producers is not acceptable to production financiers in their designated role, they should be prepared to perform another role on the production, as agreed with the production financier. In such circumstances the co-producers may agree that the rejected co-producer should receive some 'compensation' in lieu of anticipated fees, perhaps an entitlement to reimbursement of otherwise unrecouped development costs (state a fixed amount) or an enhanced profit share from the production.

Controls and approvals

Co-producers must agree a mechanism for approvals on all essential aspects of production to avoid deadlocks. The usual procedure is to provide that one individual is nominated managing producer in overall charge of production, whose decisions on key creative, artistic and financial matters will, ultimately, be final. The development agreement should either name the managing producer or set out an agreed procedure for his or her appointment by the co-producers, as and when production finance is committed.

The co-producers must agree the anticipated role of each co-producer's company on the production, for example, responsibility for filming in its territory, but the role of the company should be expressed as being under the overall control of the managing producer. If the co-producer is not successful in bringing the required amount of production funding from its territory, the company's role may be subject to variation.

Schedule

It is useful to record the anticipated length and planned timing of the production schedule and state the intention of parties relating to the whereabouts of development, recording and post-production, recognising that these matters will ultimately be subject to the financing arrangements.

Language and running time

The language in which the production is to be recorded and the running time need to be established. In settling these matters, it may prove necessary to make provision for double shooting, dubbing or sub-titling to meet the language requirements of co-producers' territories and/or different length versions for different territories. The resolution of these matters may be to provide for different versions for each territory, and it is obviously helpful if this has been anticipated (and budgeted for) from the outset.

Credits

In a creative business, credits assume great importance and emotive disputes frequently arise over the wording, size and placing of both company and individual credits. Although at the development stage there are so many uncertainties about the eventual production that it would be unrealistic to attempt to agree exact details, co-producers should, nonetheless, explore this sensitive question with a view to establishing the broad principles for their respective credit entitlements.

Budget and financing   2.3

Development budget

The co-producers should draw up and mutually agree a budget for the development work, broken down between direct and indirect costs. Any increase in the direct costs should be subject to the written approval of all parties.

Direct costs are monies payable to third parties, for example, script fees, travel expenses, legal fees. The indirect costs are the costs of the co-producers' time and office overheads and, by their nature, very hard to quantify.

The co-producers need to decide whether they agree to meet the budgeted costs out of their own resources or if they are to make approaches for development funding to third-party production financiers/subsidy boards.

If they are to meet the development costs themselves, they must specify which of these costs are to be recouped by them from the eventual production budget. It is generally accepted that the direct costs of development can be met from the production budget: it is rare for indirect costs to be recovered. Recovery will, in any event, obviously depend on sufficient production financing being secured and it is sensible to arrange that, if production funds do not extend to the repayment of development costs, they will be recouped by the co-producers from first income from sales of the production.

If the co-producers are intending to raise third-party funding for development, similar procedures should be followed as those set out below for production fund-raising.

If the co-producers are to meet the development costs from their own resources, each of them usually meets its own indirect costs in full. The arrangement for sharing the direct cost payments will be a matter for individual negotiation but an equal sharing of these costs is quite common. In this connection, the procedure for making payments to third parties needs to be agreed. It would be usual for one co-producer to be responsible for making the entire payment due to a third party, with the other co-producer being obliged to pay its share of the cost within seven days of receipt of invoice.

Production budget and funding

In addition to agreeing a budget for the development work, the co-producers should mutually agree the estimate of the anticipated costs of production and set targets for levels of this funding to be brought by each co-producer.

In this, co-producers should be aware of the need for a clear strategy for raising finance. It can be confusing and damaging to the project if the co-producers are independently pursuing the same sources of co-production finance or if they are making approaches to different financiers whose requirements are likely to conflict: for example, trying to raise finance in different countries sharing the same language, since (with the exception of the large English language market) funding from broadcasters or distributors (as distinct from subsidy funding) is nearly always contingent on the financier acquiring rights in all territories speaking that language.

Similarly, care should be taken to ensure that the criteria for a co-production treaty or subsidy grant, such as ensuring that a certain proportion of staff engaged on production are nationals of the country granting the subsidy and/or that a percentage amount of the production funding is spent within the territory, will not clash with the requirements of production financiers in another territory.

Approaches to third-party production financiers

The co-producers should agree who is responsible for approaching which potential financier/subsidy fund and who is entitled to represent the project at television markets and festivals.

They should be obliged to retain a list of individuals and organisations approached for funding and to keep the other co-producers informed of responses. (It is particularly important to have this record if and when the development agreement is terminated and one or other co-producer wants to continue to try to raise funding for production.)

Approvals to financing arrangements

The development agreement should stipulate that no agreement be entered into with third-party production financiers without prior written approval of the other co-producer(s).

This can leave open the possibility of a deadlock if one or other co-producer does not accept the terms proposed by the third party. A machinery for resolving such a situation can be to provide that, in the event that the terms proposed by a third party are not acceptable to the other co-producer, that co-producer has the right to bring an improved offer but if it is not able to do so within a period of, perhaps, 28 days, the original third-party offer may be accepted.

If funding is not forthcoming from these initial approaches, the co-producers should undertake to agree alternative strategies which should be confirmed in writing.

Contracting with third-party financiers

The development agreement should specify the arrangements for contracting with third-party production financiers.For development finance, the co-producer who originated the project or the co-producers jointly, should contract with the third-party financier.

Production budget responsibilities

As a general rule, the managing producer will be in overall charge of the entire production budget. If the co-producers wish to control certain aspects of the budget, such as the portion to be spent in the co-producer's home territory, this should be stated within the development agreement.

Division of benefits within the production budget

The extent, if any, to which the production budget will allow financial benefits for co-producers over and above payment of individual fees and overheads will vary depending on the practice of the territories and the particular financing arrangements. Whilst it may not be possible to agree definite arrangements before production finance is concluded, at the pre-production stage it is sensible to establish the principles under which the parties agree to apportion benefits accruing from the production (proportionate shares). For more information see *Chapter 21*.

Share of revenue/net profits from sales

Whilst the treatment of net profits will be subject to agreements with production financiers, it is, nonetheless, sensible to establish that any net profits remaining to the co-producers will be shared in accordance with the co-producers' proportionate shares.

Rights   2.4

Ownership of underlying literary rights in development work

Firstly, it is important for co-producers to ensure that any pre-existing agreements for underlying rights material are in order and are suitable for the proposed production.

Where the originating co-producer has acquired rights in copyright material prior to entering into the development agreement, the usual arrangement is for the development agreement to provide that the co-producer will hold these rights for the benefit of the co-producers, under such legal mechanism as is applicable to this type of arrangement under the laws of the country of the originating co-producer. As and when the actual co-production agreement is drawn up, the co-producer will assign or license these rights to the co-production under whatever arrangement is appropriate in the circumstances.

Ownership of rights in jointly created development work

Where further work based on underlying rights owned by the originating producer is to be commissioned, the originating co-producer should be the contracting party both for any third-party finance which may be available for development and for the rights to this further material. During the development period the originating producer will hold these rights for the benefit of the co-producers.

If the costs of commissioning such further work are to be shared between the originating producer and the co-producers, an arrangement is then required whereby, if the development agreement is terminated, the rights in the further work remain vested with the originating producer, subject to an obligation to reimburse the other co-producer(s) for their direct contribution to costs.

Where the co-producers own no rights prior to the development agreement but they are to be acquired during development, if the co-producers share the cost equally, it would be appropriate for the agreement for the rights to be between the co-producers jointly and the third-party rights owner. In such cases the development agreement must provide that, if the co-producers are not subsequently able to proceed jointly to co-production, one co-producer has first opportunity to mount the project (with different co-producers).

If one co-producer is contributing more than 50% of the cost it would be appropriate for the agreement to be between that co-producer and the third-party rights owner, with the co-producer holding the rights for the benefit of the other co-producers and with the majority funder being in first position to proceed with the project in the event that the development agreement is terminated.

Ownership and control of rights in the completed production

There is a common misuse in the television industry of the word 'rights'. It is frequently used to describe 'profits' or a 'share of profits', whereas correctly it means ownership of rights of copyright.

Ownership and control of rights in the completed production will ultimately be governed by the agreements with production financiers. In negotiating the development agreement, co-producers should, however, establish broad principles for the treatment of those rights in the production which are not sold off for the purposes of raising production finance. For suggestions on ways to apportion rights see *Chapter 21*.

Assignment

Co-production agreements should be personal to the co-producers: the agreement should expressly disallow the possibility of the co-producer's rights being assigned to a third party without the express prior consent of the other co-producer(s).

2.5 Termination

Procedures

One of the principal purposes and most valuable functions of a development agreement is to set out clear and orderly procedures for terminating the co-producers' relationship if it becomes apparent that they are not able to proceed to production jointly. It is hard to exaggerate the difficulties which can arise when the relationship is not working and there is a lack of clarity as to whether, how or when it can be terminated; what arrangements will prevail for the ownership of rights in material jointly developed; and the respective co-producer's entitlements to continue to try to raise funding and mount production. Further, it is often very difficult to settle such matters amicably when the parties no longer want to work together since, if that stage has been reached, it is unlikely that the co-producers' attitude to the relationship will be as noble and generous as it may have been at the outset.

Reasons for termination

The development agreement must, of course, provide grounds for terminating the agreement, generally as follows:

i   material breach of the terms of the development agreement and failure to rectify any breach capable of remedy within, say, 14 days of written notification of the breach;

ii   inability of a co-production partner to raise necessary production funding within the required time period;

iii   radical change in the circumstances of the co-producer's company, the most obvious example being insolvency, but there may be other grounds, such as the individual co-producer leaving the company or the company being taken over; and

iv   by mutual agreement.

Ownership of rights on termination

In cases where the originating producer owned or acquired rights prior to the joint development and, if applicable, owns rights in joint development, the usual position would be for these rights to be solely retained by the originating producer.

If the other co-producer(s) have shared the cost of further development material, the retention of rights by the originating co-producer would be subject to an obligation to refund the other co-producer's contribution to direct costs. The standard arrangement for such refund is that the sum becomes payable on first day of principal photography of a production based on the rights material. It is not uncommon for interest, calculated at a specified bank rate from date of payment until date of repayment, to be charged on the sum to be refunded.

It is possible that a situation could arise in which the originating producer owning the rights cannot raise co-production finance, but a co-production partner can. Whilst it might be considered unreasonable to compel the originating producer to relinquish ownership and control of rights, it is unfortunate if the co-production partner's efforts in raising finance must be to no avail. It may be possible to agree that, in such a circumstance, the originating producer assigns the rights to the other co-producer(s), subject to the other co-producer(s) reimbursing all the direct costs incurred by the originating producer in acquiring the rights and to granting the originating producer a role (or at very least a credit) on the production and a share of the net profits accruing to the co-producers.

In such a case, the date of repayment would be a matter for negotiation. The originating producer may stipulate that at least a portion of the direct costs must be paid on agreement to assign the rights, rather than on the more usual first day of principal photography.

In cases where the co-producers jointly own rights in the development work, the usual arrangement would be to provide that for a period of, say, 12 months from termination of the development agreement, co-producer X has the sole right to try to arrange financing for the project and co-producer Y will assign the benefit of its rights to co-producer X on repayment of its contribution to the direct development costs. If co-producer X does not acquire co-producer Y's rights within this period, co-producer Y then has the same window of opportunity to acquire co-producer X's rights. Unless and until one co-producer buys out the other, rights in the material remain vested with both co-producers.

The question of which co-producer should be in first position to buy out the other may be quite difficult to determine. If one has made a larger direct financial contribution to the cost of the development work, then it should be them: if the co-producers have shared the costs equally, in the absence of any obvious reason why one party or the other might be in first position, the toss of a coin could be as good a means as any of deciding!

C21

CO-PRODUCTION AGREEMENTS Chapter 21

As no two co-productions are ever quite the same, any standard form contract will need to be very carefully tailored to meet the particular requirements of the production. Not only is it obviously important for the co-producers themselves to have a comprehensive agreement, but approval of the co-production agreement is a customary pre-condition, not only of agreements with production financiers, but in order for the co-production to be accepted for subsidy funding and for it to qualify as an official co-production under a co-production treaty (see *Chapter 19*).

This chapter contains a comprehensive check list of all matters which need to be addressed in a co-production agreement and suggests ways of contractually dealing with difficult issues, such as respective rights of approval and ownership and control of the production.

KEY TOPICS & ISSUES

PRELIMINARIES   1

Financing plan   1.1

It is assumed that it is unlikely that co-producers will be entering into a formal co-production agreement unless and until all the production finance has been committed. If a development agreement did not address financing arrangements, the producers will need to establish the arrangements for contracting for production finance at the outset.

Approvals

The co-producers must mutually agree the arrangements for contracting for third-party production finance. A minimum requirement is that each co-producer must have the right to approve the contractual terms sought by production financiers, with the mechanism for avoiding deadlock being a matching offer solution, whereby the co-producer has the right to bring an improved offer, but if unable to do so within a period of, say, 28 days, the original third-party offer may be accepted.

Contracting with third parties/special purpose vehicle

The question then arises whether each co-producer individually contracts with the third-party production financier for the funding it has raised or whether the agreements are between the production financiers and the co-producers jointly; or, as frequently happens with feature film production, the co-producers set up a company for the production and that company contracts with production financiers.

There are pros and cons to all these possibilities. If each co-producer contracts independently of the others, the others may be exposed to financial risk if a co-producer defaults on the obligation to bring finance to production. It is not necessarily valid to argue, as a quid pro quo, that the other co-producer is under no liability to the co-producer's production financier. Under the laws of certain countries the other co-producers could be held liable for any default on the part of a co-producer, whether or not the others were party to the agreement.

Contracting jointly with production financiers would appear to most accurately reflect the assumption of shared responsibility which should underpin co-production. But there may be valid reasons why this is not possible; for example, certain subsidy funding may only be available to nationals of the territory granting the funding.

Setting up a special purpose vehicle jointly owned by the co-producers can be a solution and, in particular, is a means of avoiding the problems which can arise if one of the co-producers becomes insolvent. There are, however, pitfalls which need to be considered, such as the co-producers becoming liable for tax both on the company's profits in the country in which it is based and on the profits which they remit to their own country, and the responsibility and expense of continuing to make company returns to the appropriate national authorities long after production has been completed and revenues have dwindled.

In deciding which route to take, co-producers should seek specific legal advice on the advantages and disadvantages under the laws of the countries of the co-producers.

Roles   1.2

A pre-requisite of any co-production agreement is agreement between the co-producers as to the roles each are to perform on the production. Treatment of virtually every matter within a co-production agreement will relate to these respective roles and responsibilities. Key to this is selection of the managing producer who will have overall responsibility for all aspects of the production – editorial, creative, administrative, financial and legal – and who will be exclusively engaged on the production throughout pre-production, recording or filming and post-production.

1.3 Ownership and entitlements

Another pre-requisite to the agreement is the proportions in which the co-producers will share ownership and benefits. At its simplest, these can be divided in proportions equal to each co-producer's financial contributions to the production budget and certainly this formula is a useful starting point. It does not, however, necessarily take account of the effort and financial risks which the originating producer may have taken in initiating and developing the project prior to entering into the co-production agreement. Nor does it reflect that subsidy funding is readily available in some countries and easy to raise provided certain standard criteria are met, while others do not have comparable subsidies available and securing production finance from these may require a high order of contacts, skills, experience and tenacity not generally required for subsidy applications. The proportionate share of ownership should, therefore, be negotiated and agreed between the co-producers in the light of these factors. (Throughout this chapter, the agreed split is referred to as the 'proportionate share'.)

When negotiating a co-production agreement every effort must be made to provide machinery for ensuring that the production cannot be delayed or deadlocked through irreconcilable differences of view between the co-producers. Production schedules do not allow time to resolve disputes between co-producers: procedures must be agreed to ensure that, no matter what the differences, production can continue. It is frequently left that matters are 'to be agreed' which sounds very reasonable – except that when the co-producers cannot or will not agree, the contract is of no value whatsoever.

2 PREAMBLE

Co-production agreements are generally rather complex. It can be difficult to extrapolate the premise from the provisions and the basic premise may be very relevant if there were to be a dispute over the interpretation of the agreement or settlement is required of matters omitted from it. In addition to stating what the co-producers intend to co-produce, the preamble should also set out which co-producer:

i   originated the project;

ii   initially owned or acquired the underlying rights;

iii   made the initial approaches for co-production interest; and

iv   secured production funding from which source.

3 ORGANISATION OF THE CO-PRODUCTION

3.1 Production specification

In the course of setting up the production, the co-producers need to mutually agree a specification of all the key elements: administrative, creative, financial and technical. Working jointly through the specification enables the co-producers to ensure that all known elements are thoroughly explored between them in advance of commencement of production. The following list contains items to be included in the specification, although obviously not all of these may be applicable for every production. Some matters may need to be settled in the light of conditions attached to subsidy funding or a treaty application or the specific requirements of production financiers. In some cases there may be a clear division of responsibility for certain aspects of the specification and this can be recorded simply by denoting by each item whose responsibility it is.

It would be usual for the completed specification to be attached as a schedule to the agreement and detail the following:

Title
Number of programmes
Running time (and number of advertising breaks)
Source material
Script
Principal contributors: Managing producer
                          Executive producer(s)
                          Co-producer(s)
                          Director
                          Director of photography
                          Assistant director
                          Writer
                          Associate producer
                          Production manager
                          Principal cast
                          Music: Composer
                                          Performer
                          Designer
                          Lighting cameraman
                          Editor
                          Production accountant
Budget   Rights to be cleared within budget
                          Territories/markets
Production schedule   Start of pre-production
                          Commencement of filming/recording
                          Completion date
                          Post-production
Locations
Studios
Production medium   Film
                          Video tape
                          Stereo/mono
Delivery medium
Delivery requirements Stills, publicity material, synopses, music cue sheets
Facilities house
Production bank account

C21

The agreed script, or if it is not a scripted production, a detailed treatment and the production schedule should also be appended as schedules to the agreement.

3.2   The managing producer

The managing producer is the producer who has overall responsibility for all aspects of the production: editorial, creative, administrative, financial and legal, and who will be exclusively engaged on the production throughout pre-production, recording and post-production. This role differs from the role of executive producer which is generally used to describe a senior producer who is not exclusively engaged on the production, but who will be consulted about, and give advice upon, key matters relating to production and will generally oversee its progress. The role of managing producer also differs from that of line producer, which is generally used to describe a producer who is exclusively employed on the production and has responsibility for the day-to-day management of it, but is not responsible for the key creative and financial decisions.

The selection of the managing producer and key roles for the other co-producers need to be settled as a prerequisite for the co-production agreement. Where the co-production has been originated by one co-producer, they will normally be the managing producer. This may change if the originating producer contributes only a minority share of the production finance. Then, a possible solution is to provide that, although the originating producer will be the managing producer, the co-producer bringing the majority share of the funding will have final right of approval over any production decisions which vary the provisions of the agreed production budget.

Where the co-production has been jointly initiated, it would be usual for the co-producer bringing in the largest share of production finance to be (or to nominate) the managing producer.

If, for any reason, the individual named as managing producer cannot perform that function, that individual's company would generally have the right to provide a replacement, but it would be usual for the other co-producer(s) to have right of approval of the choice. To avoid deadlock it may be prudent to provide that the choice must be made out of a maximum of three nominees.

To the extent that any or all of the co-producers have to meet certain contractual obligations to third-party production financiers, the agreement must stipulate that the managing producer undertakes that, in exercising any final right of approval, due regard will be taken of these obligations.

3.3   Roles and responsibilities

The detailed responsibilities of each co-producer need to be set out clearly within the agreement. If each has responsibility for producing separate segments of the programme an additional schedule can be included. This could be a detailed specification (see *Paragraph 3.1*) of what is required of each co-producer, listing all the key elements and giving delivery dates for the material.

3.4   Rights of consultation and approval

While drawing up the production specification the co-producers will need to have agreed most key issues. It will not, however, be possible to resolve all matters in advance of finalisation of the agreement, or even commencement of production, and in any event, changes may be required during production. The following procedures for consultation and approval on key matters need, therefore, to be included in the agreement.

It may be necessary to provide that the approval arrangements between the co-producers will, ultimately, be subject to contractual requirements, which may involve right of approval of third-party production financiers.

Budget

As a general rule, the agreement must provide that any increases in the budget require the prior approval of all the co-production parties. If the increase is unavoidable, the co-producers must meet to agree means by which the increased costs can be met by savings in other budget areas, under the overall control of the managing producer (and subject to the terms of the completion guarantee, if any).

If the increased costs cannot be met from the budget and the production is not covered by a completion guarantee, the co-producers must jointly agree a strategy for finding additional financing, while in the meantime, each underwrites the additional cost in proportions equal to the shares in which they have brought funding to production.

A penalty provision can be inserted to provide that, if the managing producer or one of the co-producers incurs charges additional to the budget without going through these procedures, they will be held solely liable for financing the overcost.

Each co-producer may be entitled, within the limits of that part of the budget for which it has responsibility, to offset overcosts in one area against savings in another. However, in doing so, the co-producer must not make changes to the agreed script or treatment or production schedule. Any such changes must be made only after consultation with all the co-producers, as provided for below.

Production schedule

A detailed production schedule and, if applicable, schedules for those parts of the production for which individual co-producers have responsibility, should be drawn up in consultation with all the co-producers, be subject to their approval and be appended to the agreement as a schedule. Co-producers should be informed as soon as practicable of any proposed variations to the production schedule, with the approvals procedures exercised being in accordance with the arrangements set out in *Paragraph 3.5* below.

Script/treatment

Whilst co-producers need some latitude to make minor changes to the agreed script or treatment during the course of production, the agreement should provide that no substantive changes are to be made without the agreement of all the co-producers, with the managing producer having final approval in the event that the co-producers are unable to agree. Examples of substantive changes are, in the case of a dramatic script, changes to the characters and/or storyline which necessitate variations to the scene-by-scene breakdown. In the case of non-fiction programmes they might be such matters as alterations to the programme's approach to the subject, the film material to be included in it or the replacement of an on-screen presenter.

Appointment/replacement of production personnel

If an individual co-producer is unable to perform their agreed role, they will be responsible for supplying a replacement and will be placed under an obligation to consult with the other co-producers about the choice of appointee. It may be thought appropriate that the managing producer should have a right of veto on the selection. If so, it would be reasonable to provide that, if approval is withheld of the co-producer's first choice, the managing producer is required to make the choice out of a maximum of three nominations.

Co-producers should agree between themselves which roles are so key that no appointment/replacement appointment should be made without consultation with, and the prior approval of, all the co-producers. Such roles are generally those of writer/director/director of photography/principal casting/presenter/production accountant. If the co-producers are unable to reach agreement between themselves the managing producer should have the right to make the final choice, but only after consultation with the other co-producers as to the choice of appointee.

Aside from the procedure for key appointees described above, co-producers should each be entitled to make their own selection/appoint replacements for individuals rendering services on those aspects of production for which they are responsible.

Rough cut/fine cut

The agreement must provide procedures for the viewing and approval of rough cuts and fine cuts, stipulating the physical arrangements for the material to be viewed and, if changes are required, to be reviewed. Timescales should be specified for such viewings in accordance with the production schedule. As with approvals for other procedures (and subject to the rights of the director as outlined below) it would be sensible to provide that the managing producer has final right of approval, although this may be tempered by providing that the co-producers have the right to edit or reversion the programme to meet the requirements of their respective territories/production financiers.

In this connection it is quite common for co-production agreements to provide for different versions of the programme for different territories, with the costs of reversioning being met either from the overall co-production budget, or by the individual co-producer responsible for the different version.

Directors' rights

In a number of European countries it is accepted practice, and in some countries an inalienable legal right under the moral rights laws, for the director to have final right of approval of fine cut, over and above the rights of approval of the producer and/or production financiers. In other European countries there is no such legal right, or the right may exist but it may be the custom for it to be waived and the director would usually be contractually bound to accept the producer's/production financiers' final right of approval and be under an obligation to comply with their requirements.

Co-producers should be sensitive to these significant cultural/legal differences and explore in advance the director's likely expectations in this respect particularly since, when they relate to the inalienable moral rights laws of the director's country, they may not be specifically referred to in the director's agreement.

If, for example, it were unacceptable to a co-producer/production financier that the director had final right of approval, the most extreme remedy would be to provide for the appointment of a director who did not enjoy such rights. Alternatively it may be possible to provide a mechanism which could avert deadlock by allowing the co-producer to reversion the programme or make changes not exceeding a certain number of minutes and remove the director's credit if requested to do so.

3.5 Procedures for exercising rights of approval/consultation

The agreement should provide clear procedures for consultation/approval on the matters set out above. The co-producers should be obliged to e-mail all the co-producers details of the matter to be resolved, proposing a solution. During recording and post-production the other co-producers should be obliged to respond within a period of 24 hours: outside the recording and post-production period responses should be received within 72 hours. If no response is received within the applicable period the co-producer is entitled to assume tacit acceptance of the proposed solution and proceed accordingly. If the proposed solution is not accepted by the other co-producer(s) they should notify all co-producers of their objections in writing and the co-producers should endeavour to settle the matter between them with, if necessary, the managing producer exercising final right of approval, within the applicable timescale set out above.

To avoid misunderstandings, the co-producer who sought approval must be responsible for promptly sending to the other co-producers a written record of the agreed arrangements.

Production credits 3.6

The co-producers need to mutually agree the wording, size of type and placing of the credits for their companies, their individual credits, and also those sought by key creative talent, such as the director and the writer, and by third-party production financiers who are not parties to the co-production agreement, but who have an entitlement to be accorded credit on all versions of the programme.

As a means of reaching agreement, it is quite common to provide that the programme may carry different credits in each co-producer's territory so as to accord the co-producers lead credits in their own territories, although this still leaves the co-producers to agree the form of the credits on the international version of the programme to be sold outside the territories of the co-producers.

If it is agreed to have different credits, provision must be made for this within the production budget, with time being allowed within the post-production schedule.

The co-production agreement should detail in a schedule the principal production credits on the versions of the programme to be shown in each territory and on the version to be sold overseas. This schedule should specify the on-screen opening and closing credits, the co-producers' credits (in the same size or larger or smaller type) and the order in which the credits will appear.

The agreement should go on to make provision for credits on advertising and publicity material: these will usually follow the same form and be subject to the same territorial variations (if any) as the on-screen credits, with the agreement stipulating that the co-producers will all be accorded credit whenever and wherever production credits are shown in publicity and promotional material.

Publicity and promotional material/trailers 3.7

The agreement should specify the arrangements for promotion and publicity. It may be that the co-producers agree to appoint a third-party publicist to handle all publicity and promotion. In which case, the terms of the publicist's engagement, which will include the co-producers' rights of approval of material, will be subject to the approval of the co-producers. Alternatively, one co-producer may take responsibility for publicity and promotion, but should be placed under an obligation to consult all the co-producers about proposed plans, with the proofs of publicity material being submitted to the co-producers for their approval. Another possibility is that, each co-producer may be entitled to prepare its own publicity and promotional material for use in its own territories and markets.

In all cases, those handling publicity should be placed under an obligation to meet the co-producers' contractual requirements to third parties in respect of credits on publicity and promotional material.

The agreement should stipulate numbers and lengths of trailers and specify whether certain approved trailers are used on all forms of exploitation or whether the co-producers have the right to prepare their own for their own territories.

When making arrangements for trailers and inserting logos and advertising breaks, co-producers should bear in mind that, under the moral rights laws of certain countries the director and the author of the work may have the right to carry out, or have prior right of approval, of all such arrangements.

4   FINANCING THE PRODUCTION

The agreement should state that the raising of the required amount of production finance is a condition precedent to the agreement.

4.1   Financing plan

The financing plan should be set out in a separate schedule, detailing such matters as the different sources of funding, the co-producers' responsibility for contracting for the funding, the currencies in which the funds are to be paid, the staging of the payments and the location of the bank account(s). It should also set out the anticipated sources of gross revenues from production, the definition of net profits and the co-producers' agreed 'proportionate shares'.

If the co-producers have contracted individually for finance (see *Paragraph 1.1* above) the co-production agreement must specify that the co-producer will hold the agreement for itself and for the benefit of the other co-producers; that the funds will be placed in a separate bank account designated for use solely by the co-production, and that they will be released for production in accordance with the agreed cash flow, with the co-producer being charged interest on any late payment.

In some countries it would be customary for the individual co-producer to provide a bank guarantee to the co-production in respect of this funding. The practice of banks to give such guarantees does, however, vary considerably from country to country: in some it is quite usual business practice; in others it is not and banks may only grant guarantees if these are backed up by potentially onerous personal guarantees from the individual co-producer. If it is the practice of banks in the co-producer's country to give guarantees, then these should be sought but co-producers should not assume that if such guarantees are not forthcoming, it is necessarily a reflection of the financial viability of the co-production partner.

4.2   Cash flow/deficit financing/currency fluctuation

However the production finance is contracted, there are logistical difficulties in ensuring that funds are remitted from production financiers in accordance with the cash flow required for production and in protecting the co-producers from fluctuations in exchange rates between entering into the funding agreements and when the funds are required. (The Euro certainly has advantages in this situation.)

So far as cash flow for production is concerned, whilst a portion of funds will normally be withheld by production financiers until the programme is completed and delivered, it is usually possible to negotiate arrangements whereby funding from subsidy grants and from financiers will be staged so that regular payments will be made during the course of production: for example, on commencement of pre-production; commencement of recording; completion of recording; completion and delivery. In the case of pre-sale funding, the entire sum may only be payable on delivery of the programme. In preparing the production budget provision should be made to cover the costs of financing any such temporary shortfalls in the cash flow.

Whilst in some countries banks are prepared, subject to their usual interest and other charges, to deficit finance production against signed agreements for production finance, in others they are not, and co-producers must negotiate financing deals accordingly (see *Chapter 18*).

In the case of protection against foreign exchange fluctuations, the usual means of guarding against this is to buy forward and place the currency in a foreign account. Interest charges will, of course, be incurred on sums purchased and provision will need to be made for these within the production budget. The benefit of any fluctuations in exchange rates should firstly be set against any budget overspends and thereafter form part of any underspend, to be shared between the co-producers.

The cash flow should be appended as a schedule to the agreement and should specify the timing for remittance of funds to the production by the co-producers/ production financiers.

Production budget   4.3

Firstly, the appointment of the production accountant should be subject to the prior approval of the co-producers, with the managing producer's decision being final. If a replacement is required this is subject to the procedures set out in *Paragraph 3.4*.

Depending on the nature of the co-production it may also be necessary for each co-producer to appoint a production accountant for the proportion of the budget to be spent in their territory, but this arrangement would not obviate the requirement to appoint a production accountant in overall charge of the production budget, working to the managing producer.

The production budget must be drawn up in consultation with all the co-producers, be subject to their approval and be appended to the agreement as a schedule. Points specific to a co-production budget which need to be taken into account are:

i   costs of financing and, if necessary, provision for a contingency against fluctuations in exchange rates and late payments;

ii   the number of transmissions and area of transmission (which basic fees for services may cover) and provision for the cost of any additional clearances which may be needed to meet the requirements of co-producers/production financiers;

iii   the 'welfare' or 'social taxes' which co-producers may be obliged to pay on production salaries, which are additional to salary (in some countries these may be four or five times higher than in other countries);

iv   the level of Value Added Tax and the arrangements which exist for charging and reclaiming for goods and services supplied across national boundaries;

v   withholding tax which may be charged on payments for services across national boundaries;

vi   the costs of supplying the different delivery materials which may be required by the various production financiers; and

vii   the amount of development costs which the co-producers may be entitled to recoup from the budget or which, if the budget cannot cover these, are to be recouped from sales revenues.

4.4 Production bank account/cheque signing

The co-producers should mutually agree and record in the agreement the location of the production account(s), which should be set up under whatever banking mechanism is customary in the country in which the bank is located as being for use solely and exclusively in connection with the funding of the co-production.

The co-producers should be obliged to place all sums not immediately required for production funding in an interest bearing account: the interest can firstly be used to defray any overcost on production; thereafter it should form part of the underspend.

Cheque signing arrangements will vary depending on whether there is one production account or if each co-producer is responsible for certain aspects of production, they each have a separate production account. Whatever the arrangements, the individuals with cheque signing powers should be nominated in the agreement and as a general rule, two people should be signatories to cheques with a value over a certain amount. All the co-producers, or their nominated representatives, should be signatories on cheques with a value over a higher amount (the exact amounts to be determined in accordance with the size of the budget and the level of individual payments to be made from it).

All the co-producers should be entitled to receive copies of the bank statements for production accounts, as and when these are issued.

4.5 Accounting reports and final cost statement

Provision should be made for accounting reports to be prepared and submitted to all the co-producers at weekly intervals throughout the production period.

The agreement should provide for a final cost statement to be drawn up and submitted to all the co-producers for approval within four weeks of completion of post-production.

4.6 Sale of properties

The agreement should specify that, on conclusion of production, the managing producer and, if applicable, co-producers responsible for particular aspects of production, should sell, for the best achievable commercial price, properties purchased for the production, with the resulting funds being remitted to the overall production account to be used to defray any overspend and thereafter to form part of the underspend.

4.7 Overspend

If the accounting statements reveal an overspend in any area which cannot obviously be corrected, the managing producer should be responsible for drawing this to the attention of the other co-producers and they should be obliged to explore ways of recovering the overspend, in accordance with the procedures set out in *Paragraph 3.4*.

4.8 Underspend

In the event that the final cost statement shows an underspend then, depending on any contractual requirements of third-party production financiers, the co-producers should firstly be entitled to recover from the underspend any unrecouped development costs. In this connection it is important that such costs should be included as a note on the production budget: major difficulties can arise when co-producers claim reimbursement of development costs which have not previously been agreed by all the co-production partners. If no such costs are to be recouped, the underspend should be split between the co-producers in accordance with the proportionate shares.

Co-producers' entitlements to benefits from the production budget   4.9

The extent to which there may be any financial benefits to the co-producers within the production budget, over and above payment of individual fees and direct costs, will depend, to a considerable extent, on the budget restrictions and on the practice for budgeting production in the territories of the co-producers. The production fee payable on productions in the UK is unique to this country, but other countries have mechanisms for providing benefits from the production budget. In Germany, for example, there is a similar provision for a production 'overhead' payment. In other countries there may be no such direct provision, but it may be custom and practice to 'weight' budget items so that there may be a financial bonus to the producer. The agreement should specify that any such benefits, which will be determined after approval of final cost statement, will be split between the co-producers in accordance with their proportionate shares, with the managing producer having the responsibility to remit payments to the co-producers within a fixed period of acceptance of final cost statement. (As a general rule, any such benefits would not form part of the revenues from the exploitation of the production and thus, would be kept separate from the treatment of gross sales revenue, as set out below.)

Gross revenues/net profits/proportionate shares   4.10

As a pre-condition of the agreement, the co-producers must agree, and the agreement must specify, the proportionate shares in which the co-producers will share revenues from the production. Gross revenues, net profits and proportionate shares all need to be defined within the agreement in relation to the definitions required by third-party production financiers.

Gross revenues is generally defined as all revenues received from sales of the production in all territories and markets not pre-sold for production finance, including gross revenues from exploitation of secondary rights (such as publishing and merchandising).

Net profits are generally defined as receipts remaining from gross revenues after recoupment of the cost of production (including any deficit finance and financing charges), payment of any deferred fees or charges, deduction of distribution commissions and costs (including any residual, repeat or copyright fees) and payment of third-party profit shares.

The net profit definition should be contained in a separate schedule to the agreement, listing the following information:

i   territories and markets pre-sold for production finance;
ii   the level of distribution commissions to be levied on gross revenues from sales to all other territories and markets and from secondary rights revenue;
iii distribution costs, including repeat and residual costs;
iv   details of all sums to be recouped by third-party production financiers and/or co-producers and/or other third parties from sales revenue, specifying interest charges (if any); and
v   the order in which the co-producers are entitled to recoup (in some cases the recoupment may be from income from all sources; in others the

recoupment may be from income from certain territories and markets only, and these arrangements should be specified).

Revenues remaining thereafter are described as net profits, and the financing plan should go on to specify:

i   the percentage net profit entitlements of third-party production financiers/other third parties; and

ii the remaining percentage pool of net profits and the percentage proportions in which it is to be shared between the co-producers (the proportionate share).

5   INSURANCE

5.1   Production insurance

The agreement must specify the production insurances which are required both in the interests of sound production management and as may be required by production financiers. It must also name which co-producer is responsible for effecting insurances and which are to be named on the policies. Each co-producer should be placed under an obligation to notify the managing producer immediately of any occurrence which might result in a claim. Examples of the type of insurances which are usual are:

i   pre-production and cast insurance;

ii   negative, faulty stock, camera, editing and processing insurance;

iii supplementary: props, set and wardrobe, equipment;

iv   third-party property damage; production office contents;

v   employers' and public liability insurance; and

vi   errors and omissions insurance (see *Chapter 22*).

5.2   Completion guarantees

Completion guarantees are a form of production insurance whereby the completion guarantor guarantees to deliver a production to financiers by a certain date. For co-productions, a completion guarantor will require approval of all the co-production agreements (see *Chapter 18, Paragraph 7*).

6   COPYRIGHT

The agreement must address ownership of the underlying rights and the copyright in the production itself:

6.1   Underlying rights

The agreement will require the co-producers owning the underlying rights to either assign or license the rights to the co-production.

The terms for such assignment or licence will, firstly, be governed by the terms and conditions of the agreement under which the underlying rights may have been acquired from the copyright owner; for example, if the underlying rights material is a novel, the rights acquired may have been restricted to a limited licence in the film or television rights.

Where the underlying rights are not exhausted by production – for example, where there may be possibilities for spin-off or sequel productions or other forms of exploitation, such as publishing, merchandising or the sale of changed format rights – the extent to which these rights are shared by the co-producers will be a matter for negotiation.

Individual agreements for production   6.2

Service agreements

The agreement must specify which co-producer is responsible for contracting with individuals rendering services on the production, with the requirement that the contracting co-producer will hold rights in the products of the services for the benefit of the co-producers.

It is usual for all service agreements, with the possible exception of the director's agreement, as explained in *Paragraph 6.3* below, to provide for a complete assignment of worldwide copyright in the services (including lending and rental rights) for the full applicable period of copyright, and that any and all necessary consents are given for the use of services/performances rendered under the agreement.

Production financiers from all English language territories will require agreements to contain a waiver of moral rights, to the extent that this may be possible under the applicable national laws.

Notwithstanding the assignment of copyright and pre-payments for the equitable and lending right, under the labour/trade union agreements operated in different countries the fees payable to those rendering services on production may cover only:

i   a certain number of transmissions of the programme; and/or

ii   transmissions in a limited number of territories; and/or

iii exploitation in certain markets only, e.g. terrestrial transmissions, satellite transmissions, cable, pay cable, video distribution, non-theatric use; and/or

iv   exploitation over a limited period only.

Co-producers must ascertain the extent of exploitation rights which the fees purchase in the co-producers' territories. If, for the purpose of raising production finance, it is necessary to acquire rights in wider territories and markets than those purchased by the basic fee, the terms of the service agreements must be negotiated accordingly and any additional costs provided for within the production budget.

Care must be taken to ensure that any obligations to make additional payments for wider uses than those paid for within the agreement fee are passed on to those responsible for the distribution of the programme.

Music

The contracting of music for the production, be it original composition and/or the use of existing music, can be complex and failure to effect the necessary clearances can jeopardise subsequent exploitation of the production. The co-production agreement needs, therefore, to be very specific as to where the responsibility lies for contracting music and the minimum rights which must be acquired.

For original compositions it is a matter for negotiation with the composer of the works as to whether the co-producers will own the music publishing rights; or own them jointly and share revenues from them with the composer; or whether the composer will retain the rights. If the co-producers acquire the music publishing rights, agreement must be reached between them as to the administration of the copyright in the music under the arrangements of the applicable collecting society. The arrangements for sharing any revenues from music publishing should also be addressed within the agreement: this would usually be in accordance with the proportionate shares.

For existing music the agreement (or production specification) should set out the minimum licence needed in order to meet the exploitation requirements of production financiers. It should also provide that, if wider clearances are required, the co-producer negotiating the agreement is under an obligation to ensure that these can be purchased for a fixed price at a later stage.

Depending who the co-production partners are, it may be possible for existing music to fall within blanket licence agreements which broadcasters may hold with the applicable collecting society, thus, reducing the cost of music clearances. It is likely that the criteria for allowing music to come within a blanket licence would include the requirement that the broadcaster must be the owner, or part owner, of copyright in the production.

In negotiating mechanical copyright licences, co-producers should bear in mind that there are some variations in the level of licence fees charged for the same licences by mechanical copyright authorities operating in different countries.

Archive and library footage

As with music, the agreement must specify where the responsibility lies for clearing the use of library and archive footage; the clearances which are to be paid from the production budget; and the obligation to ensure that the material is clearable, at fixed rates, for worldwide exploitation. If it is not possible to obtain worldwide clearance, agreement to use such material within the programme must be obtained, in writing, from all the co-producers.

6.3   Copyright in the production

Depending on the financing arrangements, copyright in the production may be wholly or partially assigned to production financiers. To the extent that it is not, the copyright may be jointly owned by the co-producers or the co-producers may split the ownership between them on a territorial basis. (Most subsidy funds and the co-production treaties require copyright to be jointly owned by the co-producers.)

For European co-productions where, under EU directives, the director of the production will be joint owner of the copyright with "the person by whom the arrangements necessary for the making of the film are undertaken" (see *Chapter 1*), it will be necessary to specifically address the question of the director's copyright. In many cases the director will be expected to assign the copyright to the co-producers, but UK-based co-producers should be aware that this could be problematic in certain European countries where directors' rights are greatly respected and, thus, handled with considerable sensitivity. In such cases it might be thought appropriate for the director and the co-producers to own the copyright jointly; in others the director might retain the copyright but assign the widest possible exploitation rights to the co-producers.

Whatever arrangements are made for the ownership of copyright, the agreement should record the copyright notice which is to appear on the production and, if the copyright is to be divided on a territorial basis between different co-producers, provision for these variations should be made in the credits.

The agreement must also specify which co-producer is responsible for registering the copyright at the US Copyright Registry and such other copyright registrations as are required under the laws of the countries of the co-producers. The cost should either be included as a budget item or the agreement should specify that the costs are to be borne by the co-producer that is required by its national laws and/or regulations to make such registrations.

Exploitation rights in the production   6.4

It is reasonable to assume that a pre-condition for securing production finance will have been the acquisition by the co-producers of worldwide exploitation rights in the production. Subject to the exploitation rights accorded to third-party production financiers, these exploitation rights may be jointly owned by the co-producers or they may be divided so that each co-producer has sole control of the rights in certain national territories and in respect of certain markets. The agreement should itemise the agreed arrangements as follows:

Division of territories and markets

The usual procedure would be for each co-producer to hold the exclusive exploitation rights to the production in its home territory and (except, perhaps, in the case of the large number of English language territories) in other territories speaking the same language. For example, German rights should cover Germany, Austria and German-speaking Switzerland; French rights France, French-speaking Belgium, French-speaking Switzerland, French-speaking Canada and the former French colonies in Africa; rights for Portugal should also cover the rights to the former Portuguese colonies in Africa, to Macao and Brazil, and so on.

In many cases the terrestrial television rights for a single national territory will extend to provide for the unavoidable simultaneous relay of the programme by cable transmission in other territories, i.e. when the national broadcasters' signal is received by cable operators and audiences for those services are able to view the programmes at the same time as they are being screened in the 'originating' territory. These overlaps should be carefully checked out when licensing rights to different territories.

The agreement must specify the particular markets which each co-producer's exploitation rights cover. In European co-productions care must also be taken to identify the entitlement to exclusive language rights for each market.

The separate markets are, generally, terrestrial broadcast television, satellite subscription services, cable, pay cable, video and non-theatric. Within Europe the grant of licences to satellite and pay cable services needs to be treated with particular care, since these services frequently overlap national boundaries.

The treatment of Internet rights needs to be resolved. For strategies see *Chapter 17, Paragraph 3*.

For video or non-theatric release, it may be of greater benefit to arrange for the licensing of these rights on a territory by territory basis (see *Chapter 22*).

In some cases production funding may have been obtained on the basis that there will be a 'holdback' on other forms of exploitation economically affecting the territory for a certain period. For example, funding received in respect of terrestrial television rights is likely to be conditional on a holdback on the exploitation on the satellite services receivable in that territory. Care must, therefore, be taken to ensure that the licensing of rights by one co-producer (or the grant of rights to a third-party production financier) will not conflict with the licensing of rights by another co-producer.

Duration of exploitation rights/licences

The duration of each co-producer's exploitation rights will be subject to negotiation in each case. The co-producer may own and control the rights in its territories for the full period of copyright and be solely entitled to retain all revenues from licences in that territory. Alternatively the co-producer, whilst retaining the rights in the territory for the full period of copyright, may be under an obligation to share revenue from sales to certain markets within that territory with the other co-producers. Yet again, the co-producer's ownership and control of rights and entitlement to revenues may terminate after a certain period (anything less than about five years would probably be too short).

Accounting responsibilities/distribution commissions and costs

The agreement should specify each co-producer's responsibility for accounting to the other co-producers for their shares of revenue from its territory and set out the accounting procedures. For the first two years of exploitation this may be quarterly, with payments being remitted within 28 days of each accounting statement; thereafter it may be limited to annual accounting, with payments being made within the same period. The agreement should also specify the agreed levels of distribution commissions and costs which may be charged by the co-producers.

Appointment of a third-party distributor

The co-producers may agree to appoint a distributor to handle sales of the production outside their own territories (or, indeed, individually within their own territories). The selection and contractual terms for a third-party distributor to handle sales from which the co-producers are jointly to share the revenues should be subject to approval by all the co-producers. In the event that approval is withheld, the co-producer withholding approval should have a period of 28 days in which to bring an improved offer. If this is not forthcoming, the co-producers may appoint the distributor originally proposed.

The agreement should specify which co-producers are to contract with a third-party distributor: it may be the co-producers jointly or one co-producer may enter into the agreement and hold it for its benefit and for the benefit of the other co-producers.

Distributors will occasionally be prepared to remit revenues from sales direct to co-producers entitled to shares of such revenues, whether or not they are party to the distribution agreement. Obviously, if such an arrangement can be agreed with a distributor it considerably simplifies accounting procedures between the co-producers. If the distributor is not prepared to make such an arrangement (and many will not) the co-producers must agree between them either to appoint a collection agent (see *Chapter 22, Paragraph 3.6*) or to establish which co-producer will receive the revenues on their behalf. This places that co-producer under a contractual obligation to remit payments to the co-producers within a fixed period of, say, 14 days of receipt by the co-producer of statements and revenues from the distributor.

Withholding tax on sales revenues

If revenue to be shared by the co-producers is subject to withholding tax, the co-producers should either arrange for the revenue to remain in a bank account held in their joint names in the territory in which the sale has taken place or agree between themselves the most tax-efficient method of treating the retention of withholding tax and passing the benefit of any consequent reductions in the co-producer's liability for national tax on to the co-producers, in accordance with their proportionate shares.

Festival entries

To avoid confusion, the agreement should nominate only one co-producer to have responsibility for entering the co-production in television award festivals. This would normally be the managing producer. It should, however, be recognised that completing applications and meeting delivery requirements for entries to festivals can be both time-consuming and costly and it may be sensible to provide that, if the nominated co-producer declines to enter the programme at a festival if requested to do so, the other co-producer may be entitled to submit the entry at his or her own expense.

Any prize money awarded to the production should be shared in accordance with the proportionate shares, after recoupment of direct costs incurred in making the entry.

MASTER NEGATIVE 7
Ownership 7.1
The agreement should address the question of physical ownership of the master negative and unused footage and this would generally follow the agreement on ownership of copyright in the production.
Storage 7.2
The co-producers should agree the location of the laboratory at which the masters are to be stored and the agreement should provide a mechanism for co-producers to have appropriate access to the material for the purpose of obtaining duplicate copies.
Secondary uses/unused footage 7.3
The extent to which the individual co-producers may or may not be entitled to reversion master material and/or use unused footage for other types of programme should be specified. This is rarely of consequence in the case of drama production, but documentary material such as travel, environmental or nature footage might have some long-term commercial value, particularly when combined with other footage. The agreement should specify the respective rights and entitlements of co-producers to reversion the masters and make provision for the arrangements under which the co-producers may share in any benefits from such secondary use of the material.

WARRANTIES AND INDEMNITIES 8
The agreement will require customary legal warranties and indemnities in respect of the following matters:

i   performance of the agreement;
ii   financial responsibilities;
iii rights ownership (if applicable);
iv   infringement of copyright;
v   obligations to third parties; and
vi   inclusion of libellous, obscene or defamatory material.

TERMINATION 9
The agreement must specify the grounds for termination, generally breach of agreement or insolvency.
Breach 9.1
Provision should be made for co-producers jointly to give written notice to a co-producer of any breach of the agreement, specifying the breach and, if the breach is capable of remedy, with the co-producer in breach having a period of 14 days (five days during production) in which to remedy it.

If the breach is not remedied or is not capable of remedy, the co-producers must have the right to terminate the agreement with the defaulting co-producer. On termination, the defaulting co-producer's entire rights and interests in the co-production, together with any production funding held by the co-producer, must, so far as possible, be transferred to the other co-production partners who should be entitled to take over the co-producer's role on production and proceed to completion.

9.2 Insolvency

The most difficult problems to deal with in a co-production agreement are those that arise when one of the co-production partners becomes insolvent. The extent to which the agreement can provide legal mechanisms under which the co-production itself and/or the other co-producers individually and/or the underlying rights in the co-production and/or the exploitation rights in the co-production which may be owned by the insolvent co-producer can be protected against claims by the creditors of that co-producer will vary greatly. How things work will depend on the national laws of the countries of the co-producers in relation to allowable mechanisms for isolating assets from insolvency procedures, the rights and entitlements of creditors, and the extent to which the co-production and co-producers will be deemed to be a single legal entity.

This is, therefore, a matter on which co-producers must seek specialist legal advice in relation to the laws of their respective countries to determine the best method of providing, ideally, that in such circumstances the other co-producers are entitled to assume the co-producer's rights and interest in the co-production, take over that part of the production for which the insolvent co-producer has responsibility and proceed to completion.

If it is not possible to safeguard the co-production itself from the claims of creditors, at the very least the agreement should aim to ensure that the other co-producers cannot be held liable for the debts of the insolvent co-producer.

9.3 Substitution of a co-production partner

In the event that the agreement with one of the co-production partners is terminated, the co-producers should be entitled to appoint a substitute co-producer. The appointment of the substitute will be negotiated by the managing producer in consultation with the other co-producers and the terms and conditions of the appointment will be subject to their approval, not to be unreasonably withheld or delayed.

9.4 Force majeure

The agreement should provide that if production is delayed by events outside the control of the co-producers (acts of war, riots, civil disturbance, labour disputes, natural disasters, etc.) production may be suspended. If the conditions giving rise to the suspension prevail for longer than, say, three weeks (a shorter or longer period may be specified, depending on the nature of the production) then, subject to any contrary requirements of third-party production finance, the co-producers, individually or collectively, may have the right to abandon production. If one co-producer wishes to continue and the other(s) to abandon production, the co-producer continuing with production should be entitled to have assigned to it all the rights and interests of the co-producers abandoning production, subject to an obligation to meet their obligations to third parties.

MISCELLANEOUS 10
Disputes procedures 10.1

The co-producers may agree a mechanism for arbitration in the event of a dispute, undertaking to abide by the decision of a mutually agreed third-party arbitrator to be nominated within the agreement. It is not, however, suggested that any such procedure be adopted in place of the various mechanisms proposed for avoiding deadlocks on production which are contained within this checklist. Although arbitration can be quicker and simpler than taking a dispute to court, costs are involved and there is no procedure for appeal against an arbitrator's decision. Further, if the co-producers are in such fundamental disagreement that a third-party arbitrator has to be brought in to resolve the matter, it is likely that one or other of the co-producers is going to be unhappy about the arbitrator's decision and the good working relationship which is essential for successful co-production will have been seriously damaged.

Variations to the agreement 10.2

The agreement should specify that any variations to the agreement must be confirmed in writing and signed by all co-producers.

No partnership 10.3

Under the laws of certain countries, a co-production agreement would, de facto, constitute a partnership between the co-producers. To the extent that it is possible (or applicable) under the laws of the countries of the co-producers, the agreement should specify that the agreement between the co-producers only relates to the co-production. It does not constitute a partnership between the co-producers or have any bearing on their respective business activities outside the co-production agreement.

Notices 10.4

The agreement should specify the customary conditions under which notices under the agreement are to be given.

Registration of the agreement 10.5

In certain countries it is necessary for all agreements to be registered and the agreement should specify the co-producer responsible for making such registration, including responsibility for the cost of the registration.

Duty of confidentiality 10.6

The co-producers should be bound to a duty of confidentiality about the co-production agreement, the co-producers' business and the co-production itself.

ASSIGNMENT 11

A co-production agreement must be personal to the parties and should not be capable of assignment without the express prior consent in writing of the other parties.

GOVERNING LAW/JURISDICTION 12

The agreement must specify under the laws of which country it is to be governed since, if a dispute arises between the parties, failure to have so specified can result in protracted and complex legal wrangling on this question alone, before the dispute itself can be resolved. Determining factors in making the decision will be the relative levels of funding brought by each of the co-producers and the territory in which the agreement is to be principally performed.

Similarly the agreement should also stipulate under the courts of which jurisdiction disputes between the parties will be heard. It need not necessarily be the case that the country under whose laws the agreement is governed has jurisdiction over the agreement. A method of reaching agreement on this question is to provide that, in the event of a dispute, the choice of jurisdiction lies with the defendant to the action.

It is emphasised that co-producers should seek specialist legal advice when determining these matters.

TELEVISION, THEATRICAL AND VIDEO DISTRIBUTION

C22

Chapter 22

In many respects the arrangements for the production of feature films and television programmes are much the same, the differences being more of scale than of substance. These similarities do not, however, extend to distribution where the roles of the distributor and distribution practices are very different. These variations reflect the fundamentally different processes by which television programmes and theatrical films reach their audiences. The sale of a single television print ensures the transmission into millions of homes and, therefore, the physical aspects of distribution are not an issue. For feature films they are critical, since the distributor must be set up to ensure that prints and other materials will be screened in individual cinemas around the world. This process is likely to undergo radical change as digital technology makes it possible for cinemas to download films at a technical quality suitable for showing on the big screen.

Distribution of videos is a very different business. They have to be physically distributed into retail outlets, a process much more akin to book distribution. But as video distribution relates to the exploitation of the actual production, be it a feature film or television programme, as distinct from exploitation of secondary rights, the procedures are also dealt with here.

This chapter explains the customary arrangements for distribution and the key commercial terms.

KEY TOPICS & ISSUES

TELEVISION DISTRIBUTION

A glance through the catalogue for MIP TV, the largest television programme market, gives the producer a good idea of the number and diversity of television distributors: they range from multinational companies to one man and an answering machine. In the UK some of the major distributors were originally the in-house selling arms of various broadcasters, but these have now become free-standing distribution operations charged with being profitable companies in their own right. Whilst their main client may still be the original parent broadcaster, they are intent on building up sales catalogues and contacts over as wide a range of sources as possible and handle programme material from all sources.

Some of the largest distributors (as well as the smaller ones) are completely independent of broadcasters and a number of the larger independent production companies now have their own distribution arms. Television distribution is very much a free market economy and a highly competitive business.

Uses of a distributor   1.1

Producers need to build up relationships with distributors for two main reasons: firstly, because producers need to be able to bring funding to productions (see *Chapter 18*); and secondly, they must maximise all possible sources of revenue to stay in business and grow and this means exploiting the rights they have been able to retain in productions to the fullest effect.

Many producers question the necessity to use a distributor at all but, if in the past it was possible to secure television sales with nothing more or less sophisticated than a decent expense account and a good line in sales patter, this is no longer the case. To achieve sales in a complex and overcrowded market calls for a high degree of professionalism. Knowledge of the worldwide marketplace, the prices which are paid, contacts, presence at the various international programme markets and the ability to administer sales (i.e. the licence agreement, freighting the prints and publicity material, collecting revenues, paying clearance costs, dealing with issues such as withholding tax) are all essentials which distributors are equipped to deal with and producers, generally, are not.

It is for good reason that broadcasters may allow a producer to retain rights only on condition that the exploitation is handled by a professional distributor. This is not to say that if the programme has obvious appeal for a particular territory or market in which the producer has direct contacts, the producer should not try to make a sale direct, but for any wider distribution it is essential to use the services of a distributor.

How to choose a distributor   1.2

It is notoriously difficult to obtain objective recommendations about distributors and their operations. If a programme does not sell well it has everything to do with the distributor and nothing to do with the programme; if it does sell well, this position is reversed!

Asking to see the distributor's catalogue to assess its style and presentation can be a useful starting point. It is also advisable to attend the international sales markets occasionally and visit distributors' stands to see how professionally they operate.

Probably the best approach is 'horses for courses'. Whilst some of the largest distributors may claim to handle (almost) anything and everything, most distributors have some particular speciality and will be keen to acquire programming in that subject area and have the contacts to be able to sell it effectively.

Many producers feel more comfortable working with smaller distributors, believing, perhaps rightly, that their programme will get more individual attention and have less chance of being lost in the catalogue than with a large distributor. This needs to be weighed against the likelihood that the larger the distributor, the wider their range of contacts and the greater the possibility that they will have funds to pay distribution advances and produce high-quality sales promotion material. It is very much a matter for individual judgement, to be made in the light of the type of programming which is on offer.

2 TELEVISION DISTRIBUTION AGREEMENTS

Distributors generally have their own standard form contracts which they issue when they are being granted a licence to distribute a completed television production. This licence agreement is drawn up in such a way that the terms mesh with the terms of the distributor's sales licence agreements which the distributor will issue when making sales of the programme. In practical terms it is, therefore, rather difficult for a distributor to accept a different form of licence agreement. However, as the licence agreement is drafted by the distributor rather than by the grantor of the rights, i.e. the producer, it is important to check the provisions very carefully.

Further, there are a number of key deal points which are negotiable in any licence agreement and these should be discussed and agreed in advance of the producer granting the distributor a licence. These key points are as follows:

2.1 Distribution territories

Although many distributors prefer to be granted a worldwide licence, distribution rights can be licensed to different distributors for different territories and markets. The following is a brief description of how the various territories are generally broken down.

The main sales territories are generally divided as follows:

Europe; North America; Central America; Caribbean; South America; Asia/ Australasia/The Far East; Middle East; Africa.

Within these some sub-divisions are quite usual, as the following examples indicate:

Europe

Scandinavian rights – Norway, Sweden, Denmark and Finland – are often sold as a block;

French rights frequently include French-speaking Belgium and Switzerland (probably French Canada and sometimes French-speaking African countries);

German rights will usually include German-speaking Switzerland and Austria;

The 'Latin countries' – Spain, Portugal and Italy – are frequently grouped together (often with Spanish-speaking South American rights); and

Russia and the former Soviet bloc states come within Europe.

North America

This will usually be divided between the USA and Canada, with Canada often being divided between French- and English-speaking Canada. (Sales to the USA may be conditional on a 'holdback', i.e. an undertaking not to sell for a certain period, on sales to Canada.)

Asia/Australasia/The Far East

Of these markets Australia, New Zealand and Japan, are frequently sold separately.

Distribution markets (outlets) 2.2

This use of the word 'markets' means the different types of outlets to which programmes can be licensed. With technological advances, new outlets are being created all the time. The Internet opens up a whole range of different uses: simultaneous and non-simultaneous screenings; video-on-demand; programme-related websites with interactive features. Definitions will be required for the coming reception of programmes on, for example, mobile phones, digital watches and fridge doors.

The principal outlets are as follows. Each is capable of being licensed independently of the others, although any such licensing of individual outlets is likely to carry a holdback on the licensing to other outlets in the same territory.

Standard television/free television

The exhibition of the programme through terrestrial and satellite transmissions and by basic cable and by analogue or digital means which can be received by viewers without charge – i.e. generally transmissions by terrestrial broadcasters.

Non-standard television/pay television

Transmissions of the programme on subscription services, whether by satellite or cable, where the viewer has paid a separate fee to be able to receive the programme broadcast by these services. These rights may be subdivided between satellite and cable:

i   Satellite subscription – broadcasts of the programme by satellite for reception directly into the home by means of a satellite receiver where the signal is encrypted and the viewer has paid a charge for the privilege of receiving the signal; and

ii Pay cable – relays of the programme by way of a cable programme service where the viewer has paid a fee for receiving the service.

On-line rights

The showing of the programme on Internet services; the storing, reproducing or transmitting of the programme within databases, computer programmes and files; the streaming and downloading of the programme.

Closed circuit

Transmissions of the programme by individually wired systems which do not in themselves constitute cable programme services and in which programmes are relayed to an audience which is confined to a limited area, such as hotels, oil rigs and aircraft.

Non-theatric

The exhibition of the programme to non-paying audiences in educational institutions, charities, prisons, business and industry, film societies or to any private audience where any fee which is paid by all or any such viewers or audience is not paid primarily or principally for the purpose of viewing the programme.

Home video

The sale or hire of the programme by means of magnetic tape or disc for showing through a playback device for sound and visual images for private home use only. Home video generally includes DVD.

CD-i

The exploitation of the programme through any multimedia software programme for simultaneous interactive presentation on video, audio, graphics, animation, text and data which is designed for use with the laser optical compact disc interactive hardware.

C22

2.3   Distribution advances

A distribution advance is a sum of money which the distributor is prepared to advance to the producer in return for acquiring the exclusive licence to handle sales of the programme. When a distributor is paying an advance it would be usual for them to be granted distribution rights worldwide, although these could be limited to certain territories. The distributor will expect to deduct standard distribution commissions and direct costs and expenses from first sales revenue and will then retain all the revenue until the sum of the advance (possibly with interest) has been recouped. Thereafter, the distributor will continue to sell the programme but after deduction of commissions and expenses, the revenue will be paid to the producer (or whomsoever is licensing the rights to the distributor). In some cases, if the advance has been significant, the distributor may also be entitled to receive a profit share from sales, once the advance has been recouped.

Advances are non-returnable so, if the programme does not sell well enough for the distributor to recover the sums advanced, the loss is the distributor's.

The level of advance will obviously depend on the number of territories and markets for which distribution rights are being acquired, the nature of the programme and the largely subjective assessment of its likely sales performance. The real risk factor for the distributor is whether the programme will sell at all, not the price that will be paid for it. Although sales cartels are denied, experienced distributors know that for finished product they can expect X price for Y type of programme in Z territory or market and only the most exceptional programmes will attract any more.

As explained in *Chapter 19, Paragraph 3.3*, distributors will sometimes agree to pay advances before production has been mounted and these advances may partially fund production. In most cases, however, advances will only be offered when the distributor has had an opportunity to view the completed programme.

Distributors do not always agree to pay advances: it all depends how keen they are to control the rights. However, it is obviously a sound commercial principle never to give something away for nothing and even if a distributor is only prepared to offer a modest advance, it is worth a producer's while to make it a condition of a grant of a licence, otherwise the distributor has less incentive to make sales of the production.

Distribution guarantees

If a distributor is not prepared to offer an advance, an alternative means of ensuring that the distributor has an incentive to sell the programme is for the producer to ask for a guarantee, whereby the distributor guarantees that certain sums will be achieved from sales within, say 12 months of commencement of the licence. If this sum is not returned to the producer from sales revenue, the distributor has to pay the producer the sum of the guaranteed amount.

Commitment to costs

Failing agreement to obtain a distribution advance or guarantee, a third strategy to ensure that the distributor is incentivised to make sales is to negotiate that the distributor will undertake to spend a certain amount on promotion and publicity to generate sales of the programme (see *Paragraph 2.5* below).

Sometimes distributors seek to make the producer liable to pay costs of promotion and publicity. This comes from feature film distribution, where, unlike television deals, the costs of prints and advertising are hugely significant. This type of arrangement should be resisted on television deals where the distributor should be expected to make a certain level of expenditure in return for the right to represent the programme.

If the distributor is not prepared to offer either an advance or guarantee, the producer must ensure that the distributor's licence for the programme should, initially, run for a fairly limited period, say two years, and, if a certain level of sales has not been achieved within that period, the producer should have the right to terminate the licence.

Distributors' commissions 2.4

When selling finished product, all distributors charge a commission on gross revenues, i.e. a percentage of the actual sums paid by the buyers for the programme. Distributors' commission generally covers all the fixed office, staff and overhead costs, including all legal, accounting and other services which may be required to effect sales and collect revenues. When checking the form of licence agreement, care should be taken to ensure that there can be no double charging for the services which the distributor should pay for out of revenues from commission and those services which generally fall within the category of direct costs and expenses, as outlined below.

Distributors' commission levels vary and, although each distributor will have standard rates which they aim to get on all deals, the rates are negotiable. The levels also vary for certain markets and territories. The following example shows the approximate range of commission levels customarily charged:

	% of Gross Revenue
Sales throughout the world other than to the United States:	25-35
Sales in the United States: Primetime network	10
PBS Network	20
Any other network sale	20
Syndication sales (including PBS single station)	35
Cable syndication	35
Top cable	10
Secondary cable	20
Video release	20
Non-theatric release	40

Sub-agents' commission

Many distributors use sub-agents in certain parts of the world and the producer should check the contract carefully to ensure that it specifies either that the commission rates include any commissions for sub-agents or, more usually, that it provides for a fixed, albeit higher rate of commission in territories where a sub-agent is employed, generally 5% higher than the standard commission. Do not accept wording which allows for an unspecified rate of commission to be charged when sub-agents are used.

Whilst producers should always aim to negotiate a reasonable commission level, it is not necessarily advisable to press for low commission levels: the higher the distributor's commission level, the greater the incentive for the distributor to sell the programme.

Distribution costs 2.5

After deducting the appropriate commission from gross revenue the distributor will then recoup the direct costs incurred in making the sale. These include the cost of making prints, mastering materials, advertising costs, shipping, freight, insurance etc.

Direct costs need to be watched closely. They are genuine costs which the distributor has to expend and some, such as prints and advertising, have to be incurred speculatively, in advance of any sales. If the programme does not sell well, all these costs might have to be set against a small number of sales and the distributor can incur a loss (and the producer receive no profit at all). There is no doubt, however, that some distributors abuse the direct costs provisions and accounting statements can all too frequently show that commissions and costs neatly equate to the revenue earned from sales.

To avoid this risk, the producer should try to negotiate a 'cap' on direct costs, expressing them as being up to between 5% and 10% of gross revenue. Any expenditure above this should be made subject to the producer's prior agreement and the distributor will then have to demonstrate that the costs are reasonable and necessary.

Publicity and promotion

As part of the overall deal for distribution rights, it is often worthwhile to obtain a guarantee from the distributor that a certain amount of money will be spent on sales promotion for the programme. These costs will generally be excluded from the 'cap' on distribution costs, but the sums to be spent will be pre-agreed between the distributor and the producer. The loss will be the distributor's if the programme sales fail to generate sufficient revenue to cover these costs.

2.6 Term of licence

The length of time for which a producer grants a distributor a licence to exploit the rights is negotiable. Anything shorter than about 18 months to two years is unlikely to allow a distributor sufficient time to capitalise on a sales effort: the usual term of licence period is about five years. Where an advance has been paid, the licence runs until expiry of the term or date of recoupment of the advance, whichever is the later date.

It may be sensible to build in a review point whereby, if certain sales have not been achieved within a specified period – say three years – there might be a reversion of rights in those territories to which sales have not been made, to allow the producer to see if sales can be achieved there.

Since the producer is likely to be responding to the distributor's own licence agreement, it is particularly important to check the provisions for termination of the licence closely since they are sometimes rather ambiguous. The licence agreement must clearly stipulate that the licence terminates at the end of the agreed period: any provisions for extension must be at the producer's sole discretion. The licence agreement must also contain termination provisions if the distributor in any way defaults on any of its terms and conditions (in particular the accounting provisions and obligations to make payments).

Sometimes a distributor will enter agreements for sales towards the end of a programme's licence period, whereby the licence period granted to the end-user purchasing the programme extends beyond the term of the distributor's own licence to handle the rights. In these circumstances, the producer is generally under an obligation to honour the terms of sales licence agreements entered into by the distributor, who remains responsible for collecting any further revenues from the sales licence and is entitled to deduct commission and direct costs from it. It is a sensible precaution to provide in the distributor's licence agreement that the distributor cannot enter into agreements for sales of the programme where the term of any sales licence is longer than a certain fixed period, say three years – or at least not without the prior consent of the producer.

Option on future programmes   2.7

It is usual for licence agreements to provide that the distributor has first opportunity to obtain distribution rights in any sequel production. As a general rule, it is usually better for all the programmes to be sold by one distributor as a block of programming, rather than having the distribution split. Whilst it would, therefore, be sensible to grant a distributor rights in sequels, this must be made conditional on the producer being satisfied with the distributor's performance with the original programmes.

Distributors' licence agreements may be worded in such a way that the distributor has first opportunity to obtain distribution rights in subsequent programmes of any sort made by the producer! This should not be accepted unless the distributor is offering some payment or other consideration in respect of a 'first look' deal.

The above points are generally negotiable when entering into an agreement with a distributor for a licence of rights. The following ones are not generally negotiable, but do need to be carefully studied when granting rights.

Clearances and residual payments   2.8

To make overseas sales, the producer will be responsible for ensuring that all the agreements for services and materials (such as stills, library footage and music) used on the production provide for clearance for worldwide use. Some of these clearances may have been bought out at the outset; others may have been cleared for an additional payment on first sale to a particular territory or market. For talent union agreements, royalty or residual payments may fall due on sales to certain territories or markets.

The distributor's licence agreement will specify the clearances which the distributor requires to have been made. Care needs to be taken to ensure that the distributor is aware, firstly, if it has not been possible to obtain clearances for any particular territory or market; and thereafter which clearances have been paid for and which have not. In the latter case the payment will need to be met from revenues remaining after deduction of commissions and direct costs. The producer should ensure that the distributor is under an obligation to advise immediately of any sales which trigger payments and that the sale generates sufficient revenue to cover the residual costs involved. (If the residual costs are very high the value of the sale may not exceed the residual costs.)

Whilst some distributors may be prepared to administer these payments (and may seek to charge a higher commission for doing so), it is quite common for the producer to be responsible. In any event the producer remains primarily liable to the party granting the rights or services if a sale is made without the necessary clearances having been effected or paid for. He or she will also be required to give the distributor warranties that the necessary clearances are obtained. It is, therefore, very important to ensure that there is absolute clarity in the distribution licence agreement as to the arrangements for dealing with these payments, since the producer's contractual liabilities can be onerous if they are not made (and in the case of the talent unions, and in particular Equity, it may have a bearing on the producer's ability to contract with talent in the future).

Accounting provisions   2.9

The agreement must provide that the distributor has to account to the producer regularly, usually quarterly, commencing with first overseas sale. The accounting statements should give a complete breakdown of gross sales revenue and deductions of commission, direct costs, residual payments and, if applicable, withholding taxes (see below).

The contract must go on to provide that the producer will receive any revenues due within a certain period (often 28 days, but it can sometimes be as long as 90 days) of receipt of each accounting statement. (A sneaky trick is sometimes employed whereby the contract makes provision for dates on which accounting statements are issued, but does not specify the date on which payments fall due: these dates are not the same thing, although it is often assumed that they are, and the contract, therefore, needs to be checked closely to ensure that the dates by which payments are made is clearly stated).

It is quite customary for accounting statements/payments to be issued less frequently after the programme has been on sale for two or three years: quarterly accounting might be varied to annual accounting.

Withholding tax

In some territories there is a tax on revenues to be remitted overseas, calculated as a percentage of the revenue. As a general rule, distributors can claim a rebate on their UK taxes in respect of such taxes levied overseas and the contract should provide that the benefit of any such rebate (after deduction of the distributor's usual commission and costs) is passed to the producer. Alternatively, the money may be left in the territory to which the sale has been made and, in this instance, should be paid into a bank account in the territory in the name of the producer.

2.10 Errors and omissions insurance

Errors and omissions insurance is insurance against claims for infringement of copyright, defamation and so forth. Most UK broadcasters self-insure for errors and omissions on programmes which they are wholly or partially financing. This cover does not, however, extend to overseas sales of the production. For sales to stations in the USA, the stations require a warranty from the distributor that errors and omissions insurance is in place and the distributor will, in turn, pass this obligation on to the producer.

In some cases the distributor may be prepared to effect the cover. In others, the producer will be expected to do it. Either way, the cost should be treated as a direct distribution cost. If, in the first instance, the charges are to be met by the producer, it is important to clarify the treatment of the charges when negotiating the distribution licence agreement. As a general rule, it is easier to obtain reasonable quotations for errors and omissions insurance after the programme has been completed and transmitted in the UK without any objections being raised from any source.

2.11 Termination

In addition to the usual provisions for termination if the distributor defaults on any of the obligations within the contract, the contract should also provide that materials, such as prints and publicity, must either be destroyed or returned to the producer.

3   THEATRICAL DISTRIBUTION

There is no question that the world of feature films is far less structured and far more difficult for a producer to navigate than television. State broadcasters in all countries have given the television industry an infrastructure which the feature film business entirely lacks: it is full of the widest possible range of different operators, from those with the most serious and committed artistic intent through to ladder climbers in large corporations, small entrepreneurs, bankers, agents, lawyers, chancers, bounders and assorted gangsters, all drawn by the lure of glamour, fame and money. It is a jungle which only the most intrepid and tenacious producers should attempt to enter.

Pivotal to any feature film deal is a sales agent and/or theatrical distributor. Without a commitment to the film, either from a sales agent to find a distributor or from a distributor direct, it is likely to be extremely difficult for the producer to raise finance. Nearly all potential financiers will need not only sales estimates but assurances that a distributor will be in place since without one the film will not be released for showings to cinema audiences. Distribution of feature films is a complicated business, requiring the machinery for the physical distribution of prints and publicity materials to 'exhibitors' (i.e. cinemas) and access to the cinemas. With the exception of a handful of 'art-house' cinemas which are independently owned, cinemas are grouped on circuits which are either owned by or linked to the major theatrical distributors. How then to find a distributor?

Sales agents   3.1

The usual route for finding a distributor is to find a theatrical sales agent who will agree to take on the film. This is not always easy. Sales agents are extremely selective as to which films they are prepared to represent as the work and expense involved in marketing the film to distributors is extensive.

In return for a commission from the subsequent deals with distributors, usually of about 15% for the USA and 20-25% outside the USA, the sales agent will seek out distributors by attending the major markets and festivals, releasing publicity materials and so forth and negotiate the agreements for the licence of distribution rights.

Sales agents do sometimes invest in the development of the screenplay and give advice to producers on development of the film to maximise its possibilities for attracting distributors and may invest in the production itself. They can also act as collection agents for revenues from the films (see *Paragraph 3.6*).

Distribution territories and markets   3.2

Theatrical distribution rights can be licensed territory by territory, in much the same way as television territories can be divided. The rights to distribute a film in North America are known as 'domestic rights'; rights outside North America are collectively 'foreign rights'. The extent to which a distributor will take rights in a number of different territories will be negotiable, dependent on its capacity for releasing films in various territories and the amount being paid for the distribution licence. The major distributors will unquestionably require all distribution rights in the film worldwide. The film will need to be released theatrically, prior to any exploitation of the television rights in the territory and/or to the release of the film on video. Where film financing has been put together through a variety of distribution, television and video deals, the release pattern will need to be very carefully worked out.

Gross box office revenues/distributor's commissions/producer's net profits   3.3

Gross box office revenues from distribution are subject to the following deductions:

i   exhibitor's share: approximately 40% of box office;

ii   balance remaining (known as rental) subject to distributor's commission
        of approximately 30%, followed by deduction by the distributor of the
        agreed cost of P&A (prints and advertising);

iii   from the remaining balance is deducted the cost of the film plus interest and other financing charges (i.e. recoupment by distributors and other investors of their contributions to the overall cost of production); and

iv   the balance remaining constitutes producer's net profits.

If fees have been deferred they will be recouped in first position from producer's net profits. Any shares of net profits offered to the writer, director and key cast must be defined as being of producer's net profits.

3.4   Delivery materials

The list of delivery materials required in order to fulfil a theatrical distribution licence is staggering, literally hundreds of items, ranging from the physical materials for the film to promotional and publicity materials and all the contracts, certificates and other documentation relating to the production of the film. The cost of supplying all these materials and the work involved in doing so, is extremely extensive and provision should be made for this within the production budget and/or within the deal with the distributor. And there are no short cuts. Sales agents and distributors insist on all the materials being in place before distribution can commence.

3.5   P&A

This stands for prints and advertising. These are the costs to get the materials physically into the cinemas and to promote the film. The amount which the distributor is prepared to pay in respect of P&A is a matter of hard negotiation in the distribution deal since it is risk money: if the film bombs at the box office the P&A costs may not be recovered from gross revenues. On all feature films these costs are significant and, where the producer has to beg a distributor to handle the film, the distributor may look to the producer to meet or at least contribute to the costs. As will be seen from the breakdown in *Paragraph 3.3*, P&A costs are recovered from box office revenues in first position after deduction of the distributor's commission.

3.6   Collection agents

Collection agents, who may also be sales agents or may be set up solely to act as collection agencies, are appointed by the financiers of the film to collect all distribution revenues and distribute them amongst the financiers and profit participants according to the recoupment provisions and profit participations contained within the financing plan for the film. They generally charge a commission of up to approximately 5% of gross revenues and are responsible for taking whatever legal or other action may be required in order to ensure that revenues are remitted and paid out.

There are many publicly funded schemes (the Film Council, regional film boards, Media Plus and so forth) to help first-time film-makers to get started and to produce and exploit low-budget films. The world of higher-budget feature films is, however, unsupported and singularly unsupportive towards all but the biggest name producers. Any producer would be well advised, in the first instance, to work through an established film company with the contacts and resources to put the necessary distribution and other arrangements in place.

VIDEO DISTRIBUTION 4
Preliminaries 4.1

The home video market is now very large and as the hardware and software for DVDs become cheaper and more readily available, it is becoming even more significant. The main markets for video sales are feature films and children's programmes but high-budget television drama and/or programmes featuring well-known artistes also achieve significant sales. Of particular interest to many independent producers is the encouraging growth in the market of all forms of 'special interest' programming and this is likely to continue apace given the tremendous opportunities presented by DVD to include additional material (both audio and visual and interactive) with the programme.

There is a tendency for producers to think in terms of exploitation of video rights as being no different to other arrangements for sales of a programme. Video rights are frequently automatically licensed to distributors along with the overseas sales rights with no distinction being made between the two forms of distribution, apart from the fact that a number of distributors (but not all) charge a lower rate of commission, usually 20% of gross, in respect of video sales.

The actual procedures for exploiting video rights are, however, different in all essential respects to those for selling programmes for transmission by conventional means. For a video to be exploited, significant numbers of copies have to be duplicated, packaged and physically distributed into retail and rental shops together with publicity and display materials. Further, a video licence is not sold for a single fee, but in return for a share of revenues from sales earned throughout the course of the video's sales life.

Successful video exploitation depends on having the organisation to physically deliver videos into the largest number of appropriate shops and to have accounting systems to monitor the regular returns from sales around the country. For these reasons television distributors are rarely set up to act as video distributors: when they acquire a licence in the video rights they, in turn, license them onto a video distributor.

When producers retain video rights and elect not to license them to a television distributor, some basic research in high street video shops into the names of the distributors on the video packaging can give as good a guide as any to an appropriate video distributor. Having selected the distributor, some of the terms to be negotiated are significantly different to those for licensing sales rights in a programme to a television distributor. Key points, which apply to tape video as well as to DVD, are as follows:

Territory 4.2

With the exception of a few very large companies with worldwide operations, video distributors are rarely set up to handle video distribution in more than one major territory. Producers should be very cautious about licensing worldwide video rights, or even rights in more than one territory, to a single video distributor unless they can demonstrate that the necessary organisation in place. If a distributor is granted rights in more than one territory, it would be sensible to negotiate an advance/guarantee (see *Paragraph 4.4* below) in respect of sales from each individual territory.

Term of licence 4.3

The term of licence is negotiable, between a minimum of about five and a maximum of 15 years. (It is longer than a licence for conventional distribution because the initial costs of the operation are much higher.)

4.4 Advance/guarantee

As a matter of good practice a producer should always try to ensure that an advance/guarantee forms part of the deal, not only because it ensures an immediate financial return but because the distributor is then highly motivated to sell videos to recover its costs. An advance is a non-returnable payment to the producer, made on signature of the contract, against revenues earned from sales: a guarantee is an undertaking that, if the producer has not received a certain amount of revenue from sales within a fixed period, the distributor will pay the outstanding amount to the producer.

To arrive at an advance/guarantee it is usual to ask the video distributor for a projection of the first year's sales. Make a calculation based on 10% of revenues from projected sales and look for payment of 37.5% of this by way of an advance and 37.5% as a guarantee of return from sales, to be received by the producer 12-18 months or so after the videos have gone on sale.

There are significant costs (duplication, packaging and distribution) involved in video marketing and, if the material is not demonstrably commercial, a video distributor may be unwilling to meet these costs and pay an advance. In these circumstances it is important to ensure that the video distributor's licence can be terminated if, say, 18 months after the start of the licence they cannot demonstrate effective sales.

4.5 Revenues

There are various ways to calculate shares of revenues: as a percentage of dealer price in most cases, but sometimes they are calculated as a percentage of the distributor's net receipts from sales or as a royalty based on a percentage of the retail sales price, like books.

Dealer price

The dealer price is negotiable by the dealer but is generally between about 50-65% of the retail selling price. A mechanism should be in place whereby, even if the retailer is allowed to make discounted sales, the retail selling price cannot fall below a certain minimum. The share of dealer price returned to the producer is negotiable, between 8% and 15%, occasionally rising to 18% if the video is highly commercial. The deal should make provision whereby, when certain specified sales targets are reached, the producer's percentage share is increased by a further 1% or 2%.

Shares of net receipts

These obviously need very careful scrutiny. Definitions of net receipts are notoriously open to abuse and the producer needs to be satisfied by the explanation of the revenues, and the allowable deductions, before establishing a percentage share. Given the wide variations in practice, the share is very much a matter for individual negotiation but the bottom line is that the eventual return to the producer should be seen to come to about the same as the producer would have received from an entitlement to a percentage of dealer price, as described above.

Royalties

It is fairly uncommon for royalties to be paid on retail price, but if they are they would generally be negotiable at around 7.5-10% of retail price. As with the dealer price, the two important things to ensure, on any royalty-based deal, is that there is a percentage increase ('escalator') on the royalty after a certain level of sales has been achieved and that there is a guaranteed minimum retail price, so the videos cannot be discounted to the extent that the returns from the royalty entitlement would be negligible.

Accounting 4.6

The video distributor should be obliged to account on a quarterly basis. The producer should ensure that the contract provides for quarterly accounting statements and makes specific provision for the date by which revenues are to be paid, generally 28 days after receipt of statement. The contract must contain unequivocal termination provisions in the event of failure by the distributor to observe the accounting arrangements.

Packaging and promotional material 4.7

The producer must have a clear contractual entitlement to approve all the artwork for the video packaging and the promotional material prior to printing and the distributor must be contractually obliged to adhere to the producer's credit list on the packaging.

Clearances 4.8

When licensing video rights the producer must be careful to ensure that clearance for video release has been obtained from Equity artistes, the writers, musicians and in respect of any third-party copyright material.

C23

EXPLOITING SECONDARY RIGHTS   Chapter 23

Producers must exploit every possible means of realising revenues to generate sufficient funds so as to stay in business and develop projects in the periods between production. In addition to distribution rights, they should look to the possibility of exploiting the secondary rights, where the producer has retained control of them and where they might have commercial value.

It must be said that it is only a very small minority of productions for which the secondary rights have any real value. Although in theory secondary rights in a programme, particularly drama, may be very extensive, everything from publishing through to operatic rights, in practice it is rare for them to be exploited. The key thing is for the producer to predict accurately in which projects the secondary rights could have possibilities for commercial exploitation and in these circumstances to fight to retain control of them and exploit them as effectively as possible. Where the secondary rights have no obvious commercial possibilities, it may be better to trade off retention of secondary rights in return for securing better terms on other aspects of the production deal.

This chapter deals with the terms negotiated for the principal secondary rights, being publishing, merchandising and soundtrack rights. Although they are not strictly speaking secondary rights, it also gives some information on 'premium-rate' telephone deals on productions since these are an increasing source of 'secondary revenue'. Changed format rights, which are a form of secondary right, are dealt with in *Chapter 7*. Other examples of secondary rights are theatrical feature rights, radio rights and stage rights (i.e. the right to license a feature film and radio and stage versions of the television production).

KEY TOPICS & ISSUES

PRELIMINARIES

Producers should be aware that, except for licence fee deals, all the UK broadcasters expect to control the exploitation of secondary rights in productions for which they are the majority financier. If the producer is to retain secondary rights in such programmes, it is usually necessary for the producer to be able to demonstrate that he or she has the knowledge and expertise to be able to exploit the rights properly.

Whilst there are examples of highly lucrative books and merchandise which are spin-offs from television productions, such commercial successes are relatively rare. In many instances the returns are insignificant, particularly in relation to the amount of work which the producer may need to undertake. A producer would be well advised to take soundings from publishers or merchandisers on the likely commercial potential of a project before, for example, investing in a production in order to control the secondary rights.

As a general rule, it may be advisable for a producer to find an agent to handle the sale of publishing or merchandising rights. It is a fairly specialist business and can be very time-consuming dealing with complicated arrangements while in production.

For albums, producers are strongly advised to employ a lawyer specialising in music industry agreements to handle the deal. Although there may be exceptions, it is common for record companies' contracts to resemble those children's picture books where you have to spot all the hidden canaries – except the canaries in this case are the means by which the record company might be able to avoid ever paying any royalties to the producer and at the same time lay claim to all the producer's current and future music interests. The specialist lawyer may be expensive, but it is a necessary cost.

PUBLISHING RIGHTS

2

Publishing rights are the right to publish a book based on the production and publication of the script, newspaper serialisations and extracts.

Agents

2.1

If the producer is engaging a book agent, the agent's commission is likely to be in the region of 10-15% of gross receipts from the deal.

Timescales

2.2

Firstly, the producer should bear in mind that publishers' lead times and print schedules are generally longer and less flexible than television production and transmission schedules. Although the more go-ahead publishers can now adjust print schedules to turn books round at a speed which (for publishers) would have been unimaginable a few years ago, it is difficult and expensive to do and there must be compelling commercial reasons for giving a book priority. For TV tie-ins publishers can generally manage to have a book on sale six months from delivery of the completed manuscript. (Normally they would allow 12 months from delivery of manuscript.) Consequently, if a producer is retaining control of publishing rights in a programme, it is advisable to start pursuing publishing interest at an early stage of development. Once production is under way it will be too late to get a publishing deal and have the book written, printed and distributed in time to coincide with release of the television programme.

Producers should not, of course, give a publisher any undertakings about the likely transmission date for a production. Broadcasters will never accept any obligation to transmit a programme at, or around, a certain time (or, indeed, at all) and as a general rule, are reluctant to give firm indications of likely transmission times, certainly at the stage which publishers ideally require this information. The agreement needs to provide that producer and publisher work together to endeavour to ensure that publication will coincide with transmission. Provided the producer keeps the publisher informed as to the likely scheduling date, the publishers should be under an obligation to use reasonable endeavours to ensure that the release of the book coincides with release of the production. In some instances it would be appropriate to provide that, unless transmissions are exceptionally delayed, the book must not be on sale in advance of transmission. Here it should be borne in mind that it can sometimes take weeks for publishers to get books from the warehouse into retail outlets.

2.3   Tie-in publishing agreements

There are three principal ways of structuring tie-in publishing deals:

i   the producer can enter into an agreement whereby the publisher acquires publishing rights in the material being originated for the television programme in return for paying an advance and royalty to the producer. The publisher, at its own additional expense, engages a writer to write the book; or

ii   the producer may obtain a (higher) advance and royalty from the publisher and be responsible for engaging the writer to write the book; or

iii   a co-publishing deal, whereby the producer and the publisher will jointly share the cost of producing and publishing the book and jointly share in the proceeds from it. This obviously requires considerable financial input from the producer and as a general rule, any such deal should be regarded as a long-term and slightly risky financial investment. The arrangements for structuring any such deal should be handled through an agent experienced in dealing with this type of agreement.

2.4   Writer's agreement

In many cases the writer of the television programme will have the right to be given first opportunity to write any book based on the programme. Whether the writer is contracted to do so by the publisher or the producer, and on what terms, will be a matter for individual negotiation. If there is no such obligation, it will be for the publisher and the producer to agree on the arrangements for commissioning the manuscript.

If a writer is being engaged to novelise existing scripts, it is fairly usual for this to be contracted on a buyout basis, i.e. the writer receives a flat fee for the novelisation and does not receive royalties. In most cases, however, the writer will require an advance and a royalty.

2.5   Stills/visual materials

Although the producer may have reserved the publishing rights it is, nonetheless, likely that either the producer or the publisher will need to enter into an agreement with the broadcaster for the use of visual material from the programmes in which the broadcaster owns the copyright, for use either within or on the cover of the book. They will also need to obtain the broadcaster's agreement to promote the book on-screen after the programmes. Broadcasters will usually expect either a royalty direct from the publisher or a share of the producer's receipts in return – something approximating 25% of royalties/revenues is usual.

Artistes' likenesses

The producer should bear in mind that under the provisions of the Equity agreements, if an artiste's likeness is being used for a commercial activity linked to the programme (as distinct from promotion of the programme itself), this is subject to payment of an additional fee to the artiste. If, therefore, the producer wishes to use stills featuring the artiste(s) on the cover and inside the book, terms for this must be negotiated with the artiste(s) concerned. This is a charge which should be passed on to the publisher (although the producer is primarily liable to make the payment and effect the clearance).

On-screen promotions

2.6

On-screen promotions for books are very valuable. With the BBC these promotions are only allowed for books published by BBC Books since promotions for other publishers' books would constitute advertisements, which the BBC is not permitted to carry. Channel 4 and ITV can promote books by any publisher under guidelines laid down by the ITC, a cardinal rule being that the book can be promoted on-screen only if it has been published as a result of the programme/series; existing books on which the programme is based cannot be promoted. The style, length and number of promotions have to be agreed with the broadcaster in each case.

Advances and royalties

2.7

Advances are sums of money paid by a publisher to fund the writing of the book and are set against the royalties from sales of the book which are paid to the author. Advances are usually non-returnable, i.e. if the book is never published or never achieves sufficient sales to cover the level of advance, the advance, or the balance of it, is not paid back to the publisher. (If the writer never delivers the manuscript that may be a different matter!) Advances are generally paid in stages from commission of the book to delivery of the manuscript to the publisher.

Occasionally a publisher may seek to make the size of the advance conditional on the book being closely tied to the release of the television production. So if, for any reason the two do not coincide, the advance (and sometimes royalty level) paid by the publisher will be reduced.

Royalties are a percentage of the retail price of the book. Paperback royalties are customarily between 7.5% and 10% of the retail selling price: for hardback books, they are between 10% and 15%.

Many commercial and artistic factors govern the level of advance offered by a publisher and the level of the royalty. As a starting point publishers calculate an advance on the basis of royalties accruing on the sale of between half and two-thirds of the first print run of the book, e.g.

Retail selling price –	£4.95
Royalty –	7.5% (37p per copy)
Initial print run –	25,000
Advance 50% of 25,000 x 37p =	£4,625.

It is advisable to negotiate an 'escalator' on the royalty after a certain number of sales have been achieved; the usual escalator is to increase the royalty percentage by 2.5% and there may be two such increases. The point at which the escalator is triggered is a matter for individual negotiation: for hardback books it will be after far fewer copies have been sold than for mass-market paperbacks.

Publishers' agreements generally provide for reduced royalties to be paid on discounted and book club sales. In some cases the royalty may be reduced by 50%; in others the publisher may provide for the payment for such sales to be of a share of net receipts, as distinct from royalties for each book sold. These provisions need to be particularly carefully checked, to ensure that the publisher's right to sell discounted books is not too open-ended.

2.8 Copyright

A publisher will not normally acquire the copyright in the book but will expect an assignment of the exclusive publishing rights. The usual territories for division of publishing rights are the English language rights, which are often split between British and Commonwealth territories, the USA (it is a matter for negotiation whether Canada is included within the USA for a North American territory, or whether it is included in the Commonwealth) and foreign language rights. The territories the producer grants to the publisher will obviously depend on the nature of the deal. If the programme is to be a co-production, it is obviously advisable to reserve the publishing rights in the co-producer's territory.

Publishers will generally require the licence for the full period of copyright, with the contract making provision for a reversion of rights in the event that the book goes out of print and, if requested to do so, the publisher declines to re-issue the publication.

3 MERCHANDISING RIGHTS

Merchandising rights are the right to license characters and images from the production such as toys, games, articles of clothing and foodstuffs.

3.1 Agents

Unless a programme is a 'natural' for merchandising spin-offs, it may be quite difficult to find a reliable merchandising agent prepared to take on the licensing. Experience has shown that the fact that something is going out on television to millions of homes is not enough to persuade people to buy merchandise associated with the programme, or at least not at the marginally higher price which must be charged for such merchandise in order to cover the licensor's royalty. For example, many of the most popular and long-running series, such as the soap operas, have rarely generated any lucrative merchandising spin-offs and this is not for want of trying on the part of the broadcasters. A programme has to have an extra commercial dimension to make it 'merchandisable' and this dimension is virtually impossible to identify and deliberately create.

If an agent is found, their commission levels are very high – between 40% and 60% of gross revenues. This is because, although a good merchandising property once established on the market can represent (for the licensor) one of the easiest ways of making money known to man – no capital outlay, staff or premises – the initial work of promoting the merchandising possibilities (producing selling brochures, trips to different manufacturers all over the country, representation at trade and toy fairs, trade mark registration) can be very costly.

3.2 Timescales

One of the most difficult logistical problems with setting up merchandising deals is to align the timescales of manufacturers with those for television production. This difficulty is further compounded because it is hard to persuade manufacturers to enter into merchandising deals until the programme has had some exposure. Manufacturers' lead times are such that it can easily take 18 months from signature of a licensing agreement for merchandising to reach the shops. Therefore, for all but the most long-running and frequently repeated series, serious merchandising is unlikely to be achieved.

Whether working through an agent or licensing merchandising direct, the following are the key provisions for any merchandising deal:

Advances/royalties   3.3

It is usual for the manufacturer being granted a licence to pay an advance against royalties or alternatively be required to give a guarantee of certain revenues from royalties within a given period. Royalties are usually based on the wholesale price of the licensed goods. The level is negotiable but it rarely exceeds 10%. The agreement should provide for an escalator on the royalty after a certain level of sales have been achieved.

Term of licence   3.4

The minimum term is about five years but the manufacturer must be placed under an obligation to meet a release date by which the licensed goods are on sale, usually two years after signature of the agreement, or the licence terminates. Any renewal of the licence term should be left to negotiation at the time.

Territories   3.5

Although, under EU rules, manufactured goods can be made freely available across territorial borders, it is, nonetheless, usual merchandising practice to confine the licence to specific territories and such limitations are generally respected by manufacturers.

Approvals   3.6

The producer (licensor) must ensure that the licensee obtains written approvals at every stage of the merchandising process, from first artistic concept through prototype to the point immediately before manufacture commences. This should include approval of the manufacturing materials, samples of the designs for each product and for the wrapping, containers and display materials. The producer should also have the right of approval of all publicity and advertising campaigns. These approvals must be at the producer's absolute discretion and rigorously applied, since the producer must not run the risk of the programme being associated with sub-standard merchandise.

Accounting   3.7

It is usual for accounting statements to be issued quarterly and revenues should be payable within 28 days of each statement. The licensor must have the clear entitlement to terminate the licence agreement if there is any failure by the licensee to account and/or pay revenues.

SOUNDTRACK RIGHTS/ALBUMS   4

Soundtrack rights are the right to issue sound recordings of the music and the soundtrack itself (this would normally only arise in the case of situation comedy series). (These rights, unless dealt with separately, can also be deemed to fall within most definitions of merchandising rights.)

Music can be a very effective means of promoting a programme. When the first series of *Auf Wiedersehn Pet* was transmitted, the ratings for the early programmes were disappointing but the single that had been released of the theme tune, *That's Living Alright*, started climbing the charts and by the time it reached No.2, the ratings

C23

for the programmes had dramatically improved. No detailed research was carried out to ascertain the extent of the correlation between the popularity of the theme music and the series, but it can reasonably be assumed that it may have been very significant.

4.1 Agent or 'fixer'

Unless a producer has particular experience of the record industry, it would be sensible to find a music 'fixer' to assist with setting up the deal. These fixers will approach record companies and may be involved in the production of the record. They may work to a commission or, depending on the extent of their involvement, take a small percentage of the royalty paid for the record. It is advisable to use a lawyer specialising in music industry agreements to handle the contract. It really isn't a business for amateurs.

4.2 Types of deal

There are three principal ways of setting up a spin-off album:

i   find a record company prepared to fund (or partially fund) the recording of music for the programmes in return for having the right to release the album of the music;

ii grant the record company the right to re-mix the music tracks for the programme for release, in return for an advance against sales; and

iii grant the record company a licence to re-record the music completely at the record company's expense and with the record company paying a royalty in return for the right to promote the album as being the music of the series, using stills and graphics from the production on the packaging.

4.3 Agreements with musicians, composers and Equity artistes

So far as licensing the use of the soundtrack for the production is concerned, the producer must ensure that the following obligations are met:

Musicians

Under the Musicians' Union agreements there are fixed levels for additional payments which fall due to the musicians who originally recorded the music, in respect of the release of the soundtrack.

Composers

Under the Mechanical Copyright Protection Society (MCPS) agreement the record company is obliged to pay a fixed statutory royalty based on retail selling price to the composer in respect of all sales of the record.

Equity artistes

If an Equity artiste's performance on the soundtrack of the programme is included on the album, this will require the negotiation of an additional fee for the artiste. As with books, if an artiste's likeness is to be shown on the sleeve, this is subject to the negotiation of an additional payment.

4.4 Advances/royalties

The arrangements for payments of advances and royalties will vary depending on whether the record company is using the soundtrack of the production or re-recording the music at its own expense. In the former case, the producer should negotiate an advance against royalties, and might expect to negotiate a royalty of approximately 10% of 90% of the retail selling price in respect of singles and of approximately 13-15% of 90% of retail selling price in respect of albums. From these advances/royalties the producer will be expected to meet the payments due to the musicians and to other artistes whose performances on the soundtrack of the production are being included. The record producer will normally receive a 2-3% royalty which will be payable out of these revenues.

In cases where the record company is re-recording the music, the royalty payable in respect of the use of stills and graphics from the series would obviously be at a much lower level – probably about 2% of 90% of retail selling price.

Packaging design 4.5

The producer should ensure that there will be full consultation on design for the packaging of the album and proof-read the credits to be included on it. If the record company requires photographs and graphics from the production for inclusion on the packaging, it should pay for direct costs and for the cost of clearances of the artistes' likenesses for use on the packaging.

On-screen promotions 4.6

A limited number of on-screen promotions for the music from the series are usually allowed, although the broadcaster may expect a share of the producer's profits from the album – usually about 25% – in respect of its agreement to promote on-screen.

PREMIUM-RATE TELEPHONE CALLS 5

Following the enormous success of *Who Wants To Be A Millionaire?* and the mechanism for viewers telephoning to participate on premium-rate phone lines with the revenues being used to fund the winners' prizes, more and more programmes are being devised to allow viewers telephoning in to participate in the programme. Many different ways will undoubtedly be found of using premium-rate telephone lines, since the revenues can be very considerable.

The ITC Programme Code sets out specific conditions which are attached to any premium-rate telephone service used or promoted in or around programmes. The code also specifies that its licensees must retain control of and responsibility for the service. Therefore, if an independent producer proposes to include a premium-rate phone line element within the programme, this must be done in full collaboration with the broadcaster. For ITV licence fee deals this would be done through the compliance company (see *Chapter 16*). (For details www.itc.org.uk.)

All premium-rate telephone services must comply fully with the code of practice issued by the Independent Committee for the Supervision of Standards of Telephone Information Services (ICSTIS). Detailed information can be obtained from the ICSTIS website www.icstis.org.uk

To set up a premium-rate telephone line service in connection with a programme, it is essential to obtain a prior permission certificate from ICSTIS to be a 'service provider', who is then placed under an obligation to observe the ICSTIS code which ranges from issues relating to the protection of children to taste, decency, gambling and so forth.

The services are set up with network operators, principally British Telecom, or through a bureau which may offer a wider range of facilities than network operators. If a bureau is used it will be responsible for obtaining the prior permission certificate and observing the ICSTIS Code of Practice.

Rates for premium-rate calls have to be approved and revenues earned are shared between the network operators and the service provider in proportions to be negotiated, but about 45% is payable to the network operator and 55% to the service provider.

C24

NEGOTIATING TACTICS Chapter 24

The ability to handle the deal-making side of productions competently is crucial to survival as an independent producer. The necessity to raise production funding from a number of different sources has vastly increased the variety and complexity of deals which a producer must negotiate in order to mount production. However distasteful it may be to a creative person to have to learn to cope with commerce, in the interests of furthering their art and making a living, it has to be done. Key to this is the conduct of negotiations. Many producers tend to take a pessimistic view of their ability to negotiate. There is a myth that negotiators are born, not made and that unless the producer has a natural aptitude for it, it is inevitable that the producer will come off worse.

This is dangerously negative thinking. Whilst some people do undoubtedly relish negotiations, regarding them as a challenging game which it is important to win, the strategies, skills and tactics required to conduct successful negotiations can all be learnt relatively easily. Probably the most important criterion is careful preparation; to have worked out more thoroughly than the other side what is at stake, what you want to achieve and what arguments and strategies you are going to adopt to do so. It is surprising that producers spend weeks, months, even years working up a programme proposal but will frequently embark on negotiations for deals which are integral to its eventual control, ownership and profitability without any preparation at all. "I thought I'd hear what they had to say" is the usual comment. To some extent this is valid. It is always important in negotiation to appear to be prepared to meet the other side's requirements but it does not alter the fact that before embarking on any negotiation it is vital for the producer to have a very clear idea of what he or she wants to achieve from it. This chapter aims to give a few guidelines for strategies.

KEY TOPICS & ISSUES

C24

HOW TO PREPARE FOR A NEGOTIATION   1

Firstly, it is useful to do a bit of research amongst colleagues as to the identity of the individual the producer is likely to be facing over the negotiating table and the stance they usually adopt. If they are known to be tough negotiators, work out ways in which they might have the satisfaction of winning without actually doing so. For example, ask for a far higher fee than you expect to receive so that they can be seen to beat you down.

For co-production deals, it is sensible to find out as much general information as possible about production arrangements in the co-producer's home territory as well as specific information about the co-producer's company and the individuals involved. (A friendly distributor may well help on this.) Also, be sensitive to different conventions. For example, in Spain it is apparently the worst possible form to negotiate other than in the brief moments between the second cup of coffee and the settlement of the bill, after a lunch or dinner at which everything and anything except the real business has been discussed. (This explains a great deal about the success rate for Spanish co-production deals!) In Japan the conventions of exchanging compliments, politenesses and gifts must all be time-consumingly observed and the terms which are eventually negotiated will then almost certainly be referred through a hierarchical structure before any deal can be taken as agreed. In the USA a typically modest, low-key British approach can appear very negative to an American negotiator accustomed to US producers doing well-rehearsed pitches on the wonders of their programme, their company and the reasons why they should be entitled to the best possible terms.

Careful research is also required to work out terms to be negotiated for various types of deals. This book contains guidelines on structures for many different types of production deals; media lawyers can obviously give valuable advice; and it may be helpful to consult colleagues who have negotiated similar deals. But do not rely too heavily on what others may say; no two deals are ever quite the same and it can be misleading and dangerous to assume that just because so-and-so got such-and-such a deal, you can expect the same thing. You may reasonably be entitled to do better, or worse; there are always variable factors.

Obviously approaches will be slightly different, depending on whether the producer is negotiating to buy or sell, i.e. acquiring rights in programme material or negotiating the terms for the producer's own participation and rights in the programme.

BUYING STRATEGIES   2

Although it may be sensible first to ask a price rather than offer one, the producer should, nonetheless, have worked out in advance the key parameters for the deal, as follows:

Payments   2.1

Estimate:

i   the opening price;

ii   the price you hope to pay; and

iii   the highest price you are prepared to offer.

Rights   2.2

Note:

i   all the rights you will ask for;

   ii   the rights you are prepared to dispense with;

   iii   the rights you would like to keep; and

   iv   the minimum rights you must acquire.

2.3   **Term**

Estimate:

   i   the maximum term you could hope for (an assignment);

   ii   the licence period you would be prepared to accept; and

   iii   the minimum period you could accept.

Having, thus, got a clear idea of the essentials, it is possible to work out a strategy. The starting point for the negotiations is to offer the three (**i**)s: if that is met with outrage and derision, the producer can offer, say, 2.1 (**i**) and 2.2 (**ii**) and 2.3 (**ii**); if that is not acceptable 2.1 (**ii**) and 2.2 (**i**) and 2.3 (**i**) and so on through the various permutations, bearing in mind that if you are pushed to offering 2.1 (**iii**) you should try to do better than 2.2 (**iv**) and 2.3 (**iii**).

3   SELLING STRATEGIES

Similarly with selling deals for production or co-productions, the producer can work out a strategy, as follows:

3.1   **Production fee**

   i   maximum production fee;

   ii   hoped for production fee; and

   iii   minimum acceptable production fee.

3.2   **Profit share**

   i   maximum profit share;

   ii   hoped for profit share; and

   iii   minimum acceptable profit share.

3.3   **Control of rights**

   i   maximum control;

   ii   hoped for control; and

   iii   minimum acceptable control.

Again, (**i**) is the starting base; 3.1 (**i**) and 3.2 (**ii**) and 3.3 (**i**) second permutation, and so forth.

All this may sound extremely theoretical, even technical, and to some extent it is, for negotiations are not (generally) conducted in a clinical fashion. Psychologically, however, it is very important to approach a negotiation from the secure base of being confident that you know what you can offer and what you are prepared to accept. With these goal posts and lines firmly in place you can then play around with the various balls the other side may lob into the field.

Think through the deal, anticipate resistance and work out an argument, selling point or reason to back up each and every term you are seeking. Don't use these devices unnecessarily or all in one go, but have them ready to bring into play as and when it seems appropriate. For example, if you are wanting to control certain rights, be able to explain how you plan to exercise them; if you want to pay a low fee for rights, or claim a high fee for yourself, have some plausible reasons for suggesting the particular amounts. It is not enough to say "I want this"; you must be able to say "I should have this because…".

It can sometimes look unduly heavy to take a lawyer to negotiations, at least in the early stages. If, however, you intend ultimately to bring one in on the deal, it is sensible to run your proposed deal terms by them in advance of opening negotiations: some salient points of advice at that key stage can be extremely valuable.

HOW TO CONDUCT A NEGOTIATION   4
Telephone negotiations   4.1

It is very common for even extremely complex deals for rights or services to be conducted with agents entirely by telephone. If this is the case, the producer should:

i   bear in mind that oral agreements are as legally binding (if more difficult to prove) than written agreements;

ii   make (and keep) careful notes of what is said by both sides throughout the conversation; and

iii   follow up with a fax or e-mail confirming the main points of the discussion and noting any outstanding points which need to be resolved. If a draft contract is to follow, make this clear in the e-mail.

Meetings   4.2

Who to take

Unless the producer is a very experienced negotiator, it is always wise to take a colleague along to a negotiation. As a general rule, it is better to take a lawyer only when the other side has a legal representative and detailed terms of contracts are being worked out. The colleague may not be able to contribute to the actual negotiation but can take notes, confirm impressions or recollections and generally give moral support. It can be very daunting to go into a negotiation alone, only to find that the other side has fielded what appears to be a team of representatives.

'Power dressing'

This largely American and 1980s concept of dressing to impress or even intimidate the other side is abhorrent to many producers. It is, however, worth bearing in mind that the kind of person who is employed to negotiate contracts is more than likely to be a lawyer or accountant by training, conservative by nature, mistrustful of obvious non-conformity and consequently instinctively unwilling to grant monies/rights/ownership to someone wearing jeans, T-shirt and trainers and carrying papers in a carrier bag. However much it may go against the grain, in the interests of getting the best possible deal, it is worth going to the trouble of looking the part of someone who can be relied upon to deal responsibly with whatever business matters are under negotiation.

Opening negotiations

Notwithstanding the preparation of deal parameters, if the producer can engineer it, it is always preferable to get the other side to make the opening offer. This can be tricky: conversations along the lines of "What do you want?", "Well, what do you have in mind?", "It all depends on what you are intending to do with the project" can go round in circles. But sometimes what the other side is expecting you to offer (buying) /accept (selling) may be more favourable to you than you had anticipated, so it's always worth a try.

If you are placed in the position of having to open the negotiation, put forward your prepared minimum (buying)/maximum (selling) position, from which you know you can negotiate upwards or downwards as appropriate.

If the other side opens the negotiation, remember that it is likely that they too will probably be prepared to improve on the opening offer. Stay calm, don't accept the first thing that's offered (even if it exceeds your wildest dreams): you can almost certainly do better.

Continuing negotiations

If you are buying, it can be quite a delicate matter not to volunteer too much but, at the same time, ensure that you get all the rights you want. Some things may have been granted to you automatically but by specifically asking for them, you end up having to pay extra for them. In the initial stages offer an overall payment, define it as covering maximum ownership and wait for the other side to start reserving certain rights and then negotiate these individually.

If you are selling, don't lose your nerve if you meet resistance to your asking price: offer to drop certain terms which are not so important to you, before you start negotiating down on the key provisions.

Do not finally agree anything until all the principal points of the deal have been settled. You can, of course, indicate that certain things are likely to be acceptable, subject to agreement on the other terms under discussion.

Do not be drawn into agreeing terms which you don't understand. Although many producers are reluctant to ask for explanations for fear of looking inexperienced and ignorant, different deal terms are used by different organisations and negotiators and it is sensible to ask for clarification of what they mean by the term being used. If you still can't understand what is being proposed, or you can, but can't immediately work out the implications of it on your deal, say you need time to consider it and undertake to get back to them.

Unless negotiations have been dragging on over several meetings, never be pressed into agreeing terms on the spot (and similarly do not expect a seller to do so). It is rare for there to be such urgency about a deal that it has to be settled there and then and great caution should be taken in dealing with anyone who insists on an immediate decision: even 24 hours reflection can be very useful and it would be unreasonable for this to be refused.

It is always a useful device to have in the background a (possibly fictitious) business associate who is not present at meetings but who, it is made clear, also has to approve deal terms. This can provide a means of allowing more time to consider the terms: "It seems OK to me, but I must run it past my business associate before accepting". It can also take the personal confrontation out of a negotiation: "I understand what you are saying, but I will never be able to get my business associate to agree it".

Try to stay calm and keep the heat out of the debate. Aggressive tactics are usually counterproductive because they generally lead to a hardening of attitude on the other side's part.

Never play brinkmanship unless you really intend to go through with it: if you say "If that's the best you can offer, we have no deal", mean it. There will inevitably be a 'next time' with the same negotiator and if they have successfully called your bluff once they will try it again.

Be prepared to offer the other side something: work out in advance what it might be. There must be give and take in a negotiation: if the other side thinks it is doing all the giving and you are doing all the taking, resentment builds up.

C24

Recognise the need to close a negotiation: don't allow it to drag into a war of attrition over points which are not of fundamental importance. Offer a few concessions, hope the other side might be prepared to do the same, and call it a day.

CLOSING THE NEGOTIATION 5

During the course of negotiations always make notes of what is said (the colleague you take along can do this for you, if you are too preoccupied with the discussion). Keep the notes on file.

At the end of the meeting always recap on what has been resolved, point by point. It is extraordinary how frequently it happens that the two sides might have an entirely different understanding of what was settled and it is much easier to sort it out there and then, rather than leaving the misunderstanding to come to light at a later stage.

Immediately follow up each meeting by sending a fax/e-mail setting out the points which have been resolved and the matters which have still to be settled. It is very important that there should be a complete written record of the negotiation and there are advantages in this record being written from your standpoint.

Unless circumstances change and, as a consequence, there are valid reasons for seeking variations to a deal, be prepared to live with the terms which have finally been negotiated, even if you realise that they are even less favourable to you than you thought they were. Put it down to experience: don't keep going back and trying to tinker with a deal once it has been set. It looks unprofessional and can damage chances for more successful dealings in the future.

USEFUL ADDRESSES

UK BROADCASTERS

Anglia Television
Anglia House
Norwich NR1 3JG
Tel: 01603 615151 Fax: 01603 615151
www.angliatv.co.uk

BBC
BBC TV Centre
Wood Lane
London W12 7RJ
Tel: 020 8743 8000 Fax: 028 9032 6453
www.bbc.co.uk

Border Television
The Television Centre
Carlisle CA1 3NT
Tel: 01228 525101 Fax: 01228 541384
www.border-tv.com

British Sky Broadcasting
Grant Way
Isleworth
Middlesex TW7 5QD
Tel: 0870 240 3000 Fax: 020 7705 3030
www.sky.com

Carlton Broadcasting
Central Region
Gas Street
Birmingham B1 2JT
Tel: 0121 643 9898 Fax: 0121 634 4898
www.carlton.com

Carlton Broadcasting
West Country Region
Langage Science Park
Plymouth PL7 5BQ
Tel: 01752 333333 Fax: 01752 333444
E-mail: westcountryregion@carlton.co.uk

Carlton Television
101 St Martin's Lane
London WC2N 4RF
Tel: 020 7240 4000 Fax: 020 7240 4171

Channel 4
124 Horseferry Road
London SW1P 2TX
Tel: 020 7396 4444 Fax: 020 7306 8347
www.channel4.com

Channel 5
22 Long Acre
London WC2E 9LY
Tel: 020 7497 5225 Fax: 020 7497 5222
www.channel5.co.uk

Channel Television
Television Centre
St Helier
Jersey JE1 3ZD
Tel: 01534 816816 Fax: 01534 816817
www.channeltv.co.uk

GMTV
London Television Centre
Upper Ground
London SE1 9TT
Tel: 020 7827 7000 Fax: 020 7827 7001
www.gmtv.co.uk

UA

Grampian Television
Queen's Cross
Aberdeen AB15 4XJ
Tel: 01224 846846 Fax: 01224 846800
www.grampiantv.co.uk

Granada Television
Quay Street
Manchester M60 9EA
Tel: 0161 832 7211 Fax: 0161 827 2029
www.granadatv.co.uk

HTV Wales
Television Centre
Culverhouse Cross
Cardiff CF5 6XJ
Tel: 029 2059 0590 Fax: 029 2059 9108
www.htvwales.com

HTV West
Television Centre
Bath Road
Bristol BS4 3HG
Tel: 0117 972 2722 Fax: 0117 971 7685
www.htvwest.com

ITV Network Centre
200 Grays Inn Road
London WC1X 8HF
Tel: 020 7843 8000 Fax: 020 7843 8158
www.itv.co.uk

London Weekend Television
London Television Centre
Upper Ground
London SE1 9LT
Tel: 020 7620 1620
www.lwt.co.uk

Meridian Broadcasting
Television Centre
Southampton SO14 0PZ
Tel: 023 8022 2555 Fax: 023 8033 5050
www.meridiantv.com

Scottish Television
200 Renfield Street
Glasgow G2 3PR
Tel: 0141 300 3000 Fax 0141 300 3030
www.scottishtv.co.uk

Tyne Tees Television
The Television Centre
City Road
Newcastle upon Tyne NE1 2AL
Tel: 0191 261 0181 Fax: 0191 261 2302
www.tynetees.tv

Ulster Television
Havelock House
Ormeau Road
Belfast BT7 1EB
Tel: 028 9032 8122 Fax: 028 9024 6695
www.utvplc.com

Yorkshire Television
TV Centre
Kirkstall Road
Leeds LS3 1JS
Tel: 0113 243 8283 Fax: 0113 244 5107
www.granadamedia.com

DIGITAL CHANNELS
BBC Choice
BBC4
BBC News 24
BBC Parliament
Television Centre
Wood Lane
London W12 7RJ
Tel: 020 8743 8000
www.bbc.co.uk/news

E4
Channel 4 Television
4 Ventures Ltd
124 Horseferry Road
London SW1P 2TX
Tel: 020 7396 4444
www.channel4.com

SDN Ltd
The Media Centre
Culverhouse Cross
Cardiff CF5 6XJ
Tel: 029 2040 5600
Fax: 029 2040 5625

Sky Digital
British Sky Broadcasting Ltd
6 Centaurs Business Park
Grant Way
Isleworth TW7 5QD
Tel: 020 7705 3000
www.sky.com

UK Food
UK Style
UK Horizon
2nd Floor
160 Great Portland Street
London W1W 5QA
Tel: 020 7765 0725

UK Gold
UK Drama
UK Gold Broadcasting
2nd Floor
160 Great Portland Street
London W1W 5QA
Tel: 020 7765 0553

UK Play
UK Channel Management Ltd
2nd Floor
160 Great Portland Street
London W1W 5QA
Tel: 020 7765 5805

NOTE: A Fact File containing a
comprehensive list of names and
addresses of all types of television
channels operating from the UK can
be obtained from the Independent
Television Commission on 020 7255
3000/www.itc.org.uk

FILM FUNDING
Film Council
10 Little Portland Street
London W1W 7JG
Tel: 020 7861 7861 Fax: 020 7861 7862
www.filmcouncil.org.uk

Scottish Screen
2nd Floor
249 West George Street
Glasgow G2 4QE
Tel: 0141 302 1700 Fax: 0141 302 1715
www.scottishscreen.com

Sgrîn, Media Agency For Wales
The Bank
10 Mount Stuart Square
Cardiff Bay
Cardiff CF10 5EE
Tel: 029 2033 3300 Fax: 029 2033 3320
E-mail: sgrin@sgrin.co.uk
www.sgrin.co.uk

The Northern Ireland Film
and Television Commission
21 Ormeau Avenue
Belfast BT2 8HD
Tel: 028 9023 2444 Fax: 028 9023 9918

The Irish Film Board
Rockfort House
St Augustine Street
Co Galway
Ireland
Tel: (353) 91 561 398
Fax: (353) 91 561 405
E-mail: info@filmboard.ie

South West Screen
59 Prince Street
Bristol BS1 4QH
Tel: 0117 377 6066 Fax: 0117 377 6067

Yorkshire Media Production Agency
The Workstation
15 Paternoster Row
Sheffield S1 2BX
Tel: 0114 249 2204 Fax: 0114 249 2293
www.ympa.org.uk

OVERSEAS BROADCASTERS/ CO-PRODUCTION FINANCIERS
Australia
Australian Broadcasting Corporation
GPO Box 9994
Sydney NSW 2001
Tel: (61) 2 9333 1500 Fax: (61) 2 9333 5305
www.abc.com.au

Australian Film Finance Corporation Limited
Level 12, 130 Elizabeth Street
Sydney NSW 2000
GPO Box 3886
Sydney 2001
Tel: (61) 2 9268 2555 Fax: (61) 2 9264 8551
www.ffc.gov.au

Network Ten
1 Saunders Street
Pyrmont NSW 2009
Tel: (61) 2 9650 1010 Fax: (61) 2 9650 1456
www.ten.com.au

Nine Network Australia
24 Artarman Road
Willoughby
Sydney NSW 2068
Tel: (61) 2 9965 2538 Fax: (61) 2 9965 2119
www.ninemsn.com.au

Seven Network Australia
TV Centre
Mobbs Lane
Epping NSW
Sydney 2121
Tel: (61) 2 9877 7777 Fax: (61) 2 9877 7892
www.seven.com.au

Canada
Alliance/Atlantis Communications
121 Bloor Street East
Suite 1500
Toronto
Ontario M4W 3M5
Tel: (1) 416 533 4700
Fax: (1) 416 967 5884
www.aactv.com

Nelvana International
32 Atlantic Avenue
Toronto
Ontario M6K 1X8
Tel: (1) 416 588 5571
Fax: (1) 416 588 5588
www.nelvana.com

Telefilm Canada
360 rue Saint-Jacques
Bureau/700
Montréal
Quebec H2Y 4A9
Tel: (1) 514 283 6363
Fax: (1) 514 283 8212
www.telefilm.gc.ca

Japan
NHK (Nippon HosoKyokai)
2-2-1 Jinnan
Shibuya-ku
Tokyo 150-8001
Japan
Tel: (81) 3 5455 5873
Fax: (81) 3 3481 1453
www.nhk.or.jp

USA
A&E Television Network
235 East 45th Street
New York NY 10017
Tel: (1) 212 210 1400
Fax: (1) 212 850 9304
www.aetv.com

CNN
One CNN Centre
PO Box 105366
Atlanta
Georgia 30343

Discovery Communications Inc
7700 Wisconsin Avenue
Bethesda
MD 20814-3579
Tel: (1) 301 986 0444 Fax: (1) 301 652 7154
www.discovery.com

Discovery Networks Europe
160 Great Portland Street
London W1W 5QA
Tel: 020 7462 3600 Fax: 020 7462 3700
www.discoveryeurope.com

The History Channel
235 East 45th Street
New York NY 10017
Tel: (1) 212 210 1400 Fax: (1) 212 907 9476

Home Box Office
1100 Avenue of the Americas
New York NY 10036
Tel: (1) 212 512 1000 Fax: (1) 212 512 5102
www.hbo.com

Library of Congress
Public Affairs Office
101 Independence Ave. SE
Washington DC 20540-1610
Tel: (1) 202 707 2905 Fax: (1) 202 707 9199

**Motion Picture Association
of America (MPAA)**
15503 Ventura Blvd
Encino, California 91436
Tel: (1) 818 995 6600

National Geographic Channel
1145, 17th Street NW
Washington DC 20036-4688
Tel: (1) 202 912 6500 Fax: (1) 202 912 6602

PBS/US Public Television
1320 Braddock Place
Alexandria VA 22314
Tel: (1) 703 739 5000 Fax: (1) 310 234 4057

WGBH Boston
125 Western Avenue
Boston MA 02134
Tel: (1) 617 300 5400 Fax: (1) 617 300 1026
www.wgbh.org

WNET
13 WNET New York
450 West 33rd Street
New York NY 10001
Tel: (1) 212 560 1313 Fax: (1) 212 560 1314
www.thirteen.org

UK TELEVISION DISTRIBUTORS
BBC Worldwide
Woodlands
80 Wood Lane
London W12 0TT
Tel: 020 8433 2000 Fax: 020 8433 0538
www.bbcworldwidetv.com

Carlton International Media
35-38 Portman Square
London W1H 6NU
Tel: 020 7224 3339 Fax: 020 7486 1707
www.carltonint.co.uk

Channel 4 International
124 Horseferry Road
London SW1P 2TX
Tel: 020 7396 4444 Fax: 020 7306 8364
www.channel4.com

Chatsworth Television Distributors
97/99 Dean Street
London W1D 3TE
Tel: 020 7734 4302 Fax: 020 7437 3301
www.chatsworth-tv.co.uk

Chrysalis Distribution
The Chrysalis Building
Bramley Road
London W10 6SP
Tel: 020 7465 6274 Fax: 020 7221 6286
www.chrysalis.com

Entertainment Rights
Colet Court
100 Hammersmith Road
London W6 7JP
Tel: 020 8762 6200 Fax: 020 8762 6299
www.entertainmentrights.com

Fremantle International Distribution
1 Stephen Street
London W1T 1AL
Tel: 020 7691 6000 Fax: 020 7691 6100

Granada Media
London Television Centre
Upper Ground
London SE1 9LT
Tel: 020 7620 1620
www.granadamedia.com/international

HIT Entertainment
5th Floor
Maple House
149-150 Tottenham Court Road
London W1T 7NF
Tel: 020 7554 2500 Fax: 020 7388 9321
www.hitentertainment.com

Minotaur International
160 Great Portland Street
London W1W 5QA
Tel: 020 7299 5000 Fax: 020 7299 5777
www.minotaur.tv

Southern Star Sales Limited UK
45-49 Mortimer Street
London W1W 8HX
Tel: 020 7636 9421 Fax: 020 7436 7426
E-mail: sales@sstar.uk.com

Target
41-42 Berners Street
London W1T 3NB
Tel: 020 7323 7900 Fax: 020 7323 7933
E-mail: info@target-tv.com

**UK THEATRICAL SALES AGENTS
AND DISTRIBUTORS**
Sales Agents
Alliance Atlantis
184-192 Drummond Street
London NW1 3HP
Tel: 020 7391 6935 Fax: 020 7383 0404

FilmFour International
124 Horseferry Road
London SW1P 2TX
Tel: 020 7396 4444 Fax: 020 7306 8361/2

First Independent Films
69 New Oxford Street
London WC1A 1DG
Tel: 020 7528 7767 Fax: 020 7528 7770

Myriad Pictures
5 Percy Street
London W1T 1DG
Tel: 020 7467 6880 Fax: 020 7467 6890

Universal Pictures International
Oxford House
76 Oxford Street
London W1D 1BS
Tel: 020 7307 1300 Fax: 020 7307 1301

The Sales Company
62 Shaftesbury Avenue
London W1V 7DE
Tel: 020 7434 9061 Fax: 020 7494 3293

THEATRICAL DISTRIBUTORS

Artificial Eye Film Company
14 King Street
London WC2E 8HR
Tel: 020 7240 5353 Fax: 020 7240 5242

Buena Vista Home Entertainment
3 Queen Caroline Street
Hammersmith, London W6 9PE
Tel: 020 8222 1000 Fax: 020 8222 2795

Feature Film Company
4th Floor
68-70 Wardour Street
London W1V 3HP
Tel: 020 7734 2226 Fax: 020 7494 0309

Universal Video International
Oxford House
76 Oxford Street
London W1D 1BS
Tel: 020 7307 1300 Fax: 020 7307 1301

Twentieth Century Fox
31-32 Soho Square
London W1D 3AP
Tel: 020 7437 7766 Fax: 020 7434 2170

United International Pictures (UK)
12 Golden Square
London W1A 2JL
Tel: 020 7534 5200 Fax: 020 7534 5202

GOVERNMENT/QUANGOS

Advertising Standards Authority
2 Torrington Place
London WC1 7HW
Tel: 020 7580 5555 Fax: 020 7631 3051
www.asa.org.uk

Department of Culture Media and Sport
Creative Industries Division
2-4 Cockspur Street
London SW1Y 5DH
Tel: 020 7211 6433 Fax: 020 7211 6417
www.culture.gov.uk

Her Majesty's Stationery Office (HMSO)
St Clements House
2-16 Colegate
Norwich NR3 1BQ
Purchase legislation: 0870 600 5522
Copyright and licensing: 01603 621000
Other enquiries: 01603 723011

Home Office Immigration and Nationality Department
Lunar House
Wellesley Road
Croydon CR9 2BY
Tel: 0870 606 7766
www.ind.homeoffice.gov.uk

Independent Committee for the Supervision of Standards of Telephone Information Services (ICSTIS)
4th Floor, Clove Building
4 Maguire Street
London SE1 2NQ
Tel: 020 7940 7474 Fax: 020 7940 7456
www.icstis.org.uk

Independent Television Commission (ITC)
33 Foley Street
London W1W 7TL
Tel: 020 7255 3000 Fax: 020 7306 7800
www.itc.org.uk

Registrar of Companies
Companies House
Crown Way, Cardiff CF14 3UZ
www.ws4.companies-house.gov.uk

**TRADE ASSOCIATIONS,
ORGANISATIONS AND UNIONS**
BECTU
111 Wardour Street
London W1F 0AU
Tel: 020 7437 8506 Fax: 020 7437 8268

**British Academy
of Film and Television Arts (BAFTA)**
195 Piccadilly
London W1J 9LN
Tel: 020 7734 0022 Fax: 020 7734 1792

British Actors Equity Association
Guild House
Upper St Martin's Lane
London WC2H 9EG
Tel: 020 7379 6000 Fax: 020 7379 7001

**Directors' and Producers'
Rights Society**
Victoria Chambers
16-18 Strutton Ground
London SW1P 2HP
Tel: 020 7227 4757 Fax: 020 7227 4755

Directors Guild of Great Britain
Acorn House
314-320 Grays Inn Road
London WC1X 8DP
Tel: 020 7278 4343 Fax: 020 7278 4742
www.dggb.co.uk

**Internet Corporation for Assigned
Names and Numbers (ICANN)**
4676 Admiralty Way, Suite 330
Marina del Rey, CA 90292-6601
USA
Tel: (1) 310 823 9358
www.icann.org
www.nominet.net/howto/domainreg.html

**MCPS (Mechanical
Copyright Protection Society)**
Elgar House
41 Streatham High Road
London SW16 1ER
Tel: 020 8769 4400 Fax: 020 8378 7300

Musicians' Union
60-62 Clapham Road
London SW9 0JJ
Tel: 020 7582 5566 Fax: 020 7582 9805

**PACT (Producers Alliance for
Cinema and Television)**
45 Mortimer Street
London W1W 8HJ
Tel: 020 7331 6000 Fax: 020 7331 6700
E-mail: enquiries@pact.co.uk

**Producers Rights Agency
(formerly PIRS)**
45 Mortimer Street
London W1W 8HJ
Tel: 020 7830 6600 Fax: 020 7830 6611

PRS (Performing Rights Society)
29/33 Berners Street
London W1T 3AB
Tel: 020 7580 5544 Fax: 020 7306 4455

Writers' Guild of Great Britain
430 Edgeware Road
London W2 1EH
Tel: 020 7723 8074 Fax: 020 7706 2413

FINANCE/BANKS
Bank Leumi Ltd
20 Stratford Place
London W1C 1BG
Tel: 020 7907 8000 Fax: 020 7797 8001

Barclays Bank Media Business Centre
27 Soho Square
London W1A 4WA
Tel: 020 7445 5700 Fax: 020 7445 5784

Coutts & Co
440 Strand
London WC2R 0QS
Tel: 020 7753 1000

Film Finances Limited
14-15 Conduit Street
London W1S 2XJ
Tel: 020 7629 6557 Fax: 020 7491 7530

EUROPEAN ORGANISATIONS
Eurimages
Council of Europe
67075 Strasbourg Cedex
Tel: (33) 3 88 41 26 40
Fax: (33) 3 88 41 27 60
E-mail: eurimages@coe.int

UK Media Desk
66-68 Margaret Street
London W1W 8SR
Tel: 020 7343 9733 Fax: 020 7323 9747
www.mediadesk.co.uk

**EUROPEAN INDEPENDENT
PRODUCER ORGANISATIONS**
CEPI Members
ANEPA Spain
C/ Luis Bunuel 2, 2o Izqda.
Ciudad de la Imagen
28223 Pozuelo de Alarcon
Madrid
Tel: (34) 91 711 08 08
Fax: (34) 91 518 46 98
E-mail: anepa@anepa.org
www.anepa.org

APIT Portugal
R. D Pedro V, No 60, 1oDto
Sala.33, 1250 Lisboa
Tel: (351) 21 343 30 23
Fax: (351) 21 347 43 03
www.apit.pt

APT Italy
Via F Corridoni, 15
00195, Roma
Tel: (39) 06 370 02 65
Fax: (39) 06 372 30 77
E-mail: apt-info@wing.it

BVDP Germany
Widenmayerstraße 32
80538 München
Tel: (49) 89 286 28 385
Fax: (49) 89 286 28 247

DFTP Denmark
Allégade 24A, 2nd Floor
DK-2000 Frederiksberg
Tel: (45) 33 86 28 80
Fax: (45) 33 86 28 88
www.dftp.dk

FAFO Austria
c/o Satel-Film
Wiedner Hauptstraße 68
1040 Wien
Tel: (43) 1 588 72 100
Fax: (43) 1 588 72 106

Film Makers Ireland
c/o The Studio Building
Meeting House Square
Temple Bar
Dublin 2
Tel: (353) 1 671 35 25
Fax: (353) 1 671 42 92
www.filmmakersireland.ie

OTP The Netherlands
PO Box 27900
NL-1202 KV Hilversum
Tel: (31) 356 23 11 66
Fax: (31) 356 28 00 51

Produsentforeningen Norway
Filmens Hus
Dronningens gt. 16
0152 Oslo
Tel: (47) 23 11 93 11/12
Fax: (47) 23 11 93 16
www.produsentforeningen.no

SAPOE/SPET Greece
30, Aigialias Str.
Marousi
Tel: (30) 1 68 33 212
Fax: (30) 1 68 33 606

SATU ry Finland
Fabianinkatu 4B 14
00130 Helsinki
Tel: (358) 9 6840 610
Fax: (358) 9 6221 860
www.satu.fi

SPI France
1 Bis, rue du Havre
75008 Paris
Tel: (33) 1 44 70 70 44
Fax: (33) 1 44 70 70 40

Sverige TV-Producenter ek för Sweden
P E Wallin
Box 27 298
102 53 Stockholm
Tel: (46) 8 665 12 55
Fax: (46) 8 665 12 04
E-mail: info@frf.net
www.frf.net

USPA France
5, rue Cernushci
F-75017 Paris
Tel: (33) 1 40 53 23 00
Fax: (33) 1 40 53 23 23
www.uspa.fr

VOTP Belgium
Ransbeekstraat 230
1120 Brussels
Tel: (32) 15 23 00 32
Fax: (32) 15 23 06 66

GLOSSARY

Aggregation – Where a company has more than one production commissioned by the same broadcaster at any one time and where the broadcaster may require the production fee to be calculated on the basis of total combined cost of the productions

Bandwidth – The amount of data that can be transmitted within a fixed amount of time

BECTU – Broadcasting Entertainment Cinematograph and Theatre Union

Bible – Specification for a programme: setting out, in the case of a drama, characters, backgrounds to the characters, situation and storyline; in the case of a game show, game play, rules, questions and timings

Blanket licence – A licence agreement between a music organisation (PRS/MCPS/BPI/PPL) and a broadcaster or service operator which allows the unlimited use of music on the broadcaster's channel

Blood chit – Form signed by a contributor or interviewee in a programme confirming their agreement to the inclusion of their contribution

BPI – British Phonographic Industry

Broadband – Communication lines or services that allow high-bandwidth transmissions, including high-speed Internet access and video-on-demand

Buyout – A payment to talent which covers all forms of exploitation of a production around the world, with no further payments accruing to the talent

Cash flow – Stage payments for the production budget

Catch-up service – Service in which broadcasters repeat programmes shortly after their initial transmission

CDPA 1988 – Copyright, Designs and Patents Act 1988

Ceiling – The highest fee payable in respect of rights/services

Chain of title – All the agreements relating to copyright materials which form the underlying rights in a production, such as a book on which it is based and the screenplay

Changed format rights – The right to adapt an existing format for production in another territory

CNC – Centre National de la Cinematographie

Collecting societies – Organisations set up for the purpose of collecting revenues in respect of exploitation of copyright materials and dispersing the revenues to the copyright owners

Combined use – Fee payable to members of the Musicians' Union which covers the use of their performances by a number of different means

G

Completion guarantee – Completion guarantees (sometimes called completion bonds) are a form of insurance whereby the completion guarantor guarantees to take over and complete production if, for any reason at all, it becomes apparent during the course of production that the production cannot be completed within the approved total budget

Cost of money – Bank charges (interest, arrangement fees) levied on borrowed money

Cybersquatting – Registering another company's trading name as a domain name

Deficit finance – A shortfall between the budget for the production and the available funding

Direct access route – Commissions obtained direct from the ITV Network Centre

Direct costs – Monies payable to third parties, for example, script fees, travel expenses, legal fees

Domain name – Name/address of a website

DPRS – Directors' and Producers' Rights Society

EEA – European Economic Area: Austria, Belgium, Denmark, Finland, France, Germany, Greece, Iceland, Republic of Ireland, Italy, Liechtenstein, Luxembourg, Netherlands, Norway, Portugal, Spain, Sweden, UK

Errors and omissions – Insurance against issues such as breach of copyright, libel, defamation

Equity – British Actors Equity Association

Escalator – A contractual provision whereby a purchase price is subject to a percentage increase related to a production budget

Escrow account – Bank account into which funds are remitted for payment for a specific purpose, usually used for payments due to actors under the terms of Equity agreements

Favoured nations – The right to have the same entitlement to a share of net profits as others engaged on a production

Finder – Individual who seeks financing for productions

First opportunity/first option – To have the right to make an offer to acquire rights before any other party is given the opportunity to make an offer

Fixed price deal – Where the price for the programme is pre-agreed with no provision made for overspend or underspend

Floor – Lowest fee payable in respect of rights/services

Framing – Displaying another website in a smaller window

Holdback – Agreement not to exploit certain rights for a fixed period of time.

Hybrid deal – One where the broadcaster and the producer are jointly bringing funding to the production

ICANN – Internet Corporation for Assigned Names

ICSTIS – Independent Committee for the Supervision of Standards of Television Information Services

Indirect costs – The costs of the co-producers' time and office overheads

ISDN (Integrated services digital network) – An international communications standard for sending voice, video and data over digital telephone lines or normal telephone lines. Offers high-speed access to the Internet

ISP – Internet Service Provider

Limited rights material – Existing copyright material to be used in a programme where it is only possible to secure a limited licence in the rights

Linking – Providing a click-through from one website to another

Matching rights – The right to acquire rights by offering the same terms as those proposed by a third party

MCPS – Mechanical Copyright Protection Society

MIP – Marché International des Programmes (International Television Programme Market)

MPAA – Motion Picture Association of America

MU – The Musicians' Union

Music cue sheet – Form completed on delivery of a production giving all information about the composer, length and type of music included in the production

Overspill – Satellite transmissions receivable in territories outside the territory of the satellite service

P&A – Prints and Advertising

PBS – Public Broadcasting System

Personal guarantee – When an individual's personal assets are used to underwrite a loan or an overdraft

Picture deal – Where a fee is in full payment of all work on a production from completion to delivery, regardless of the length of time taken

PIRS – The Producers Industrial Relations Service (now Producers Rights Agency)

Polish – Writer's further work on a script or screenplay which is not as extensive as a new draft or a revision to a draft

PPL – Phonographic Performance Ltd

Prequel – A second production in which the storyline is about events and characters which preceded the storyline of the original production

Programme compliance – Supervision of a production by a broadcaster to ensure that it complies with the provisions of the Broadcasting Act

PRS – Performing Rights Society

Public domain – Material which is not protected by copyright law

Re-make – The right to make another version of the production using the original script or screenplay

Residuals – Fixed additional payments laid down in agreements with the talent unions which are payable to the talent on sales of a production in overseas territories

Right of cut-off – The entitlement to terminate a writer's contract at certain stages during the writing of a script or screenplay

Rolling licence – The term of a licence in a programme or a format which is automatically extended on commission of each new series

Royalties – Payments which are computed as a percentage share of revenues earned from exploitation, or, in the case of format royalties, which may be computed as a percentage of the writer's fee

Sequel – A sequel to a production where the storyline continues the storyline of the production

SOFICIAS – Sociétés pour le Financement des Industries Cinematographiques et Audiovisuelles

G

Source code – Computer software code for interactive programmes

Spin-off – A production which features the original characters in a new storyline which is not a sequel or prequel to the storyline of the original production

Tie-ins – A book or item of merchandise which is promoted for sale as being "from the production" using graphics and visual images from the production

Turnaround – The right an author (or producer) may have to reacquire rights in a copyright work if it has not gone into production within a certain fixed time period

UCC – Universal Copyright Convention

UK Secondary Market – UK television channels other than the main terrestrial broadcasters and BSkyB

Umbrella deal – One production company enters into an agreement to oversee a production by another, usually smaller and less experienced, production company.

URLs – Uniform Resource Locators (website addresses)

Video-on-demand – Service where programmes can be ordered on payment of a fee

Web-casting – Transmission of a broadcaster's service on the Internet

WIPO – World Intellectual Property Organisation

Withholding tax – A tax on revenues to be remitted overseas, calculated as a percentage of the revenue

INDEX

I

I

N

notes

N

N

N